M000168249

How to Use
Adobe®
Photoshop® Elements 2

Lisa Lee

201 W. 103rd Street
Indianapolis, Indiana 46290

How to Use Adobe® Photoshop® Elements 2

Copyright © 2003 by Que Publishing

All rights reserved. No part of this book shall be reproduced, stored in a retrieval system, or transmitted by any means, electronic, mechanical, photocopying, recording, or otherwise, without written permission from the publisher. No patent liability is assumed with respect to the use of the information contained herein. Although every precaution has been taken in the preparation of this book, the publisher and author assume no responsibility for errors or omissions. Nor is any liability assumed for damages resulting from the use of the information contained herein.

International Standard Book Number: 0-7897-2803-6

Library of Congress Catalog Card Number: 2002-111095

Printed in the United States of America

First Printing: April 2003

06   05   04   03   4   3   2   1

Trademarks

All terms mentioned in this book that are known to be trademarks or service marks have been appropriately capitalized. Que cannot attest to the accuracy of this information. Use of a term in this book should not be regarded as affecting the validity of any trademark or service mark.

Warning and Disclaimer

Every effort has been made to make this book as complete and as accurate as possible, but no warranty or fitness is implied. The information provided is on an "as is" basis. The author and the publisher shall have neither liability nor responsibility to any person or entity with respect to any loss or damages arising from the information contained in this book.

Acquisitions Editors
Betsy Brown
Candy Hall

Development Editors
Nick Goetz
Laura Norman
Alice Martina Smith

Managing Editor
Charlotte Clapp

Project Editor
Elizabeth Finney

Production Editor
Seth Kerney

Indexer
Erika Millen

Proofreader
Kellie Cotner

Technical Editor
Elizabeth Bulger

Team Coordinator
Vanessa Evans

Interior Designer
Anne Jones

Cover Designer
Anne Jones

Page Layout
Stacey Richwine-DeRome

Contents at a Glance

Introduction 1

1 Getting Around in Photoshop Elements 2 2

2 Getting Started with Color Management 26

3 Basic Image Editing Techniques 38

4 Image and Color Correction Techniques 58

5 Fine-Tuning and Repairing Images 80

6 Correcting Images of People 94

7 Combining Images and Creating Panoramas 116

8 Creating Animation 138

9 Adding Filters and Effects 152

10 Typing Text and Adding Text Effects 166

11 Creating Custom Graphics and Using Layers
and Brushes 182

12 Publishing to the Web and Printing 206

A Installing Photoshop Elements 2 228

B Command and Tool Matrix 232

C Supported File Formats 242

Glossary 246

Index 254

Contents

Introduction 1

1 Getting Around in Photoshop Elements 2 3

How to Create a New Document .4

How to Browse Files 6

How to Navigate and View a Document 8

How to Acquire Images 10

How to Grab a Frame of Video 12

How to Use Help 14

How to Use the Work Area .16

How to Set Preferences 18

How to Copy and Paste Images 22

How to Use File Options 24

2 Getting Started with Color Management 27

How to Use the Adobe Gamma Control Panel 28

How to Use Color Management 32

How to Work with Color Spaces 34

How to Change Image Modes 36

3 Basic Image Editing Techniques 39

How to Select Pixels 40

How to Create a Mask 42

How to Resize an Image 44

How to Crop an Image 46

How to Work with Layers 48

How to Remove Objects 50

How to Scale an Image 52

How to Straighten an Image .54

How to Enhance Perspective 56

4 Image and Color Correction Techniques 59

How to Correct Tonal Range 60

How to Adjust Brightness and Contrast 62

How to Brighten or Darken an Image 64

How to Use Color Variations 66

How to Correct Color 68

How to Remove a Color Cast .72

How to Use Adjustment Layers 74

How to Quick Fix Images 78

5 Fine-Tuning and Repairing Images 81

How to Salvage a Portion of an Image 82

How to Remove Glare from Glass 84

How to Warm Up Lighting 86

How to Repair Torn Areas 88

How to Remove Scratches, Mold, and Stains 90

How to Replace Missing Areas 92

6 Correcting Images of People 95

How to Fix a Smile 96

How to Remove Red Eye 98

How to Change a Hair Style .100

How to Remove Blemishes 102

How to Counteract Aging in a Subject 104

How to Change Facial Expressions 106

How to Modify Eyes, Nose, and Mouth 108

How to Reshape a Physique .110

How to Construct a Portrait .112

**7 Combining Images and Creating
    Panoramas 117**

How to Create a Composite .118

How to Organize Layers 120

How to Transform Selections .122

How to Fine Tune Composites 124

How to Create a Reflection 126

How to Select Photos for Panoramas 128

How to Create an Outdoor Panorama 130

How to Create an Indoor Panorama 132

How to Manually Arrange Photos 134

8 Creating Animation .139

How to Pick Images for Animation 140

How to Create Animation Frames 142

How to Preview Animation 144

How to Animate People 146

How to Animate Shapes 150

9 Adding Filters and Effects 153

How to Apply a Filter or Effect 154

How to Use the Liquify Filter 156

How to Add Clouds 158

How to Apply Artistic Filters 160

How to Apply Destructive Filters .162

How to Add Lighting Effects 164

10 Typing Text and Adding Text Effects 167

How to Add Text to an Image 168

How to Create a Type Mask 170

How to Modify Text 172

How to Combine an Image with Text 174

How to Warp Text 176

How to Create Text Effects 180

11 Creating Custom Graphics and Using Layers and Brushes 183

How to Use Brush Tools 184

How to Apply the Shape Tools 188

How to Blend Graphics with Images 190

How to Create a Web Button 192

How to Change the Welcome Screen 194

How to Apply a Pattern 196

How to Add a Picture Frame Effect 198

How to Use Layer Style Commands 200

How to Create Custom Brushes 202

How to Create a Pattern 204

12 Publishing to the Web and Printing 207

How to Send a Photo in Email .208

How to Optimize an Image 210

How to Choose a File Format 212

How to Create a Web Photo Album 214

How to Create a Slideshow 218

How to Print a Picture Package 220

How to Print a Contact Sheet 224

How to Resize a Photo to Fit on a Page 226

A Installing Photoshop Elements 2 228

Macintosh System Requirements 229

Windows System Requirements .229

Installing Photoshop Elements 230

B Command and Tool Matrix 232

Toolbox Tools 233

The Shortcuts Bar 234

Menu Commands 236

C Supported File Formats 242

File Formats for the Web 243

Supported File Formats 244

Glossary 246

Index 254

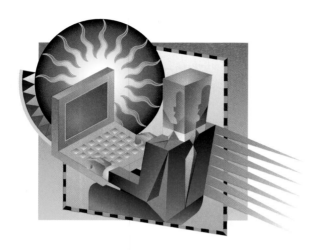

About the Author

Lisa Lee is the author of several best-selling computer books about Adobe Photoshop Elements, Adobe Photoshop, and Macintosh computers. She has written more than a thousand online tutorials about digital cameras, computers, handhelds, and multimedia applications. Her writing efforts are especially tailored to beginners and intermediate computer users.

When she's not authoring books, Lisa works at Microsoft as a software test engineer. She has more than ten years of experience developing hardware and software products for Macintosh and Windows computers. When she's not working, she is an amateur photographer, artist, musician, and Web designer.

Dedication

*This book is dedicated to
Jenna Kiyoko Lee.*

Acknowledgements

Thanks to all my fellow photographers who contributed to this book. Laura and Jason Lee, Sairam Suresh, Neal Tucker, and Julie Ann Lee, this book wouldn't be the same without your photos. Thanks for your photo permissions! Also, thanks to Marta Justak for being a wonderful agent.

A big thank you to the super, fantastic team at Que Publishing for being so helpful and for helping me put together such a great book. Thanks to Laura Norman, Nick Goetz, Candy Hall, Alice Martina Smith, Elizabeth Bulger, Elizabeth Finney, and Betsy Brown for all your awesome skills and team work. Finally, thanks to all the folks at Que who helped put this book together to get it out into the world.

We Want to Hear from You!

As the reader of this book, *you* are our most important critic and commentator. We value your opinion and want to know what we're doing right, what we could do better, what areas you'd like to see us publish in, and any other words of wisdom you're willing to pass our way.

You can email or write me directly to let me know what you did or didn't like about this book—as well as what we can do to make our books stronger.

Please note that I cannot help you with technical problems related to the topic of this book, and that because of the high volume of mail I receive, I might not be able to reply to every message.

When you write, please be sure to include this book's title and author as well as your name and phone or email address. I will carefully review your comments and share them with the author and editors who worked on the book.

Email: feedback@quepublishing.com

Mail: Mark Taber
          Associate Publisher
          Que/Sams Publishing
          201 West 103rd Street
          Indianapolis, IN 46290 USA

Reader Services

For more information about this book or others from Que Publishing, visit our Web site at www.quepublishing.com. Type the ISBN (excluding hyphens) or the title of the book in the **Search** box to find the book you're looking for or to download the image files shown in this book.

The Complete Visual Reference

Each part of this book is made up of a series of short, instructional tasks, designed to help you understand all the information you need to get the most out of your computer hardware and software.

 Click: Click the left mouse button once.

 Double-click: Click the left mouse button twice in rapid succession.

 Right-click: Click the right mouse button once.

 Drag: Click and hold the left mouse button, position the mouse pointer, and release.

 Pointer Arrow: Highlights an item on the screen you need to point to or focus on in the step or task.

 **Selection:** Highlights the area onscreen discussed in the step or task.

 Type: Click once where indicated and begin typing to enter your text or data.

 **Drag and Drop:** Point to the starting place or object. Hold down the mouse button (right or left per instructions), move the mouse to the new location, and then release the button.

Each task includes a series of easy-to-understand steps designed to guide you through the procedure.

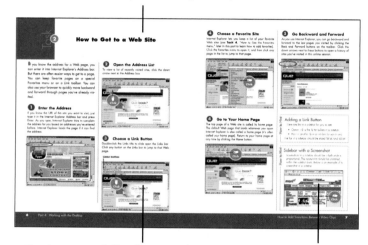

Each step is fully illustrated to show you how it looks onscreen.

Extra hints that tell you how to accomplish a goal are provided in most tasks.

 Key icons: Clearly indicate which key combinations to use.

Menus and items you click are shown in **bold**. Words in *italic* are defined in more detail in the glossary. Information you type is in a `special font`.

Introduction

Photoshop Elements 2 is the latest version of Adobe's popular, affordable image-editing software adapted from Photoshop. Photoshop Elements 2 is available in retail stores as well as bundled with digital cameras, scanners, and printers. You can also try a 30-day free trial that you can download from Adobe's Web site, `http://www.adobe.com`.

Photoshop Elements 2 has several new additions since the 1.0 release. In addition to an updated look and support for Mac OS X and Windows XP, it has a new Selection Brush tool, Quick Fix window, support for the JPEG 2000 file format, and a new, easy-to-use File Browser window.

Photoshop Elements 2 also has the same great tools that were in the previous version. The Red Eye Brush tool, originally introduced with version 1.0, is also in version 2.0. The panorama-creating Photomerge command has been updated, as has the Liquify and the Web Photo Gallery commands. You can download recipes from Adobe's Web site and access solutions for common issues from the newly designed Welcome window, too!

Although Photoshop Elements isn't as powerful as Photoshop, it contains most of the tools you'll need to perform a broad range of photo-editing tasks, such as removing red eye, correcting color, applying special effects, and preparing an image for the Web or print. What's most important, Photoshop Elements enables you to apply many of the same top-notch photo-editing techniques that make Photoshop so popular.

How to Use Photoshop Elements 2 is designed for use with version 2.0 of the program. However, most of the features in version 2.0 work nearly the same in version 1.0. Although this book doesn't come with a CD-ROM filled with the sample images used in the tasks in this book, you can follow along with the steps in each task by downloading images from `http://www.flatfishfactory.com/pse2home`. You can also download images from the Que Publishing Web site at `http://www.quepublishing.com`. Type this book's ISBN number (`0789728036`) into the **Search** field to locate the files. Then download the files to your computer.

You can go through this book sequentially from beginning to end, or find the tasks that are interesting to you and walk through each one step by step. The tasks in the first parts introduce you to the basic features in Photoshop Elements; everything that follows builds on tasks from previous parts.

As you spend time working with digital images, you'll find that some tasks are extremely easy, and others seem impossible. If you're not working with damaged images and simply want to print or publish a photo as is, jump to the task you're interested in to get fairly quick results using Photoshop Elements. On the other hand, you can spend an extraordinarily long time working on a digital image if you want perfection. Working with color and creating high-resolution images is a tedious task. If you don't get the results you're expecting the first time, be patient and try again, or try a different approach to solving the problem.

One way to improve your skills as a photographer is to join a photography club or participate in photography contests. Working with an online or local community will introduce you to other photographers and provide an education on a wide range of photography topics—along with critical feedback on your work. Visit `http://www.photo.net` or `http://www.psa-photo.org` to find out more about photography. Adobe's Web site is also a great resource for learning more about digital photography. Visit `http://www.adobe.com/photoshopel` and join the Photoshop Elements forum to participate in Photoshop Elements discussion topics.

May your digital photo adventures with Photoshop Elements be fun-filled and enjoyable!

① How to Create a New Document 4

② How to Browse Files 6

③ How to Navigate and View a Document 8

④ How to Acquire Images 10

⑤ How to Grab a Frame of Video 12

⑥ How to Use Help 14

⑦ How to Use the Work Area 16

⑧ How to Set Preferences 18

⑨ How to Copy and Paste Images 22

⑩ How to Use File Options 24

Task

Getting Around in Photoshop Elements 2

When you launch Photoshop Elements, it greets you with the **Welcome** screen. In addition to giving you one-click access to common issues and tutorials, the **Welcome** screen offers you three ways to open a document: You can create your own new, blank document, you can open an existing image file, or you can connect to and download an image from a camera or scanner. Opening a document, or *image window*, enables you to view a digital photo in the work area.

After you open a document, you can select a tool, palette, or command in the work area. The *work area* consists of the document window and all the palettes, toolbars, menus, and tools in Photoshop Elements. The work area is where you open images and perform digital magic.

The tasks in this part of the book show you how to use the **Welcome** screen, view documents, capture a frame of video, and use help. It also provides a brief tour of the Photoshop Elements work area, preferences, copy and paste commands, and file options.

How to Create a New Document

Images, graphics, and text are viewed and stored in an image window in the Photoshop Elements work area. This task shows you all the options available for creating a new, blank document. You start with a new document to create a photo montage, to work with custom graphics or text, or to use as a scratch pad to store interesting photo snippets.

1 Start on the Welcome Screen

The **Welcome** screen is the first window you'll see when you start Photoshop Elements. (If you have closed the Welcome screen, choose **Welcome** from the **Window** menu to open it.) To open the **New** dialog box, click the **New File** button in the **Welcome** screen.

2 Name the Document

In the **New** dialog box that opens, type the name you want to give to the new document into the **Name** field.

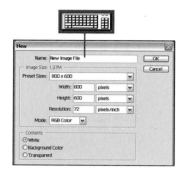

3 Set the Image Size

Click the **Preset Sizes** drop-down menu and choose a size from the list. The file size for the new document appears in the **Image Size** field of the **New** dialog box. If the size you require is not listed as a preset, type a value in the **Width** and **Height** text boxes.

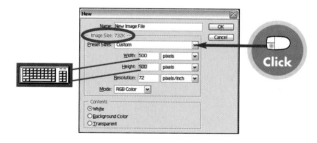

④ Set the Resolution

Type **72** (pixels per inch) in the **Resolution** text box to create a Web-ready image. Type **300**, **600**, or a higher number in the text box to create a document you want to print. (**Mode** settings are discussed in Part 2, "Getting Started with Color Management." **Resolution** settings are covered in Part 3, "Basic Image Editing Techniques.")

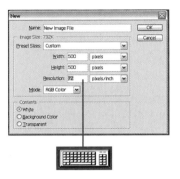

⑤ Select a Color Mode

The *color mode* determines how many colors the new document will support. Choose **RGB Color** from the **Mode** drop-down list to work with a full-color image. Choose **Grayscale** to work with 256 shades of gray. (**Bitmap** image mode supports only black and white.)

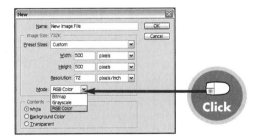

⑥ Choose Background Contents

The radio buttons in the **Contents** area determine what your document will initially display. Choose **White** to add a white background color. Choose **Background Color** to add a custom color. Select the **Transparent** radio button to exclude a background. Click **OK**. A new, blank document will open.

How-to Hint

Welcome Screen Options

Enable the **Show this screen at startup** check box in the **Welcome** screen if you want the Welcome screen to appear every time you start Photoshop Elements. Disable this check box if you do not want the **Welcome** screen to greet you so that you can go directly to the work area.

What Is Resolution?

300 dpi is a resolution supported by most printers. Some printers can print higher-quality images, such as 600 or 1200 dpi. On the other hand, if you're designing photos for the Web, you'll want to use a screen resolution of 72 pixels per inch (ppi). In the Photoshop Elements **Image Size** dialog box, the **Pixels/Inch** setting in the **Resolution** field is synonymous with dpi.

How to Browse Files

The **File Browser** dialog box enables you to preview thumbnail images of a directory of files. This can help you quickly find the image you want to open without having to open every file in a folder. You can customize the size of the thumbnails, rotate, move, and rename files from the File Browser, too.

① Open the File Browser

The **Welcome** screen is the first window you'll see when you start Photoshop Elements. (If you closed the Welcome screen, choose **Welcome** from the **Window** menu to open it.) To open the **File Browser** dialog box, click the **Browse for File** button in the **Welcome** screen. You can also choose **File**, **Browse** or click the **Browse** button in the shortcuts bar.

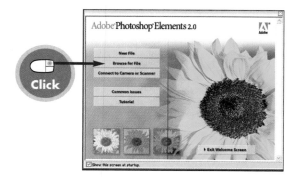

② Browse Folders and Files

View folders on your hard drive in the top-left pane of the File Browser. Click a folder to preview thumbnails of the files stored in that folder on the right side of the dialog box. Click a thumbnail to view details in the lower-left pane of the File Browser.

③ Change Thumbnail View

Click the **left drop-down** menu at the bottom of the File Browser to choose the sort order of the files. Click the **right drop-down** menu to select a thumbnail size (select **Small**, **Medium**, **Large**, or **Details**). Click the **scroll bar** area to view the different thumbnail images in a directory. Click a **thumbnail** to select it.

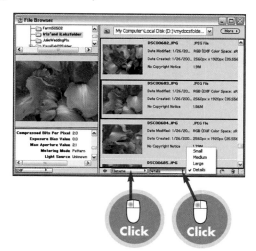

4 Rotate a Thumbnail

To change the orientation of an image, select an image in the File Browser and then click the **Rotate** button located at the bottom of the dialog box. The thumbnail rotates clockwise in the File Browser.

Click

How-to Hint

Organizing Files from the File Browser

You can move and rename files using the File Browser. Click and drag a thumbnail to a folder to move that image file to a new location. To rename a file, click the **filename** of a thumbnail. Wait for the highlight to appear over the filename. Type a new name or click to change the location of the cursor in the filename. Press **Enter** or **Return** to save the new filename.

5 Open Multiple Files

Hold the **Ctrl** key (the ⌘ key in Mac) and click to select two or more images in the **File Browser** window. Double-click one of the selected thumbnail images to open all selected images.

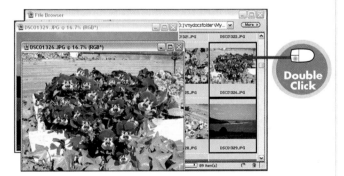

Double Click

How to Navigate and View a Document

Being able to adjust the view of an image and to view document information as you work enables you to know exactly what kind of digital image you're working with. You can use the **Navigator** palette to customize the view of the image window. You can also view or customize the information that appears in the image window and status bar, such as the image dimensions and image mode.

1 Open the Navigator Palette

Choose **Window, Navigator** to open the **Navigator** palette. Click and drag the **slider** control to zoom into or out of the document. Click the box in the **lower-left** corner of the palette and type a number to change the image window to a specific view percentage.

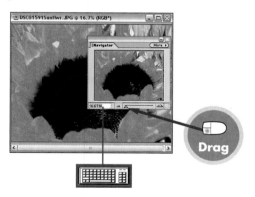

2 Navigate the Document

Click and drag the **slider** control in the lower-right corner of the palette to the **right** to **zoom into** the image window. Drag the slider control to the **left** to **zoom out**. The area within the **red square** (called the *view box*) represents what you see in the image window. Click and drag the view box to navigate the photo in the image window.

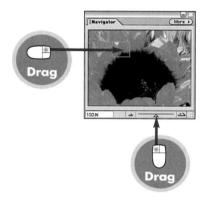

3 Change the Document View

Click the **text box** in the lower-left corner of the image window. Type a number between 1 and 999. Press **Enter** or **Return** to change the view of the image window to the specified percentage.

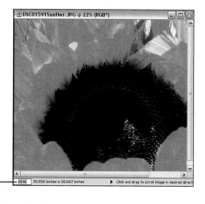

4 Display Document Information

Click the **arrow button** in the status bar to view a list of options that Photoshop Elements can display in the status bar for your convenience. You can display information about **Document Sizes**, **Document Profile**, **Document Dimensions, Scratch Sizes, Efficiency, Timing**, or the **Current Tool** in the status bar.

5 View Document Information

Click and hold the mouse button on the information located in the status bar. Information about the **width**, **height**, **channels**, and **resolution** of the current image appears in the pop-up box.

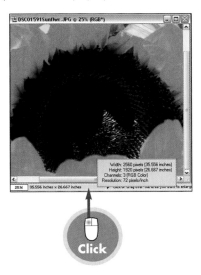

How-to Hint

Zoom Buttons

To the left and right of the slider control in the **Navigator** palette are the **Zoom Out** and **Zoom In** buttons. Click either button to zoom into or out of the red view box.

Previewing Images with the Open Dialog Box

Select **Open** from the shortcuts bar, or choose **File**, **Open** to access the **Open** window. Alternatively, press **Ctrl+O** (**⌘+O** in Mac) to open the selected image. If you select an image file in the **Open** dialog box, a preview image appears at the bottom of the dialog box. See Task 7, "How to Use the Work Area," for more information about the layout of the work area.

How to Acquire Images

Most digital cameras and scanners have a USB or serial port that enables you to connect the device to a computer. If the camera or scanner has TWAIN plug-in software, you can use Photoshop Elements to control the scanner or camera and bring digital photos directly into the work area. Before you begin this task, you must install the software for the scanner or digital camera onto your computer.

① View Import Sources

The **Welcome** screen is the first window you see when you start Photoshop Elements. (If you closed the **Welcome** screen, choose **Welcome** from the **Window** menu to open it.) Click the **Connect to Camera or Scanner** button from the **Welcome** screen. The **Select Import Source** dialog box opens. You can also choose **File**, **Import** to select a camera or scanner device.

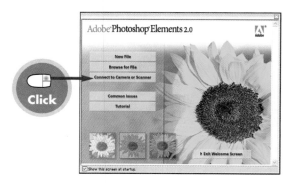

② Select a Device

Choose the name of the digital camera or scanner device from the **Import** drop-down list. The software for the selected device opens in the work area. You must close the software window for the camera or scanner before you can access any other tools or commands in Photoshop Elements.

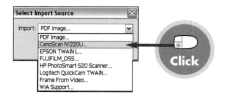

③ Preview Images

For scanners, you can click the **Preview** button to view the scanned image before running the final scan. The scanner will send a preview image to your computer. If you have a digital camera, use the device's software to preview photos stored in the camera.

④ Crop Images

Some devices have software tools that enable you to crop to the exact area of the image you want to scan. In this example, click the **Selection** tool and drag it over the preview image to select the area you want to scan. You can adjust the size of the selection area by dragging the sides of the selection marquee.

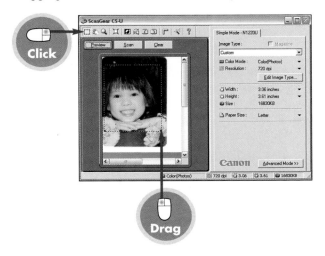

⑥ Save the File

Each scanned image or photo downloaded from a scanner or camera appears in a separate image window in the work area. Select each image window and then click the **Save** button in the shortcuts bar to open the **Save** dialog box. Type a filename and click **Save** to store the file on your hard drive.

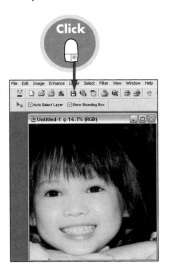

⑤ Scan an Image

Click the **Scan** button to download the digital data into Photoshop Elements. If you have a digital camera, click **Download** to send selected files from the camera to your computer.

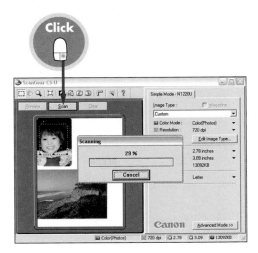

How-to Hint

Viewing Camera Settings

EXIF (**Exchangeable Image File**) is the file format digital cameras use to store the camera settings required to create digital image files. You can view EXIF information by selecting a photo in the **File Browser** dialog box. You can also open a photo and choose **File, File Info** to open the **File Info** dialog box. Choose **EXIF** from the **Section** drop-down menu to view the image description. Use EXIF information to see the file format the original image was captured in, any color profile information used to create the photo, as well as camera settings. You can use the color profile information in the EXIF data to adjust the color settings on your computer, enabling Photoshop Elements to more accurately work with color if you modify the photo.

How to Grab a Frame of Video

You can create digital video with a digital camcorder, VHS tape, or other analog video media. Each video file contains frames of video that range in size from 320×240 to 640×480 pixels. The **File**, **Import** menu enables you to capture a frame of video from a QuickTime or Windows Media Player file.

① Choose Frame From Video Command

Click the **File** menu, select **Import**, and then choose the **Frame From Video** command. The **Frame From Video** dialog box opens.

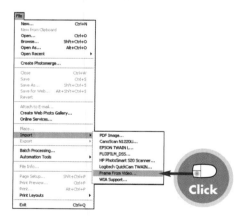

② Select a Video File

Click the **Browse** button. The **Open** dialog box appears. Navigate to the hard drive and select a **QuickTime** or **Windows Media Player** file. Select a file and click **Open**.

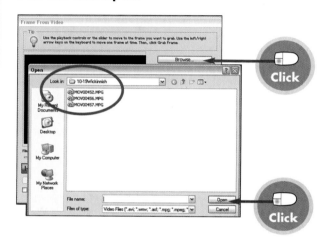

③ View Video Information

The first frame of the selected video appears in the center of the **Frame From Video** dialog box. Just below the video, you can find the filename, elapsed time, and duration of the video.

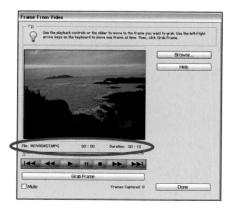

④ Preview Video Footage

Click the **Play** button to watch the video. Click the **Rewind** or **Fast Forward** button to navigate the video. When you get to the area you want to capture, click **Pause** and press the **left** and **right arrow keys** on your keyboard to step frame-by-frame through the video.

⑤ Capture a Frame of Video

Click **Grab Frame** to capture the frame of video displayed in the dialog box. Navigate to another frame of video and click **Grab Frame** again. You can capture as many frames of video as your computer's disk drive and memory can hold.

⑥ Save the Video Frame

Click **Done** to exit the **Frame From Video** dialog box and return to the work area. An image window is created for each frame of video captured. Click the **Save** button in the shortcuts bar and type a filename for the video frame in the **Save As** dialog box. Choose a file format and click **Save**.

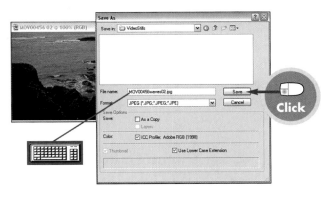

How-to Hint

Tips for Grabbing Frames

You can click **Grab Frame** while the video is stopped or while it is playing in the **Frame From Video** dialog box. Enable the **Mute** check box if you do not want to listen to the audio portion of the video.

Video Image Quality

Digital cameras can capture images with resolutions from one to six megapixels (from 1024x768 to 2000x1500 pixels). Digital camera files tend to be larger and of higher quality than a single frame of video stored in a Windows Media Player or QuickTime file.

How to Use Help

To find out more about a menu command, palette, tool, or particular preference setting, you can use the Photoshop Elements help system. You can view Help topics in a Web browser or in the work area. Common help issues can also be viewed in the **How To** palette.

① Choose Common Issues

The **Welcome** screen is the first window you see when you start Photoshop Elements. (If you have closed the **Welcome** screen, choose **Welcome** from the **Window** menu to open it.) Click the **Common Issues** button from the **Welcome** screen. Photoshop Elements opens the **How To** palette. Alternatively, you can choose **Window**, **How To** and select **Common Issues** from the drop-down menu.

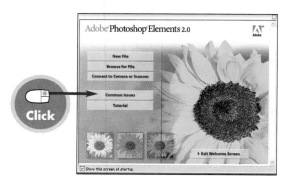

② View Common Issues

A list of common issues appears in the **How To** palette. Click an **issue** to view more information about that topic in the **How To** palette. Click the **Close** box in the upper-right corner of the palette to return the palette to the palette well.

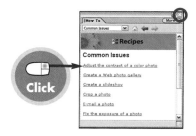

③ Navigate Help Topics

To access another form of assistance, choose **Photoshop Elements Help** from the **Help** menu. Adobe's help system for Photoshop Elements opens in a browser window. Click a help topic in the left pane; the information appears in the right pane of the browser window. Choose **File**, **Quit** to exit the browser.

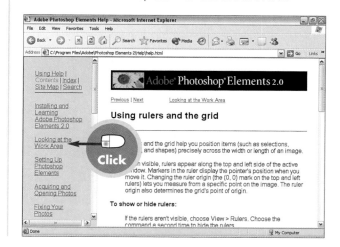

4 Search Help and Hints

To access yet another form of help, type a word or words in the **Search** text box in the shortcuts bar and click **Search**. The search results appear in a separate window. Browser-based help is identified with a square-shaped, checkmark icon. Hints are identified with a question mark icon. Double-click an item in the **Search Results** window to read the help information.

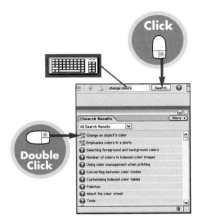

5 Contact Adobe Support

Click the **sunflower** button at the top of the toolbox. Windows machines open the **Adobe** Web page, which you can navigate for additional help. Macs open the **Adobe Online** dialog box, from which you can download updates and help information.

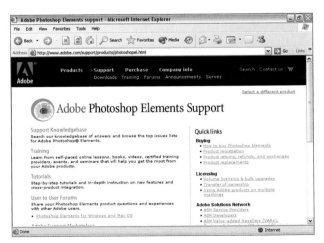

How-to Hint

More Help Online

Can't find what you're looking for in the built-in tutorials and help? Adobe sponsors a user forum for Photoshop Elements. Go to **http://www. adobeforums.com** to log in as a registered user or guest. The user forum enables you to post your question to the Photoshop Elements community and view questions and answers from fellow users.

How to Use the Work Area

Close the **Welcome** screen to enter the work area. The work area consists of the menu bar, any open palette windows, the toolbox, and the toolbar (the toolbar combines the shortcuts bar and the options bar). You create new documents, open existing image files, acquire images, and perform photo magic in the work area.

1 Access Menu Commands

Click a **menu name** to open its menu list. Then drag the cursor and select a **menu command**. Some menu commands perform a task; others open a dialog box.

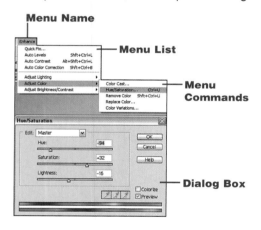

2 Use Shortcuts

The shortcuts bar appears immediately below the menu bar and contains a set of buttons you can use to quickly access a command. Use the shortcuts bar to access Adobe's online Web site or to perform some of the **File** menu commands (such as Open, Browse, Import, and so on).

3 Open and Close Palettes

On the right side of the work area, click a **tab** to open a palette. Click and drag a **palette** tab to convert it to a floating window. Click the palette's **Close** box to return it to the *palette well*. Click the drop-down arrow at the top of the palette to view the palette menu.

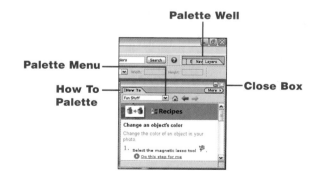

④ Navigate Palettes

Click the **More** button at the top-right of the palette to view a custom drop-down menu. Drag the **Grow box** in the lower-right corner of the palette to resize the palette. Some palettes contain drop-down menus and buttons located at the top or bottom of the palette.

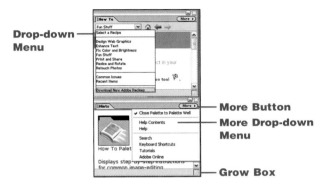

Drop-down Menu

More Button

More Drop-down Menu

Grow Box

⑤ Apply a Tool

The toolbox displays 24 tools out of a total of 40 tools. Click and hold the mouse on a tool with a triangle in the corner to view and select other related tools. Click and drag the mouse in the image window to apply the tool.

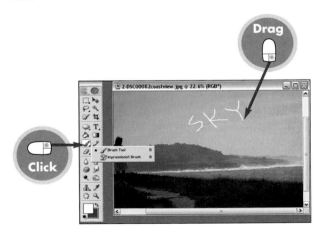

Drag

Click

⑥ Adjust Tool Options

Each tool in the toolbox has its own set of options located in the **options bar**. Type in a text box, click a drop-down list, or click a button to view additional settings for that tool in the options bar. The settings you choose remain selected and apply to that tool until you change them.

Selected Tool

Additional Options

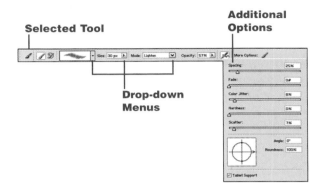

Drop-down Menus

Viewing ToolTips

You can view a ToolTip by holding the mouse pointer over a toolbox tool, shortcut, or toolbar button.

Combining Palettes

Drag and drop one palette onto another to force more than one palette to share the same window. Remember that each palette is unique; most palettes have settings located at the top and bottom of the window and a **More** button pop-up menu.

How-to Hint

How to Set Preferences

Customizing preferences enables you to streamline some of your work processes. The **Preferences** dialog box consists of eight Preferences panels: **General**, **Saving Files**, **Display & Cursors**, **Transparency**, **Units & Rulers**, **Grid**, **Plug-ins & Scratch Disks**, and **Memory & Image Cache**. Any changes you make to the preferences become the default settings in Photoshop Elements. You might find that the factory default settings work just great, but I highly recommend that you experiment with the options.

1 Choose the Preferences Command

Select the **Edit**, **Preferences**, **General** command from the menu bar at the top of the Photoshop Elements screen. The **Preferences** dialog box opens to the **General** panel.

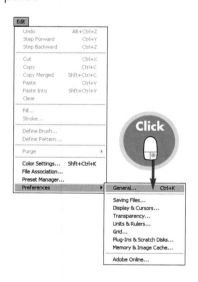

2 Choose a Screen

The name of the current panel appears at the top-left of the dialog box. Click the drop-down menu and select another panel name to open the selected panel. You can access all eight Preferences panels from this drop-down menu.

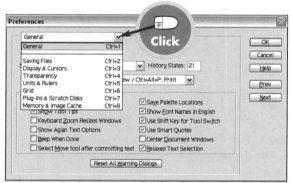

3 Set General Preferences

Click a **drop-down menu** to choose a new setting. Click a **check box** to change an option. Click **Next** to move to the next panel in the Preferences dialog box.

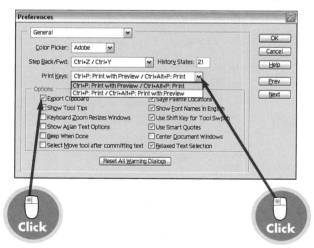

4 Set File-Saving Options

In the **Saving Files** panel, click the **Image Previews** drop-down menu and select **Ask When Saving**, **Always Save**, or **Never Save** to decide how image previews (thumbnails) are saved with a file. Choose whether to use uppercase or lowercase file extension names.

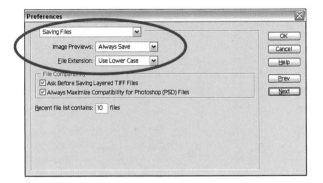

5 Set File Compatibility Options

Still in the **Saving Files** panel, select one or both of the **File Compatibility** check boxes. Type a number into the **Recent file list contains** text box to specify how many files appear in the **File**, **Open Recent** menu. Click **Next**.

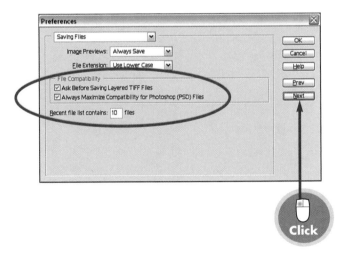

6 Set Display & Cursor Options

In the **Display & Cursors** panel, enable the **Use Pixel Doubling** check box for faster screen display. Choose **Standard**, **Precise**, or **Brush Size** to set the Painting Cursors option. Set **Other Cursors** to **Standard** or **Precise** mode. Click **Next** to move to the next panel in the Preferences dialog box.

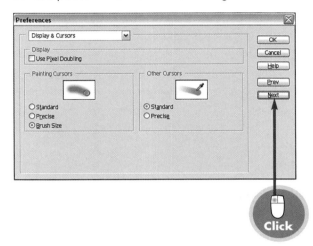

7 Set Transparency Options

In the **Transparency** panel, click the **Grid Size** and **Grid Colors** drop-down menus to customize the settings for transparency options. You can see the results in the preview pane on the right side of the dialog box. Click **Next** to move to the next panel.

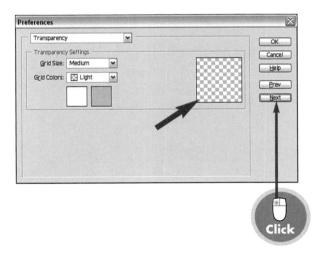

8 Set Units and Column Size

In the **Units & Rulers** panel, choose the unit you want to use for both **Rulers** and **Type** (inches, pixels, centimeters, millimeters, points, picas, or percent). Use the **Column Size** area to customize the **Width** and **Gutter** settings for your documents.

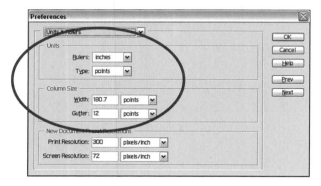

9 Adjust Preset Resolutions

Still in the **Units & Rulers** panel, modify the preset print and screen resolutions for a new document in the **New Document Preset Resolutions** area. Click **Next** to move to the next panel.

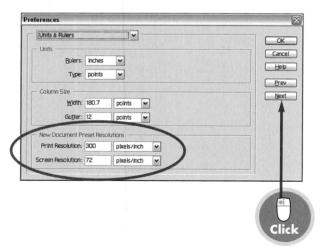

10 Select Grid Settings

The *grid* is used to help align objects in a document. In the **Grid** panel, click the **Color**, **Style**, or **Gridline every** drop-down menu, or type a number in the **Subdivisions** text box to set the grid preferences. Click **Next**.

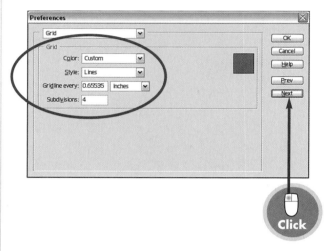

11 Choose Plug-in Settings

By default, Photoshop Elements looks in its program folder for plug-ins. If you have other plug-ins installed elsewhere on your computer, open the **Preferences** dialog box to the **Plug-Ins & Scratch Disks** panel, enable the **Additional Plug-Ins Directory** check box, click **Choose**, and locate the folder in which the plug-ins are located.

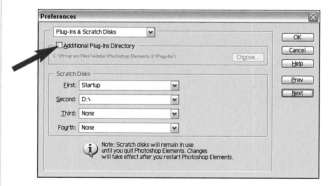

12 — Customize Scratch Disks

Still in the **Plug-Ins & Scratch Disks** panel, set scratch disk preferences in the **Scratch Disks** area. Photoshop Elements uses one or more scratch disks to keep track of the images you're working on. Click a drop-down menu to set the order in which each disk will be used. Click **Next**.

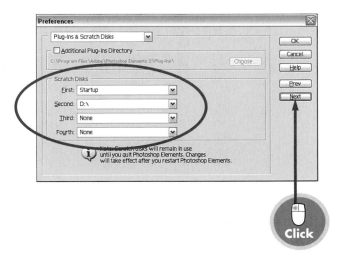

13 — Set Memory & Image Cache Options

In the **Memory & Image Cache** panel, set the number of **Cache Levels** by typing a number in the text box. Type a number in the **Maximum Used by Photoshop Elements** box to set the memory usage. Click **Next**.

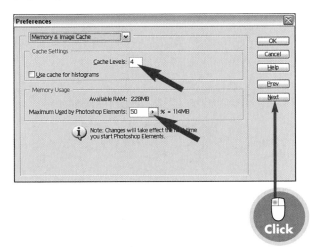

14 — Save Preferences

Click **OK** in the Preferences dialog box to save your changes. Note that you must exit Photoshop Elements and restart the program before the options you set will take effect.

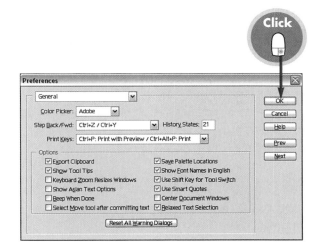

How-to Hint

Rebuilding Preferences

Hold down the **Shift+Ctrl+Alt** keys (**Shift+⌘+Option** keys in Mac) when you start Photoshop Elements; a dialog box appears asking whether you want to rebuild the preferences file. Click **OK** and your preferences settings file will be rebuilt. This keyboard command enables you to remove any previous preference settings you may have chosen, reverting all preferences to a first-time run of Photoshop Elements. If you want to restore the original palette settings, choose **Window**, **Reset Palette Locations**. The keyboard shortcut does not reset palette options.

Default Warning Settings

If you want to return all warning dialog boxes to their original settings, click the **Reset All Warning Dialogs** button in the **General** panel of the **Preferences** dialog box.

How to Copy and Paste Images

Creating a new document and opening an existing one are two ways to open an image file. The third method uses the Clipboard to store an image file. In this task, you copy and paste an image into a new document to experiment with different commands and tool settings.

1 Select an Image

Select **Open** from the shortcuts bar and open an image file. Choose a selection tool and click and drag it in the image window to select part of the image.

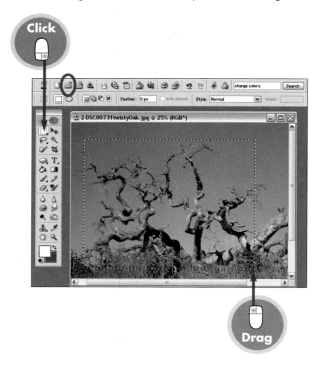

2 Copy the Image

Select **Edit**, **Copy** or press **Ctrl+C** (⌘**+C** for Mac users) to move the selected portion of the image to the Clipboard.

3 Paste in Current Document

To paste the contents of the Clipboard into the same document, select **Edit**, **Paste** or press **Ctrl+V** (⌘**+V** for Mac users). The contents of the Clipboard are inserted in a separate layer in the active image window.

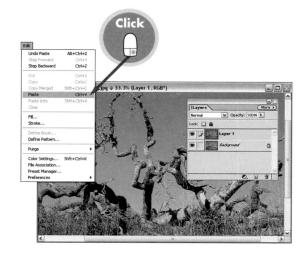

④ Paste Into a New Document

To paste the contents of the Clipboard into a brand-new document, choose **File**, **New from Clipboard**. Wait for Photoshop Elements to paste the copied image into a new window.

⑤ View the Image

A new, empty document window will open in the work area. Select the new document window. View the contents in the new image window. Here you can see the original image in the background window and the cropped and copied version in the foreground window.

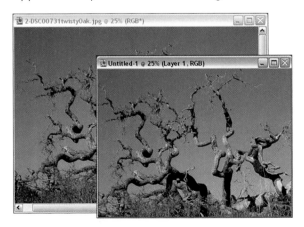

⑥ Save the Image

Choose **File**, **Save** to save the copied image in its current file. If you are saving a new document, the **Save As** dialog box opens. Type a name into the **File name** text box and click **Save**.

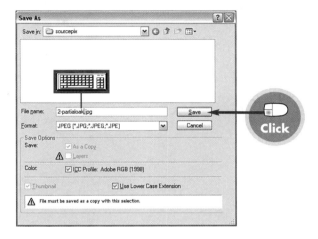

How-to Hint

Viewing the Mac Clipboard

On a Mac, you can view the contents of the Clipboard by going to the **Finder** and choosing **Edit**, **Show Clipboard**. Windows does not have an equivalent command.

How to Use File Options

File options enable you to preserve your changes to a file or save a copy of the original file before modifying it. There are fifteen different file formats to choose from; the option you choose depends on what you want to do with the image file and what applications you want to use to modify it.

1 Open an Image File

Choose **File**, **Open** and select an image file, click the **Open** button in the shortcuts bar and select an image file, or create a new document and import an image or apply the drawing tools to the document window.

2 Choose File, Save As

To access the various file formats, choose **File**, **Save As**. The **Save As** dialog box opens.

3 Name the File

Click the **Save in** drop-down menu at the top of the **Save As** dialog box and locate a folder in which you want to save the file. Type a name for the file in the **File name** text box.

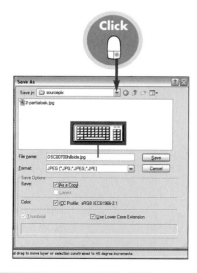

4 Select File Options

Choose a file format from the **Format** drop-down menu. Choose **JPEG** or **TIFF** if you want to compress the file. Choose **TIFF**, **PSD**, or **PDF** if you want to preserve layers within the files. For more information about file formats, see Appendix C.

5 Adjust JPEG Options

Click the **Save** button to save the file to your hard drive. If you selected the **JPEG** file format, you have additional options: In the **JPEG Options** dialog box, type a higher number into the **Quality** text box to set the quality of the JPEG file. Then click **OK** to save the file.

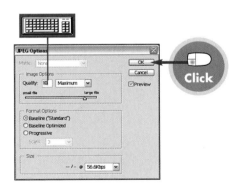

6 Adjust TIFF Options

If you selected the **TIFF** file format, the **TIFF Options** dialog box opens so that you can adjust several file options. Click an **Image Compression** radio button to choose a compression option. Click **IBM PC** or **Macintosh** to set the Byte Order of the file. If the image contains layers, choose one of the three layer compression methods.

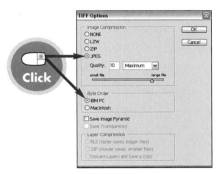

How-to Hint

Opening Files and File Associations

Windows users can set specific image file types to open automatically in Photoshop Elements 2. For example, you can choose to have JPEG, PSD, bitmap, or TIFF images open in Photoshop Elements when you double-click their file icons. Open an **Explorer** window and choose **Tools, Folder Options**. If you have Windows XP, choose **File Associations** from the **Edit** menu. Enable the check box for any file types you want to associate with Photoshop Elements.

Task

① How to Use the Adobe Gamma Control Panel 28

② How to Use Color Management 32

③ How to Work with Color Spaces 34

④ How to Change Image Modes 36

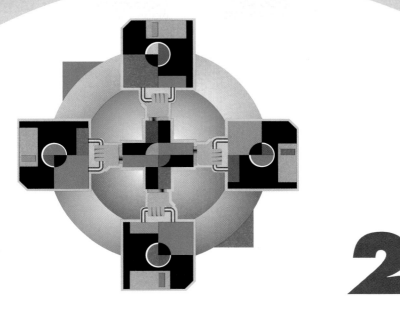

2

Getting Started with Color Management

Even if you see a perfect picture on your computer, there's no guarantee that it will look great when it prints or is viewed on a different computer. Why is color different when you see it on a screen than it is on a piece of a paper? The main reason is that computers process color differently for a monitor than they do for other peripherals, such as printers and scanners.

Digital cameras, scanners, and printers—as well as Macintosh and Windows computers—capture, display, and process colors in different ways. Color management is one way to minimize the differences between all these color systems. The tasks in this part show you how to calibrate colors for your computer, monitor, and printer; how to work with image modes and resolutions; and how to adjust settings in the Adobe Gamma control panel.

How to Use the Adobe Gamma Control Panel

Adobe installs the *Adobe Gamma control panel* in the Control Panel folder of your Windows or Mac OS 9 computer. This tool enables you to create an International Color Consortium (ICC) profile that is compatible with *ICM 2.0* for Windows or Apple *ColorSync* for Macintosh computers. Color profiles help translate color values between computers, printers, and cameras. Mac OS X users must use the **Display Calibrator** program in the **Utility** folder to calibrate color settings.

① Open the Control Panel

For best results, allow your monitor to warm up for at least 30 minutes before beginning this task. For Windows, begin the process of calibrating your monitor by clicking **Start** and selecting **Control Panel**, **Adobe Gamma**. For Mac OS 9, select the **Apple** menu, **Control Panels**, **Adobe Gamma**.

② Choose Step-by-Step

In the **Adobe Gamma** dialog box that opens, enable the **Step-by-Step** radio button and click **Next**. The wizard will suggest the best option as you navigate each page.

③ Choose a Color Profile

The **sRGB color profile** is the default profile selected in the wizard. You can modify an existing profile or create a new one. Type in the **Description** field to create a custom color profile. To choose a different profile, one more appropriate for your monitor type, click the **Load** button and choose a color profile. Click **Next**.

④ Adjust Monitor Settings

Adjust the monitor's settings (usually found at the bottom or under the edge of the monitor) to adjust the **brightness** and **contrast** of your computer screen as directed by the onscreen instructions. Click **Next**.

⑤ Select a Monitor Profile

The monitor profile listed in the **Phosphors** field identifies the type of monitor that will be used with the profile. Click the **Phosphors** drop-down menu to view a list of profile options and select the appropriate profile (if you know what it is). Click **Next** to continue.

⑥ Adjust Gamma Settings

Choose **Windows Default** or **Macintosh Default** from the **Gamma** drop-down menu. Click **Next**.

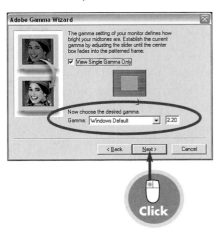

⑦ Set the White Point

Choose **6500 degrees Kelvin** from the **Hardware White Point** drop-down menu. 6500 degrees Kelvin is generally the optimal setting to make the white point of the screen work best with printed output. Click **Next**.

8 Set Adjusted White Point

Select **Same as Hardware** from the **Adjusted White Point** drop-down list. This option enables you to select a different white point setting without changing the previous settings for the color profile. Click **Next**.

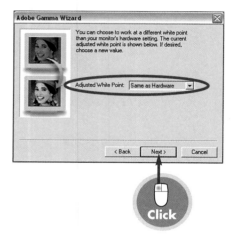

9 Finish the Wizard

Click the **After** radio button and look at the sample on the left side of the wizard and compare it with the **Before** sample. If you're satisfied with the color improvements, click the **Finish** button. In the **Save As** dialog box that opens, type a name for the color profile you've just created and click **Save**.

10 Start the Display Calibrator

For Mac OS X, double-click the **hard drive** icon on the desktop. Click the **Application** icon and then double-click the **Utility** folder. Double-click the **Display Calibrator** icon. The **Display Calibrator** application opens.

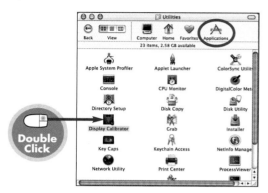

11 Set the Gamma

Click the **Right Arrow** button at the bottom of the screen until the **Select a target gamma** screen appears. Click the **1.8 Standard Gamma** radio button.

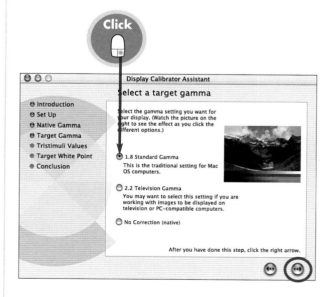

12 Set the White Point

Click the **Right Arrow** button at the bottom of the screen until the **Select a target white point** screen appears. Click **D65** as the white point setting you want to use. D65 represents 6500 degrees Kelvin, the same white point value selected in the Adobe Gamma control panel in step 7.

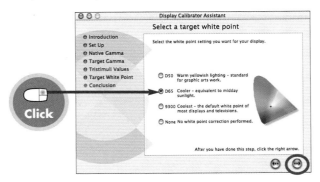

13 Exit the Display Calibrator

Click the **Right Arrow** button at the bottom of the screen until you get to the conclusion screen. In the text box, type a name for the profile you have just created and click **Create**.

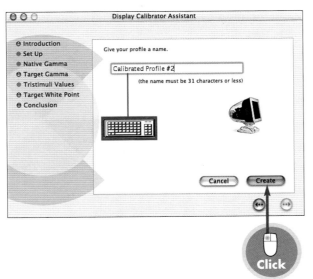

How-to Hint

Why Is Color Important?

Calibrating color enables you to create a color profile. The profile information enables your computer to translate color information between the monitor and the printer connected to your computer. It also enables you to more accurately correct colors and tweak images.

A color profile defines how color data is stored for the display and print devices connected to your computer. Creating a color profile involves identifying the type of monitor and printer connected to your computer.

How to Use Color Management

Color management settings enable you to save color profile information within an image file. You can choose color management settings when you are saving and printing your image files. Photoshop Elements lets you choose one of three options: limited, full, or no color management.

① Open Color Settings

In either Windows or Mac, choose **Edit**, **Color Settings** to open the **Color Settings** dialog box. Enable a radio button in the **Color Settings** window to select a color management setting for your image files.

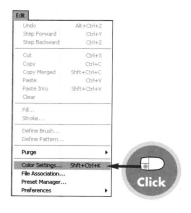

② Choose a Color Management Setting

If you want to preserve all color management data when you use the **File**, **Save** command, enable the **Full color management** radio button and then click **OK**.

③ Open an Image File

Click the **Open** button in the shortcuts bar. Select an image file from the **Open** dialog box to open that image.

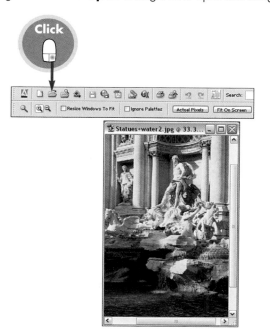

4 Choose the Save As Command

Click the **File** menu and choose the **Save As** command. The **Save As** dialog box opens.

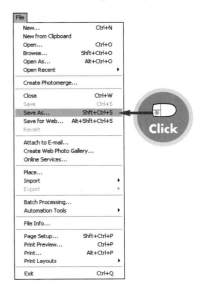

5 Choose Color Management Option

In the **Save As** dialog box, enable the **ICC Profile: Adobe RGB (1998)** check box to save that color profile when you save the image file. If you don't select the **ICC Profile** check box, the file will be saved without a color profile.

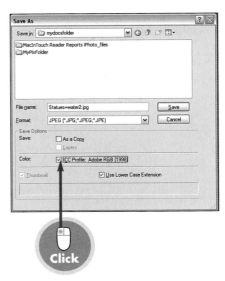

6 Save or Print a File

Type a new name for the file in the **File name** field. Navigate to the folder where you want to save the image file and then click **Save**.

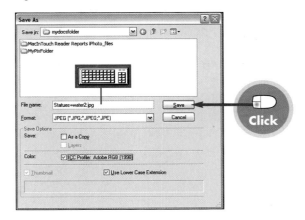

How-to Hint

Color Profiles and Image Files

When you open a color image, Photoshop Elements sets the image to the **Full color management** mode, regardless of the color setting you've selected. To save any other color profile with the image, you must choose the **Save As** command from the **File** menu as directed in steps 5 and 6.

sRGB Color Profile

If you select the **Limited color management** option in the **Color Settings** dialog box, the **sRGB Color Space Profile** color profile is used when you choose the **File**, **Save** or **Save As** command. Choosing **Full color management** configures Photoshop Elements to use the Adobe RGB color profile.

How to Work with Color Spaces

How do computer devices know what's red or blue? They use a *color space*, such as hue, saturation, and brightness (HSB) or red, green, and blue (RGB). Printers, for example, use the cyan, magenta, yellow, and black (CMYK) color space, also known as a *subtractive* color space, to create colors. Monitors, on the other hand, use an *additive* color space, such as red, green, and blue (RGB) to create the full spectrum of colors.

① Work with RGB Color Settings

Open an image file that you want to use to experiment with colors. Choose **Enhance**, **Adjust Color**, **Color Variations**. The **Color Variations** window opens. Follow the steps onscreen to see how the picture will look if you increase or decrease the red, green, or blue color level in the image. Click **OK** to accept these changes.

② Work with HSB Color Settings

Select the **Enhance**, **Adjust Color**, **Hue/Saturation** menu command to open the **Hue/Saturation** dialog box. Drag the sliders in this dialog box to adjust the **Hue** (tint), **Saturation** (intensity), and **Lightness** of the colors in the selected image window. Click **OK** to save your changes.

③ Open the Color Picker

Click the **foreground** color located at the bottom of the toolbox. The **Color Picker** dialog box opens. Enable the **Only Web Colors** check box if you want the **Color Picker** to show only the Web-safe palette of 216 colors.

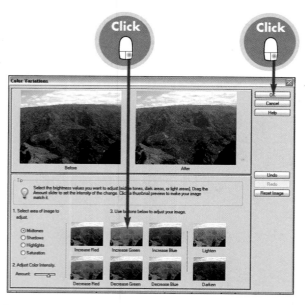

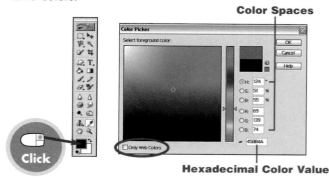

Color Spaces

Hexadecimal Color Value

4 Pick a New Color

Click a color in the **Select foreground color** area of the dialog box. The exact values of the selected color appear in the RGB and HSB text boxes. The newly selected color appears above the previous color in the dialog box. Click **OK** to accept the changes.

New Color

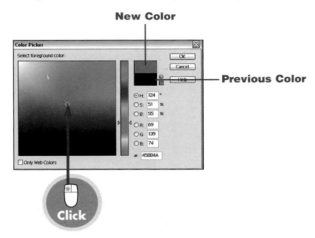

Previous Color

Click

5 View Settings in Info Palette

Click the **Info** tab in the palette well to open the **Info** palette. Select a color space from the **More** drop-down menu to choose the color readout information you want to appear in the palette. When you move the cursor over a color in an image window, its color values appear in the **Info** palette.

How-to Hint

Swapping Colors

Click the arrow icon just above the foreground and background colors in the toolbox. The foreground color moves to the background color square and vice versa. Alternatively, press the **X** key to swap the foreground and background colors. This shortcut key can come in handy if you're working with the eyedropper and want to keep or change the foreground or background color.

Additive and Subtractive Color Spaces

Printers use a *subtractive* color space to create colors. Subtractive color spaces include cyan, magenta, yellow and black (CMYK). To create additional colors, color values are subtracted. Photoshop Elements does not support the CMYK color space. Monitors use additive color spaces, such as red, green, and blue (RGB) to create color. For example, to create purple, red and blue are added together. Although the terms themselves don't affect your color space choices, they can help you understand why there are differences in colors on your various computer devices.

How to Change Image Modes

Photoshop Elements 2 supports four image modes: RGB Color, Indexed Color, Grayscale, and Bitmap. Each image mode determines how many colors, grays, or black and white appear in the selected image window. Choose RGB Color image mode if you're working with color images.

1 Choose RGB Color

Choose **File**, **Open** and open an image file. Choose **RGB Color** from the **Image**, **Mode** menu.

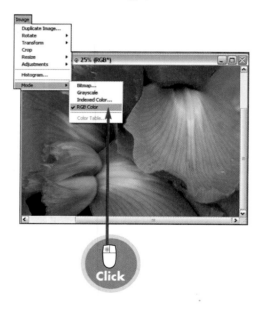

2 View Color Image

View the image in its new RGB color mode.

3 Select Indexed Color Mode

Choose **Indexed Color** from the **Image, Mode** menu. The **Indexed Color** dialog box opens. Choose **Local (Selective)** from the **Palette** drop-down menu and type **256** into the **Colors** text box. Click **OK**. Indexed Color mode preserves as much of the original color information in an image as it can while also reducing the file size of the image. You can use Indexed Color mode to reduce the file size and colors in an image. It's great for creating Web graphics and animation.

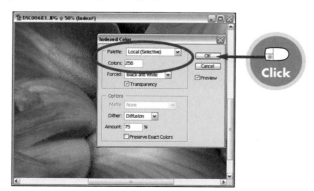

4 Choose Grayscale Mode

Choose **Grayscale** from the **Image, Mode** menu. Click **OK** in the **Discard Color Information** dialog box. When you apply the Grayscale image mode to a color image, it converts all color information to 255 shades of gray plus the color white. Grayscale mode is great if you're working with black-and-white images and don't want to save any color data with the image file.

5 Select Bitmap Mode

Choose **Bitmap** from the **Image, Mode** menu. The **Bitmap** dialog box opens. Type **72 pixels/inch** into the **Output** text box. Choose **Diffusion Dither** from the **Method** drop-down list and click **OK**.

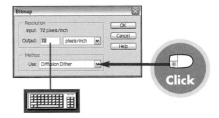

6 View Bitmap Image

Bitmap image mode supports only two colors: black and white. Bitmap mode is optimal for black-and-white graphics, text, and line art. Note that you must first convert a color image to Grayscale mode before you can convert it to Bitmap mode.

How-to Hint

Permanent Changes

One thing to keep in mind as you're experimenting with image modes: Selecting a new image mode for an image **permanently** changes the color—or lack of color—information available to an image file. You may want to save the original file with a different name before experimenting with image modes.

An Image Mode for Every Occasion

Most images open in Photoshop Elements to the appropriate image mode. Digital camera and color scanned images usually open in RGB Color mode.

No CMYK Support

Photoshop Elements does not support the cyan, magenta, yellow, and black (CMYK) color mode. This color mode is commonly used for printing color documents, books, and posters. Use Photoshop if you must print or convert RGB images into CMYK-compatible images.

① How to Select Pixels 40

② How to Create a Mask 42

③ How to Resize an Image 44

④ How to Crop an Image 46

⑤ How to Work with Layers 48

⑥ How to Remove Objects 50

⑦ How to Scale an Image 52

⑧ How to Straighten an Image 54

⑨ How to Enhance Perspective 56

Task

3

Basic Image Editing Techniques

With Photoshop Elements, you can change each pixel in a digital image. You can make grass greener, lighten or darken colors, rotate, grow, or shrink a selection, and so on. The downside is that each edit you make will remove some of the original colors or pixels. The key to productive image editing is to start with the clearest, best-quality image possible and master working with selection tools and layers.

You can use the selection tools such as the **Rectangular Marquee**, **Lasso**, **Magic Wand**, or **Selection Brush** to modify all or part of an image. You can modify a selection to add, change, or remove pixels from the selection area, enabling you to make precise edits to any photo. In addition to moving a selection, you can use the **Move** tool to grow, reduce, and rotate a selection in the image window. You can use the **Transform** commands to modify perspective, skew, or distort a selection.

Layers enable you to isolate image elements, combine images, correct color, and apply filters or effects to different parts of an image. The tasks in this part show you how to apply selection tools, work with layers, and apply automatic color correction commands. You will also learn how to scale, straighten, and work with perspectives.

How to Select Pixels

Selection tools enable you to choose a particular set of pixels in the image window. The **Marquee**, **Lasso**, **Magic Wand**, **Crop**, and **Selection Brush** tools enable you to create a selection area based on shape or color. This task shows you how to use the **Magnetic Lasso** tool.

① Open an Image File

Click the **Open** button from the shortcuts bar. Select a file that contains one or more objects and open the file.

② Choose a Selection Tool

Select the **Magnetic Lasso** tool from the toolbox. You might have to click the **Lasso** tool and choose the **Magnetic Lasso** tool from the pop-up menu.

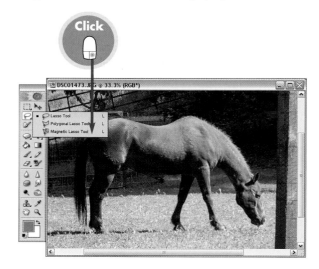

③ Define Selection Area

Click the edge of the object you want to select in the image window. Drag the mouse along the edge of the object. The **Magnetic Lasso** tool creates points to define the selection area based on the pixels located inside the selection area. You can click to create additional points to fine-tune the selection area.

4 Complete the Selection

Drag the mouse pointer around the object until you return to the first point, and then **double-click** the first point to complete the selection. The marching ants graphic appears to define the selected area.

5 Add to the Selection

Zoom into the edge of the selection area. Choose the **Selection Brush** tool and type a number into the **Size** text box in the options bar to specify a brush size (or use the default brush size). Hold down the **Shift** key and drag in an area of the image window that is not selected to increase the selection area.

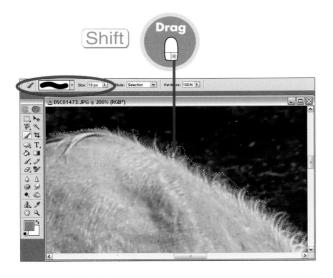

6 Delete from the Selection

Hold down the **Alt** key (the **Option** key for Mac users) and click and drag the mouse in the selection area to remove pixels you do not want selected. When you release the mouse button, the marching ants will redraw to show the new selection area.

How-to Hint

Marching Ants and Masks

The selected area of an image is surrounded by an animated set of dash-marks, also known as *marching ants*. The selected area can also be called a *mask*. The part of the image outside the selected area is protected; only the pixels within the selected area can be modified.

Selecting with Other Lasso Tools

The **Lasso** tool enables you to select pixels freehand: Just drag the mouse to define a selection area. The **Polygonal Lasso** tool enables you to define a selection area using straight lines: Each click generates a straight line between the points you've defined in the selection.

How to Create a Mask

You can use a mask to edit a specific part of an image. When you apply a selection tool to the image window, you create a mask. You can use a mask to work on an isolated part of an image, or move the masked area of the image to a new document.

1 Open an Image File

Click the **Open** button from the shortcuts bar. Select a file that contains one or more objects and open the file.

2 Choose a Selection Tool

Select the **Elliptical Marquee** tool from the toolbox.

3 Define the Masked Area

Click and drag the **Elliptical Marquee** tool in the image window to select an area. The pixels within the elliptical shape you dragged are the selected area, the masked area.

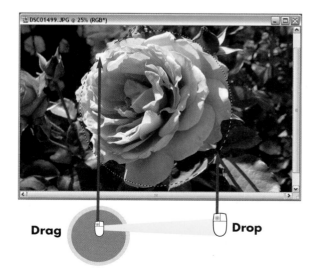

Drag   Drop

④ Remove Pixels from the Selection

Click the **Selection Brush** tool in the toolbox. To more closely follow the image outline, hold down the **Alt** key (the **Option** key for Mac users) and drag the tool to remove pixels from the selection.

⑥ Smooth Edges of Mask

Choose the **Feather** command from the **Select** menu. The **Feather** dialog box opens. Type a number into the text box to define the number of pixels that will be smoothed along the edge of the selection area and click **OK**. Copy and paste the selection into an image window to view the final mask.

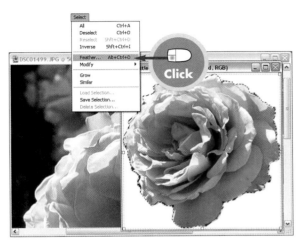

⑤ Add Pixels to the Selection

Click and drag the **Selection Brush** tool in the image window to adjust the selection outline to more closely follow the image outline by adding pixels to the selection area. Hold down the **Shift** key and click to select a straight line of pixels.

How-to Hint

More About Selection Tools

You can use any combination of selection tools to customize a selection area in the image window. Simply click a selection tool, hold down the **Shift** key, and select some pixels that aren't already selected. A plus symbol appears next to the mouse pointer as you add pixels this way. Similarly, hold down the **Alt** key (the **Option** key for Mac users) and click or drag to remove parts of a selection with the **Lasso**, **Magic Wand**, or **Selection Brush** tool. The mouse pointer shows a minus symbol as you remove pixels from the selection.

Deselecting Pixels

To remove the mask or cancel the current selection, choose the **Deselect** command from the **Select** menu or press **Ctrl+D** (⌘**+D** for Mac users).

How to Resize an Image

One of the more common tasks you'll perform on an image file is resizing it. You can resize an image by changing its dimensions or resolution settings. Decreasing the dimensions of an image creates a relatively high-quality image. After reducing the dimensions, you won't be able to modify the image or print it at larger dimensions. Increasing the dimensions of the image is not recommended; it "stretches" the existing pixels to fit in a larger space.

① Open an Image File

Click **Open** in the shortcuts bar. Select an RGB image file and open it.

② View Resolution

Click in the **status bar** located at the bottom of the image window to view the resolution of the image. The resolution of this image is 1800×1200 pixels.

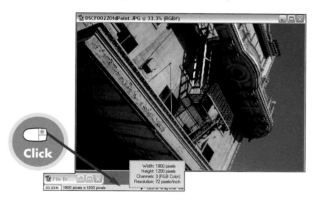

③ Copy the Image

Press **Ctrl+A** (⌘**+A** for Mac users) to select the entire image. Choose **Edit**, **Copy** to copy the image to the Clipboard. Select **File**, **New from Clipboard**. A second, duplicate image window appears in the work area.

4 Decrease Image Size

Select either image window by clicking in it. Choose **Image**, **Resize**, **Image Size** to open the **Image Size** dialog box. In the **Width** text box, type a number that's about half of the number that was originally in the text box (in this example, the value **800** is used as roughly half of the image's original dimension of 1800).

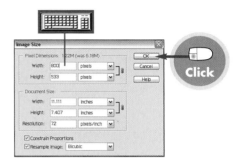

5 Compare Image Quality

Place the resized image window next to the original image window. Select the **Zoom** tool and magnify the resized image to match the general size of the original image. Note that the image quality of the smaller, resized image is worse than that of the original image when you zoom in.

Low-Resolution Image

High-Resolution Image

What's Resolution?

This task explains how you can change the resolution of an image by resizing it. You can also change the resolution of an image by changing the value in the **Resolution** field of the **Image Size** dialog box. For example, a 72 pixel per inch (ppi) image contains fewer pixels per inch than a 300 ppi image. The 300 ppi image will look sharper when you print it than the 72 ppi image.

This task explained how to resize images by specifying the width or height of the image in pixels. (Note that the width and height values are related; changing one changes the other—unless you want the image to be distorted.) If you're more comfortable working with inches than pixels or a specific resolution value, type those numbers in the appropriate text boxes in the **Document Size** area of the **Image Size** dialog box.

How to Crop an Image

With the **Crop** tool, you can preview and remove part of a photo. Cropping can come in handy when you want to change the composition of a photo to focus on a particular subject. Simply select the part of the photo you want to keep and press **Enter** or **Return**.

1 Open an Image File

Click the **Open** button in the shortcuts bar. Select a photo that contains a subject plus one or two additional objects and open the image file.

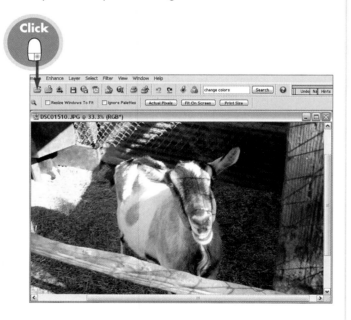

2 Select the Crop Tool

Click the **Crop** tool in the toolbox. In the options bar, click the **Front Image** button; the **Width**, **Height**, and **Resolution** text fields in the options bar are filled automatically with the dimensions of the image.

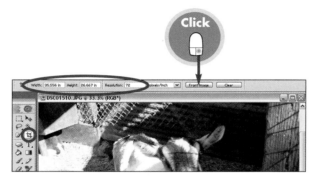

3 Select Part of the Image

Drag the **Crop** tool in the image window to select the portion of the image you want to keep. Marching ants surround the cropped area. Areas of the image window that will be removed as the result of the crop are shaded in gray.

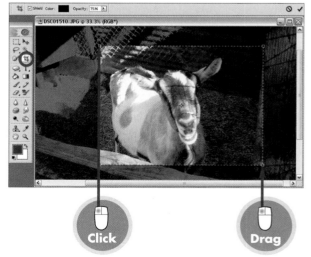

④ Resize the Cropped Area

Move the mouse pointer to one of the corners of the selected (cropped) area in the image window. Click and drag a **corner box** to resize the crop area. Alternatively, position the mouse pointer within the selected area and drag the entire selection to reposition the crop rectangle.

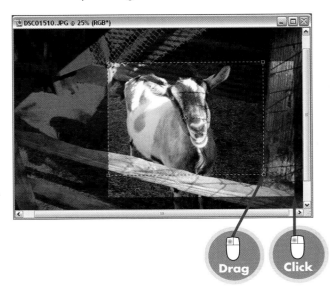

⑤ Rotate the Cropped Area

Click just outside a corner box and drag the mouse up or down to rotate the cropped area in the image window.

⑥ Crop the Image

Press **Enter** or **Return** or double-click inside the selection area to complete the crop. The selected portion of the image is resized in the image window; unselected areas are discarded.

How-to Hint

The Crop Menu Command

The **Crop** tool has a similarly named command in the **Image** menu. You can use any selection tool, such as the **Rectangular Marquee** or **Magnetic Lasso** tool, to select any part of an image. Then choose **Image**, **Crop**, and Photoshop Elements crops the image to the nearest rectangular shape based on the selection area.

Canceling a Crop

If you change your mind about a crop selection you've drawn, click the **Cancel** button (the circle–with–a–slash) in the options bar for the **Crop** tool or press the **Escape** key on your keyboard to cancel the cropping operation

How to Work with Layers

Layers enable you to make changes to the image while preserving the original image. Each layer is like a sheet of tracing paper placed over the original image. Changes you make to one layer can affect how the overall image appears, but you can select or change pixels only one layer at a time. If you want to work with text or graphics, combine images, or create composites, layers are essential. This task introduces you to the **Layers** palette.

1 Create a New Layer

Open an image file. Copy part of an image from another photo and paste it into the image window. Select the **Layers** palette from the palette well. Notice that a new layer, **Layer 1**—(containing the image you pasted)—appears in the **Layers** palette.

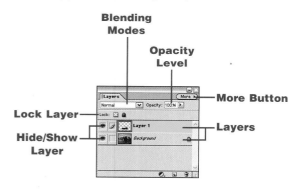

Blending Modes

Opacity Level

More Button

Lock Layer

Hide/Show Layer

Layers

2 Duplicate a Layer

Click a layer to select that layer in the image window. Use the buttons at the bottom of the **Layers** palette to create or delete a layer in the selected image window. Click and drag the layer over the **Create a new layer** button to duplicate the layer.

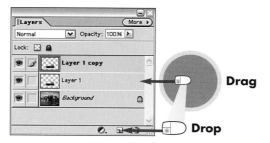

Drag

Drop

3 Decrease Opacity

Click the **Opacity** drop-down menu and drag the slider control to change the opacity value. The lower the value, the more you can see through the object in the selected layer to the layer beneath.

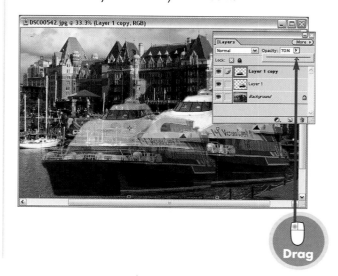

Drag

4 Move a Layer in the Layer Stack

Click a layer in the list of layers (the middle layer was selected in this example) and drag and drop it above the first layer in the list. The selected layer becomes the top layer in the image window. The image in the top-most layer covers (appears on top of) images in the lower layers.

5 Hide and Show Layers

Click the far left column in the **Layers** palette to hide or show that layer in the image window. Click the eye icon next to the layer tile to hide that layer. Click again in the blank to display the eye icon and show the contents of that layer in the image window.

6 Merge and Flatten Layers

Click the **More** button in the **Layers** palette. Choose the **Merge Down** command to combine the selected layer with the layer below it. You can choose the **Flatten Image** command to combine all visible layers into one layer. Hidden layers are discarded unless you choose the **Merge Visible** command.

How-to Hint

Copying a Layer

You can duplicate a layer by clicking and dragging it over the **Create a new layer** icon in the **Layers** palette. The duplicated layer appears in the **Layers** palette named as a *copy* of the original layer. Double-click the name of a layer and type to rename a layer. To delete a layer, drag the layer and drop it on the **Trash** icon in the **Layers** palette.

Back Up Before Flattening

When you apply the **Layer**, **Flatten Image** command to a multilayered image, all layers are merged into a single layer. Before you flatten the image, choose **File**, **Save As** and save the file as a Photoshop (PSD), TIFF, or PDF file to preserve the multiple layers (just in case).

How to Remove Objects

Some objects—such as a thumb, a tree, or a bush—might obstruct the subject of a photo. You might also want to remove man-made items such as signs, lights, or garbage from an image to clean up the composition. This task shows you how to use the **Clone Stamp** tool to remove small objects from an image.

① Open an Image File

Choose **Open** from the shortcuts bar. Select a photo that contains an object or two that you want to remove from the composition of the image and open the file.

② Zoom into the Image

Choose the **Zoom** tool and click the image to increase the magnification of the particular area you want to remove. Hold down the **Alt** key (the **Option** key for Mac users) and click to zoom out.

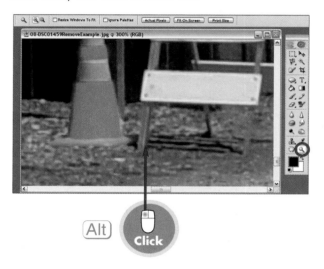

③ Select the Clone Stamp Tool

Select the **Clone Stamp** tool from the toolbox. In the options bar, choose a soft-edged brush. Click and drag the **Size** control slider to set the size of the brush. Enable the **Use All Layers** check box.

Clone Stamp Tool

Select a Brush Style

Use All Layers

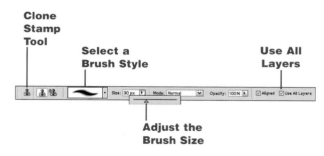

Adjust the Brush Size

4 Sample the Image

Hold down the **Alt** key (the **Option** key for Mac users) and click the **Clone Stamp** tool in the image window to sample the image. The area you sample should be a portion of the background that you can "duplicate" to cover over the offending portion of the image. Here the gravel area is sampled to help obscure the construction barrier and cone.

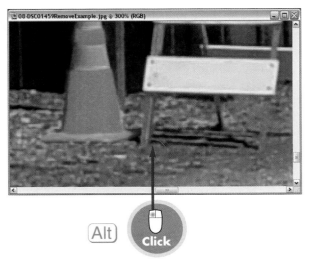

5 Apply the Sample

Drag the mouse in a new location to apply the sampled pixels to the image window. As you move the mouse, a cross-hair cursor appears in the location of the original sample. The cloned pixels duplicate any sampled pixels as you move the tool around the image window.

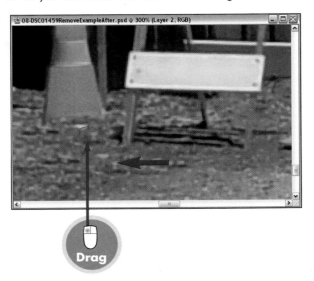

6 Remove the Objects

Apply the **Clone Stamp** tool until the entire object is removed from the image. In this example, the side of the barn was also sampled and cloned to help obscure the construction barrier and cone.

How-to Hint

Moving Instead of Removing

This task shows you how to use the **Clone Stamp** tool to remove pixels from a photo. An alternative way to remove objects from a photo is to apply a selection tool and select the part of the image you want to preserve. Then delete the rest of the photo, or copy and paste the selection into another image window.

Object Removal Check List

When you remove an object from an image, check the rest of the image for other areas that may have to change as a direct result of the removal. Look for reflections and colors that may have bounced off the object. You might want to create a short checklist of things to look for after removing unwanted pixels from an image.

How to Scale an Image

One way to add perspective to a photo is to make the subject larger. In this task, the selection and move tools are used to emphasize the subject and de-emphasize the background elements.

① Open a Photo

Click the **Open** button in the shortcuts bar. Open an image that contains at least two photo subjects.

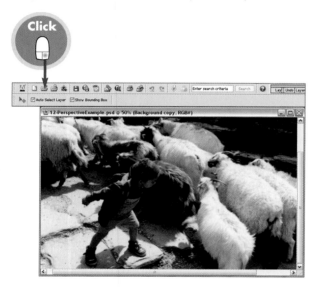

② Select the Subject

Click the **Magnetic Lasso** tool and drag to select the main subject of the photo.

③ Duplicate the Layers

Choose **Edit**, **Copy** and then choose **Edit**, **Paste** to duplicate the selection. The selection is pasted into the image on a separate layer. In the **Layers** palette, drag the **Background** layer and the layer with the pasted selection over the **Create a new layer** button to create a new layer with a copy of each of the original images.

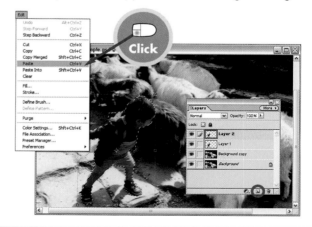

④ Delete the Subject

Hold the **Ctrl** key (the ⌘ key for Mac users) and click the layer that contains the subject. In the **Layers** palette, click the duplicate background layer (called **Background copy** in this example) to select it. Press **Backspace** (**Delete** for Mac users) to remove the subject from the background layer.

⑤ Grow the Selection

Select the layer that contains the duplicate subject from step 3. Click the **Move** tool. Click and drag a corner of the selected subject to grow the selection.

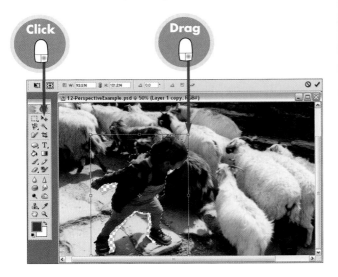

⑥ Blur Background Pixels

Blurring the background pixels makes the subject more prominent. Choose **Select**, **Inverse** to reverse the selection (so that everything *except* the subject is selected). Choose **Filter**, **Blur**, **Motion Blur** from the menu bar to display the **Motion Blur** dialog box. Type a number into the **Distance** text box and click **OK**. The larger the number, the blurrier the image will be.

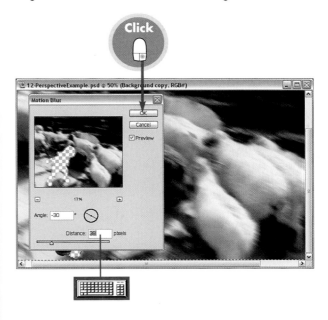

How-to Hint

What Is Pixelation?

As you increase the size of a selection, it loses image clarity. The resulting chunky, blocky look is called *pixelation*. To avoid pixelating an image, try not to grow a selection more than 10 to 20 percent of its original size.

Rulers and Grids

You can use rulers and grids to scale selections with more precision. To show the rulers in the image window, press **Ctrl+R** (**Option+R** for Mac users). To show the grid, choose **View**, **Grid**. **Ctrl**+click (⌘+click for Mac users) the layer that contains the subject. Select the **Move** tool and drag a corner to rotate the selection until a vertical or horizontal element in the subject matches the x or y axis of the grid or a background element in the photo.

How to Straighten an Image

Photoshop Elements 2 offers several ways to rotate and align an image. Tucked away in the **Image**, **Rotate** menu are several versions of the rotate command. Display the grid to help you line up a horizontal or vertical line in the image.

1 Open an Image

Click **Open** from the shortcuts bar. Select an image of a room, a building, or something that has an obvious horizontal or vertical edge. Open the file.

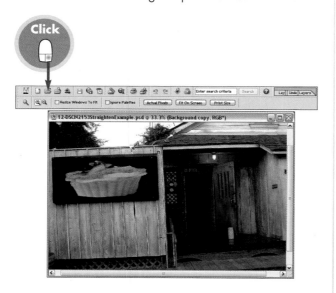

2 Display the Grid

Choose **Grid** from the **View** menu. Solid and dotted vertical and horizontal lines appear in the image window, on top of the image itself.

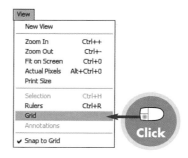

3 Duplicate the Background Layer

In the **Layers** palette, drag and drop the **Background** layer over the **Create a new layer** button to duplicate the background layer. You cannot modify the original background layer; duplicating this layer enables you to modify it. Select the duplicate layer (called **Background copy** by default).

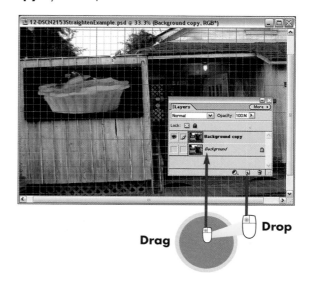

④ Choose Free Rotate

Choose **Free Rotate Layer** from the **Image**, **Rotate** menu. A rectangular box with corner and center handles appears around the selection.

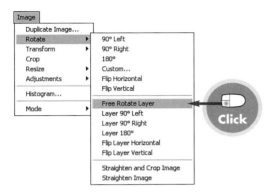

⑤ Rotate the Layer

Click a corner of the image area and drag down to rotate the image layer clockwise; drag up to rotate the image layer counterclockwise. When an important horizontal or vertical edge in the image aligns with one of the grid lines, click the **Check** button in the options bar to accept the changes.

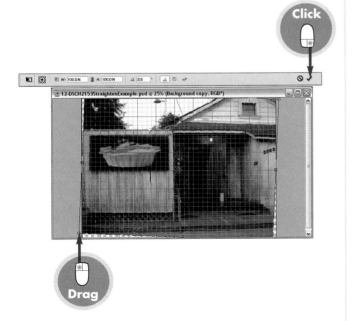

⑥ Check Alignment

Select the **Zoom** tool and click the image window to zoom into the image. The vertical lines of the image should parallel the Y axis of the grid; the horizontal lines of the image should parallel the X axis of the grid.

How-to Hint

Straighten Image Command

If you have a photo that was shot or scanned at an odd angle, choose the **Image**, **Rotate**, **Straighten Image** command to automatically rotate and straighten an image. This command works best if the canvas is larger than the image. This command takes a few minutes to complete. Watch the status bar at the bottom of the work area as this command runs through several automated tasks.

How to Enhance Perspective

You can duplicate and resize part of an image to enhance the size and scale of its subjects. Enhancing a photo can add a dramatic touch to a landscape or make the subject of a photo more prominent. This task shows you how to use the selection, duplicate layers, **Liquify**, and **Transform** commands to enhance perspective.

1 Open an Image

Click the **Open** button in the shortcuts bar. Select an image that contains foreground and background elements and open the file.

2 Choose the Liquify Command

Choose **Liquify** from the **Filters**, **Distort** menu. The **Liquify** window opens. The **Liquify** window contains several tools that enable you to stretch, move, and blur pixels.

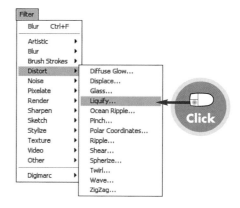

3 Apply the Warp Tool

From the left side of the **Liquify** window, select the **Warp** tool. Type a large number into the **Brush Size** text box. Click and drag using short, upward, staccato strokes to gradually stretch the pixels in the background of the image. In this example, the **Warp** tool turns the small hills into bigger hills.

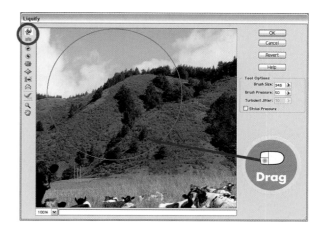

④ Apply the Bloat Tool

To make the foreground images larger, choose the **Bloat** tool. Specify an appropriate brush size by typing a number into the **Brush Size** text box (here, I use a brush big enough to encircle the cow's head). Click the subject to enlarge pixels. The longer you hold down the mouse button, the bigger the subject gets. Click **OK** to close the window and apply the effect.

⑤ Distort a Selection

Select a portion of the image and choose **Image**, **Transform**, **Distort**. Click a corner of the selection and drag it *away from the center* until the angle of the selection matches the background perspective. Select any corner and drag it in any direction to create a distortion. Click the **Check** button in the options bar when you are satisfied with the distortion.

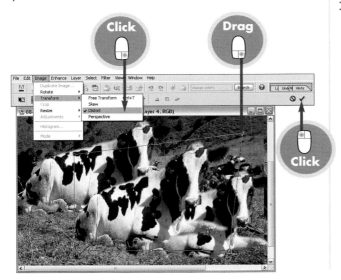

⑥ Skew the Perspective

Select a portion of the image and choose **Image**, **Transform**, **Skew**. Click a corner of the selection and drag it outward until the angle of the image matches the angle of other subjects in the photo. Select any corner and drag it to horizontally or vertically skew the image. Click the **Check** button in the options bar when you are satisfied with the skew.

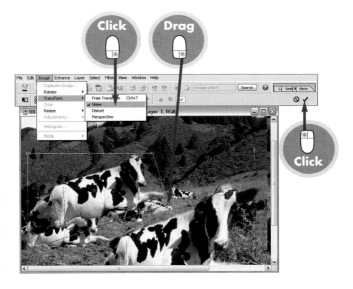

How-to Hint

Brush Skills and the Liquify Tools

When applying tools in the **Liquify** window, place the center of the brush over the area of the image you want to change. The outer edges of the brush produce slightly different effects than does the center of the brush. To experiment, choose a huge brush size (such as 75 or 150 pixels). Place the center of the brush over an image and click the mouse to see how the tool affects the pixels under the brush.

Growing Taller with Liquify

Perspective indicates how big an object is compared to other elements in a photo. If you want to make someone appear taller than other people in a photo, you can use the **Warp** tool in the **Liquify** window to stretch that person's legs or torso.

Task

1 How to Correct Tonal Range 60

2 How to Adjust Brightness and Contrast 62

3 How to Brighten or Darken an Image 64

4 How to Use Color Variations 66

5 How to Correct Color 68

6 How to Remove a Color Cast 72

7 How to Use Adjustment Layers 74

8 How to Quick Fix Images 78

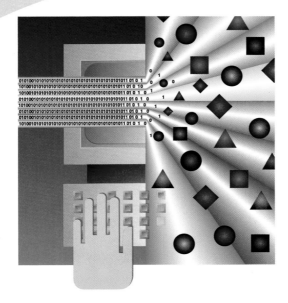

Image and Color Correction Techniques

4

If you work with images, you'll undoubtedly have issues with color. Colors might be faded, too bright, too dark, or slightly different than what you expected. The type of camera you use to take a photo, the settings you choose, and lighting conditions all play a part in creating the digital colors in a photo. There are several techniques, tools, and menu commands in Photoshop Elements that you can use to correct color problems. The automatic color correction commands are a speedy way to find out whether Photoshop Elements can fix a photo. Simply choose the menu command to see instant results.

If the color in an image can't be magically corrected with the automatic color correction commands, try one of the manual color corrections commands. The **Quick Fix** command provides a one-stop shopping dialog box for the most commonly used color correction tools. In addition, the **Color Variations** dialog box enables you to adjust color using a slightly different set of commands. The **Color Cast** command and the **Gradient**, **Levels**, and **Hue/Saturation** adjustment layers round out a powerhouse group of color correction commands for any digital image. The tasks in this part show you how to work with the **Fill Flash** and **Adjust Backlighting** commands. You will also find out how to adjust blacks, grays, and whites in images, and how to use the automatic and manual color correction commands.

How to Correct Tonal Range

Every photo has a *tonal range* of shadows, midtones, and highlights. Black, gray, and white are synonymous with *shadows, midtones,* and *highlights.* These values are built into each pixel and help determine the contrast levels in an image. The **Levels** command displays tonal range with a histogram graphic. The **Levels** command works with images in RGB, Indexed, and Grayscale color modes.

① Open an Image File

Click the **Open** button in the shortcuts bar. Select a photo that contains bright and dark areas and open the file.

② Select the Levels Command

Select the **Levels** command from the **Enhance, Adjust Brightness/Contrast** menu. The **Levels** dialog box opens.

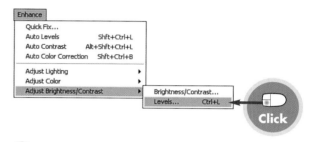

③ Adjust the Shadows

The histogram graphic shows the arrangement of tones in the image, with the dark tones on the left and the light tones on the right. Drag the left slider to the right to darken the shadow tones (the darker pixels) in the image. Move the slider arrow so that it points to the first row of pixels in the histogram.

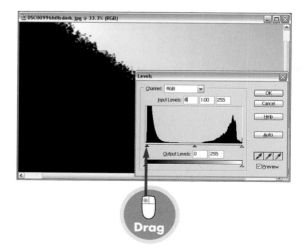

4 Adjust the Highlights

The right slider under the histogram controls the high-lights in the image (the lighter pixels). Click and drag the right slider to the left to make the image grow lighter.

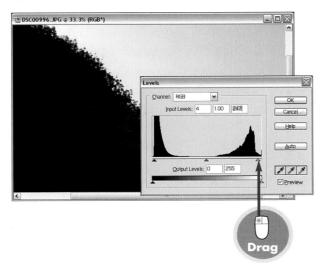

5 Change the Midtones

The slider in the middle of the histogram controls the midtones (the gray pixels, or the pixels in the middle of the color spectrum) of the image. Click and drag the middle slider to the left to lighten the midtones. Move the slider to the right to darken the midtones.

6 Set the Black Point

Hold down the **Alt** key (the **Option** key for Mac users) and click the left slider control. Notice that most of the colors in the image window disappear, leaving only the darkest pixels. These dark pixels are called the *black point*. Drag the slider to adjust the black point for the image. Repeat this step, clicking the right slider to adjust the *white point* (the lightest pixels) for the image.

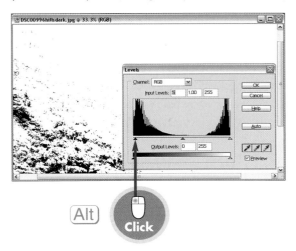

How-to Hint

Using the Eyedropper Tools

Use the eyedropper tools in the **Levels** dialog box to sample a specific pixel for the shadows, mid-tones, or highlights. Sampling pixels enables you to set accurate white and black points. Open the **Levels** dialog box and click the shadows, mid-tones, or highlights eyedropper. Click a pixel in the image window to adjust the tonal range. You can achieve some interesting color shifts in the image by sampling different areas of the image with the eye-dropper tools.

Adjusting the Output Settings

You can lighten the overall image by moving the shadow **Output** slider control (the left slider at the very bottom of the **Levels** dialog box) to the right. If the **Preview** check box is enabled, you can see the image change as you move the slider controls.

How to Adjust Brightness and Contrast

A common photo correction task is adjusting the contrast and brightness. Brightening an image involves reducing shadows and midtones and increasing highlights. Of course, you can also decrease the brightness of (or darken) an image. The *contrast* in an image is represented by the intensity of the darkest and lightest pixels in an image.

❶ Open an Image File

Click the **Open** button in the shortcuts bar. Select a file that contains both well-lit and shaded areas. Open the file.

❷ Select the Brightness/ Contrast Command

Choose the **Brightness/Contrast** command from the **Enhance**, **Adjust Brightness/Contrast** menu. The **Brightness/Contrast** dialog box opens.

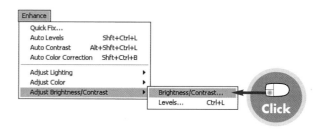

❸ Reduce Brightness

Click and drag the **Brightness** slider control to the left to decrease the brightness level in the image.

④ Increase Brightness

Drag the **Brightness** slider control to the right to increase the brightness level in the image.

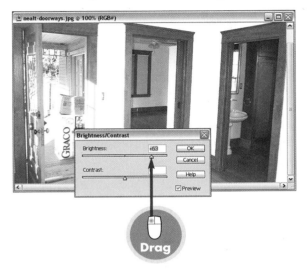

⑤ Increase Contrast

Drag the **Contrast** slider control to the right to increase the contrast level in the image. Increasing contrast tends to bring out the shadows and highlights in an image, while reducing the midtones.

⑥ Reduce Contrast

Drag the **Contrast** slider control to the left to decrease the contrast in the image. Decreasing the contrast tends to bring out the midtones in the image, while minimizing the highlights and shadows.

How-to Hint

Adjustment Layers

You can use adjustment layers to make color corrections without altering the original image, because the color adjustments are contained on a separate layer. Choose **Layer**, **New Adjustment Layer**, **Levels** or **Layer**, **New Adjustment Layer**, **Levels**, **Brightness and Contrast**. You can edit the adjustment layer at any time by double-clicking it in the **Layers** palette; you can discard the color adjustments on the layer by deleting the layer or turning off the visibility icon (the eye icon) for the adjustment layer. Task 7, "How to Use Adjustment Layers," later in this part explains how to use adjustment layers to adjust levels, hue/saturation, or add a gradient layer to an image.

How to Brighten or Darken an Image

Sometimes you can't avoid taking a picture where the light source is directly behind or above the subject of your photo, with the result that the foreground is too dark. The controls in the **Fill Flash** dialog box help you brighten photos taken in low light or lighten photos with dark foreground shadows. Conversely, you can use the **Adjust Backlight** command to darken the backlighting in an image, making the foreground appear brighter.

① Open an Image File

Click the **Open** button in the shortcuts bar. Choose an image that contains an under-lit subject in the foreground. Open the file.

② Choose the Fill Flash Command

Select **Enhance**, **Adjust Lighting**, **Fill Flash**. The **Adjust Fill Flash** dialog box opens.

③ Lighten Foreground Pixels

Drag the **Lighter** slider control to the right to lighten the pixels in the image window.

④ Adjust Saturation

Drag the **Saturation** slider control to the right to intensify the colors in the image window. Click **OK** when you are satisfied with the changes.

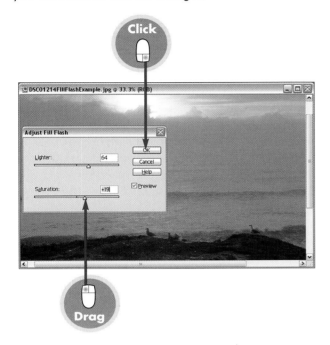

⑤ Choose the Adjust Backlighting Command

Open an image that contains a bright background light. Select **Enhance**, **Adjust Lighting**, **Adjust Backlighting**. The **Adjust Backlighting** dialog box opens.

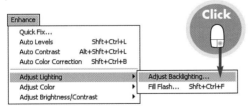

⑥ Increase the Darkness Level

Move the **Darker** slider control to the right to darken the pixels in the background of the image. Click **OK** to save your changes.

How-to Hint

Checking for Pixelation

As you lighten or darken an image, look for areas in which the pixels do not blend together with other colors. Some areas of color may stand out, causing pixilation. To avoid this, increase or decrease the lightness setting with the **Fill Flash** slider until the pixilated colors blend together with the rest of the image.

Alternative Tools

If the **Adjust Backlighting** tool doesn't have much of an effect on an image, try using the **Brightness/Contrast** and **Levels** commands, located in the **Enhance**, **Adjust Brightness/Contrast** menu. If there's a particular area of bright pixels in an image, select that area of the image and add a **Brightness/Contrast** adjustment layer to the image.

How to Use Color Variations

You can use the **Color Variations** dialog box to easily increase or decrease the amounts of red, green, and blue in an image by clicking thumbnails. You can apply color variations to an entire image or to just a selected area of the image.

1 Open a File

Click **Open** in the shortcuts bar. Open an image that contains dull or washed out colors.

2 Select a Portion of the Image

Click the **Magic Wand** tool in the toolbox. Click a washed-out color, such as the blue sky or an area of water, to select all pixels with that color. Hold down the **Shift** key and click other colors in the image window to add those colors to the selection area. Hold down the **Alt** key (the **Option** key for Mac users) and click to remove a color from the selection.

Click

3 Select Color Variations Command

Choose **Enhance**, **Adjust Color**, **Color Variations**. The **Color Variations** dialog box opens.

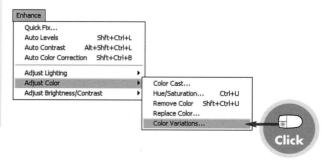

Click

④ Adjust Settings

Click the **Midtones** radio button to work with this tonal range. Drag the **Amount** slider control to the right to increase the amount of color that will change in the photo. The colored thumbnail images change as you move the slider control.

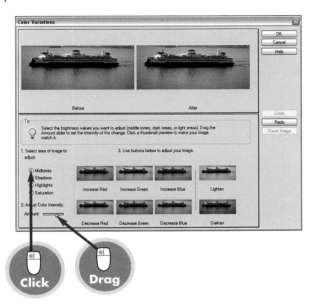

⑤ Increase a Color

Click the **Increase Blue** thumbnail to add blue to the selection in the image window. Look at the **Before** and **After** images at the top of the dialog box to see the change. Click any combination of **Increase** or **Decrease** thumbnails to modify the **After** image.

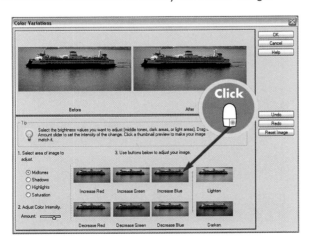

⑥ Darken Image

Click the **Darken** thumbnail to decrease the brightness level in the entire image. When you are satisfied with the adjustment you have made to the color in your image, click **OK** to save your changes.

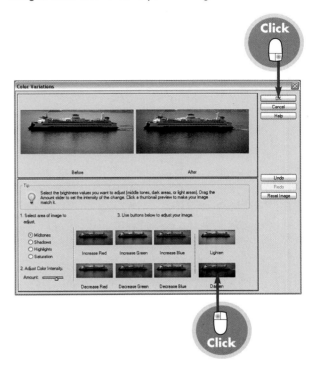

How-to Hint

Adjusting the Magic in the Magic Wand

You can adjust the range of colors the **Magic Wand** tool chooses by changing the **Tolerance** value in the options bar. Increase the value in the **Tolerance** text box to expand the color range of pixels selected by the **Magic Wand** tool. Conversely, decrease the tolerance value to select a smaller range of colors.

How to Correct Color

Get the best combination of colors in a photo by applying the automatic color correction commands. Then manually enhance colors with the **Hue/Saturation** command. For larger areas such as a sky, or ocean, add a Gradient adjustment layer to the photo to enhance colors. Intensify or reduce the amount of color in a small area of pixels by applying the **Dodge** and **Burn** tools.

1 Open a File

Choose **Open** from the shortcuts bar. Select an image that contains a landscape, flowers, trees, or other natural objects with subdued or faded color. Open the file.

2 Apply Auto Color Correction

Choose **Enhance**, **Auto Color Correction**. Photoshop Elements makes some automatic enhancements to the color in your image. Depending on the color in the original image, these automatic changes might be all you need.

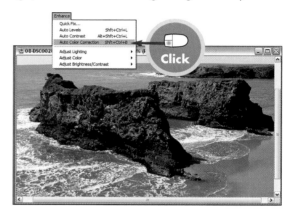

3 Apply Auto Contrast

Choose **Enhance**, **Auto Contrast**. You might see light colors become lighter, and dark colors become darker in your image. Depending on the contrast that existed in the original image, these automatic changes might be all you need.

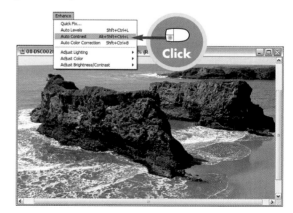

④ Apply Auto Levels

Choose **Enhance**, **Auto Levels**. Photoshop Elements automatically redistributes the tonal values (shadows, highlights, and midtones) in your image.

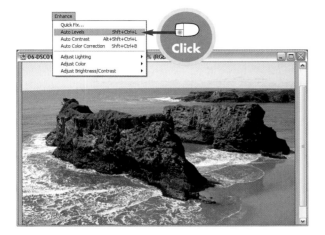

⑤ Choose Hue/Saturation Command

The auto adjustment commands are handy, but you might want more control over the changes made to your image. Open the **Layers** palette, click the **New fill or adjustment layer** button, and select **Hue/Saturation**. The **Hue/Saturation** dialog box opens as your first step in manually adjusting the image.

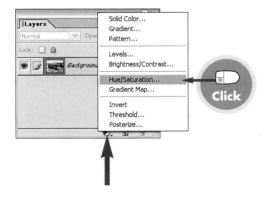

⑥ Adjust Hue and Saturation

Drag the **Hue** slider to the right to change colors. Drag the **Saturation** slider to the right to intensify the colors. Drag the **Lightness** slider to the right to lighten the entire image. Enable the **Preview** check box to preview your changes in the image window. Click **OK** when you are satisfied with the color adjustments.

⑦ Apply the Magic Wand Tool

Select the **Magic Wand** tool and select the background image in the **Layers** palette. Click a color in the image window, such as blue. Hold down the **Shift** key and click another color to select additional pixels; press the **Alt** key (the **Option** key for Mac users) to deselect a color. Here I select the sky in preparation for enhancing its color.

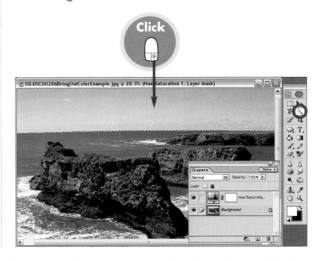

8 Create a Gradient Layer

In the **Layers** palette, click the **New fill and adjustment layer** icon and choose **Gradient**. The **Gradient Fill** dialog box opens.

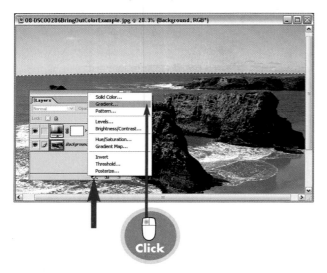

Click

9 Adjust Gradient

Click the **Gradient** color bar to open the **Gradient Editor** dialog box. A *gradient* blends two or more colors together. Depending on how you position the colors in a gradient, you can fade or blend gradient colors into other colors, adding a little realism to a photo.

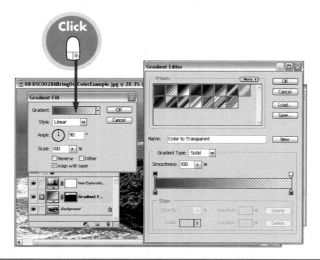

Click

10 Create a Gradient

Click the **Color** square at the bottom of the **Gradient Editor** dialog box. When the **Color Picker** opens, select a color for the gradient and click **OK**. Click **OK** in the **Gradient Fill** dialog box. The sky in the image now takes on the gradient color.

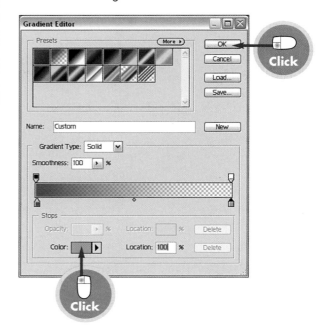

Click

Click

11 Select the Dodge Tool

Select the **Background** image layer in the **Layers** palette, and then choose the **Dodge** tool from the toolbox. The **Dodge** tool lightens pixels so that they match the surrounding pixels. Specify a soft round brush and adjust the brush size to match the area of pixels you want to modify.

Click

⑫ Lighten Colors

Select the **Zoom** tool and click in the image window to magnify the image. Select the **Dodge** tool. Click a dark area of the image and hold the mouse down to lighten the pixels. The longer you hold down the mouse, the lighter the pixels become.

⑭ Darken Colors

Drag the mouse in the image window to apply the **Burn** tool. The longer you hold down the mouse, the darker the pixels become. In this example, the sand below the surf is slightly darker.

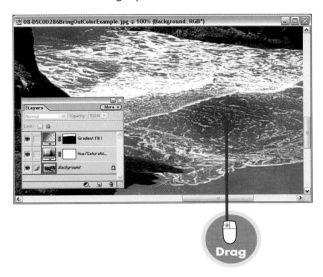

⑬ Select the Burn Tool

Select the **Burn** tool from the toolbox. The **Burn** tool darkens pixels to blend better with surrounding pixels. In the options bar, choose a soft, round brush and specify an appropriate brush size. From the **Range** drop-down menu, select **Midtones**.

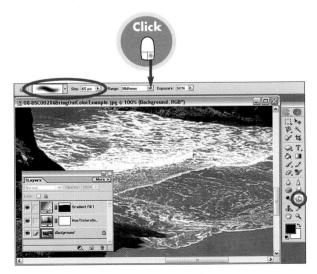

How-to Hint

Working with Color Images

While working on an image, view the full image (or as much of it as will fit onscreen). If you see areas of the image in which the colors don't look quite right, zoom into that part of the image. Adjust the size of the brush to match the number of pixels you'll be working with and see whether you can select those particular pixels using the **Magic Wand** tool. If the **Enhance** menu's color correction commands don't help, try applying the **Blur** tool to the colors you want to blend together.

When using the **Dodge** and **Burn** tools, adjust the **Exposure** setting in the options bar to a low value if you want to gradually lighten or darken the colors in the image.

How to Remove a Color Cast

Fluorescent and incandescent lights often cast a green or orange color across an image. You can use the **Color Cast** command to change a range of colors so that a slightly green or yellow image can be made whiter, bluer, or darker. Simply click the color you want to use to adjust the overall colors in the image window.

1 Open an Image

Click the **Open** button in the shortcuts bar. Choose a photo that is slightly off-color. Open the file.

2 Choose the Color Cast Command

Choose **Enhance**, **Adjust Color**, **Color Cast**. The **Color Cast** dialog box opens.

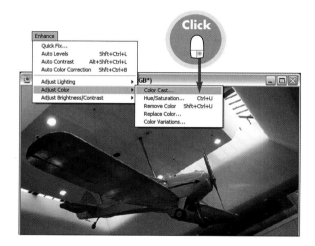

3 Click a Gray Color

Following the instructions in the **Color Cast Correction** dialog box, click a gray color in the image window, such as a shadow or a light shade of black. If a gray color doesn't jump out at you, identify a light source, and then look for an object that faces the light to find its shadow. The colors in the image window change to a slightly different hue.

4 Select White

Still following the instructions in the **Color Cast Correction** dialog box, next click a white area (or the lightest color) in the image window. The colors in the entire image should lighten.

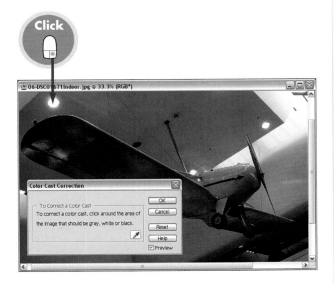

5 Select Black

Still following the instructions in the **Color Cast Correction** dialog box, finally click a black color (or the darkest color) in the image window. The colors in the entire image should darken.

6 Save Your Changes

View the corrected image. Click **OK** to save your changes.

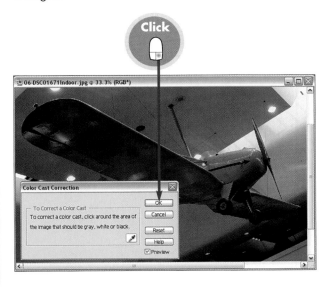

How-to Hint

Working with Light and Color

The **Color Cast** command enables you to use colors in a single image window or to sample a color from another image window. The color cast in an image can vary depending on the light sources present when the image was captured. For example, if the photo was captured with lots of red or green lights, it might be difficult to locate a white color to eliminate a particular color hue. Open a second image window that contains the color you want to use to correct the color cast in an image and click in the second window to adjust the colors in the original image.

How to Use Adjustment Layers

Adjustment layers enable you to create customized **Levels**, **Hue/Saturation**, or **Gradient** layers that can correct problems with the original image without affecting any other image layers. This task shows you how to create and modify **Levels**, **Gradient**, and **Hue/Saturation** adjustment layers.

① Open an Image File

Choose **Open** from the shortcuts bar. Select an image that contains at least one large area of color. Open the file.

② Open Layers Palette

Choose **Window**, **Layers** to open the **Layers** palette.

③ Add a Levels Adjustment Layer

Click the **Create new fill or adjustment layer** icon at the bottom of the **Layers** palette and select the **Levels** command. The **Levels** dialog box opens.

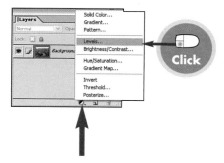

4️⃣ Adjust Levels

Drag the **Shadows** slider control (on the left side of the histogram) to the right to adjust the shadows in the image. Drag the **Midtones** slider control (in the middle of the histogram) to adjust the midtones of the image.

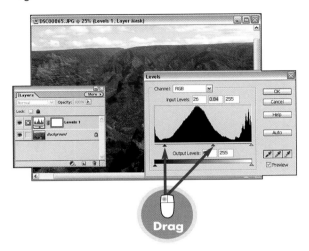

6️⃣ Edit Levels

Double-click the **histogram** icon in the **Levels 1** adjustment layer. The **Levels** dialog box opens again, ready for you to make any additional changes. Drag the **Shadows** slider control to the left to modify the dark areas in the image.

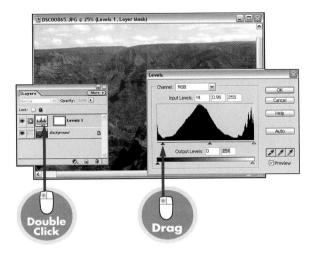

5️⃣ Apply Settings

Click **OK** to close the **Levels** dialog box. In the **Layers** palette, notice that the **Levels 1** adjustment layer shows a histogram icon and a layer mask thumbnail.

7️⃣ Select an Area of the Image

Select the **Magic Wand** Tool. Click a color in the image window to select a color range of pixels. The color selected with the **Magic Wand** tool is the color used to create the gradient in the next step.

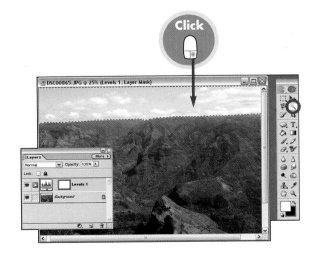

10 Edit Gradient Settings

In the **Layers** palette, double-click the **Gradient** icon in the **Gradient** adjustment layer to open the **Gradient Fill** dialog box again. Make any further adjustments to the gradient you have applied and click **OK** when you're done. You can see that the applied gradient has darkened the sky considerably.

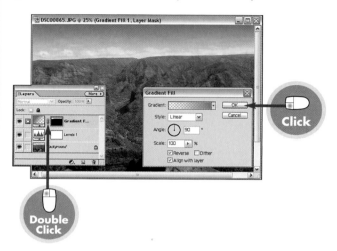

8 Add Gradient Adjustment Layer

In the **Layers** palette, click the **Create new fill or adjustment layer** icon and select **Gradient** from the menu. The **Gradient Fill** dialog box opens.

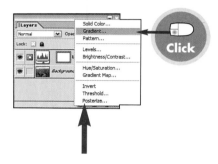

9 Apply Gradient Layer

Click the **Gradient** bar in the **Gradient Fill** dialog box. The **Gradient Editor** window opens. Click the **Color** box to open the **Color Picker**; pick the color you want to apply to the gradient you are creating and click **OK**.

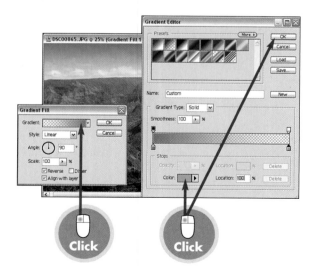

11 Add a Hue/Saturation Layer

In the **Layers** palette, click the **Create new fill or adjustment layer** icon and choose **Hue/Saturation** from the menu. The **Hue/Saturation** dialog box opens.

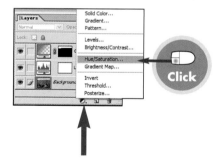

⑫ Adjust Color Settings

Type a value between –180 and +180 in the **Hue** text box. Alternatively, drag the **Hue** slider to adjust the hue of the image. Drag the **Saturation** slider control to the right to increase the color in the image. Alternatively, type a value between –180 and +180 in the **Saturation** text box. Click **OK** to apply the color changes.

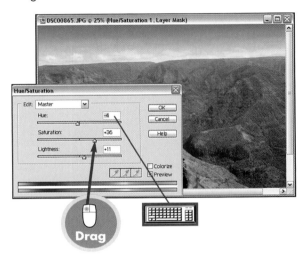

⑬ Edit Hue/Saturation Settings

In the **Layers** palette, double-click the **Hue** icon to open the **Hue/Saturation** dialog box again so that you can make additional changes to this adjustment layer. Drag the **Hue** slider control to the right to change the colors in the image. Type a lower value into the **Lightness** text box (or drag the **Lightness** slider) to lighten the overall image. Click **OK** to apply these changes.

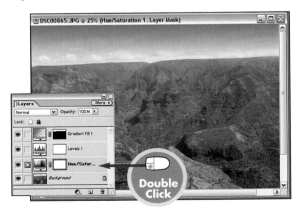

Blending Modes and Color

Blending modes enable you to blend colors between two layers in an image. The **Blending Mode** drop-down menu is located in the top-left corner of the **Layers** palette (and in the options bar for some tools). You can apply blending modes to any layer except the bottom layer (usually the **Background** layer) in the **Layers** palette. Blending modes affect how the colors in one layer mix with the colors in the layer directly below it. You can choose from 22 different blending modes. Some lighten colors, others darken, and some add or calculate the differences in color values to create the resultant blend.

Layers and PSD File Sizes

You can preserve layers by saving the image file as a Photoshop (PSD) file. Adjustment layers and image layers increase the size of a file. In addition to layers, Photoshop Elements stores a composite image along with the file. Programs such as Adobe Illustrator and Go Live use the composite information to interpret layer information from Photoshop files. If you want to decrease the overall file size, deselect the **Always Maximize Compatibility for Photoshop (PSD) File** check box located in the **Saving Files** panel of the **Preferences** dialog box.

Customizing Gradients

In addition to choosing the colors in a gradient, you can use the **Gradient Editor** window to customize other options. Several preset gradients are located at the top of the **Gradient Editor** window. Click the **More** button to choose a different set of presets. Click a preset to apply the gradient colors to the selected gradient. Type a new name for the gradient in the **Name** field. Click underneath the gradient bar to add additional colors to the gradient. Conversely, drag a color square away from the gradient bar to remove a color from the gradient. Drag each color marker along the bottom of the gradient bar to adjust how much of each color appears in the gradient. Drag the black and white colors at the top of the gradient bar to modify the opacity stop points (end points) of the gradient. Preview each change you make in the **Gradient Editor** window in the image window. Click the **Save** button to save a custom gradient. Finally, click **OK** to save the changes to the image.

How to Quick Fix Images

You can use the **Quick Fix** dialog box to try a wide range of image correction tools without having to open more than one dialog box. All the instant color correction menu commands and some of the most commonly used manual color correction commands are stored in the **Quick Fix** dialog box. You can view the image as you make changes and compare the **Before** and **After** thumbnails as you work.

① Open an Image File

Click the **Open** button in the shortcuts bar. Select an image that has some color problems and open the file.

② Choose Quick Fix Command

Choose **Enhance**, **Quick Fix** to open the **Quick Fix** dialog box. To correct the brightness of the image, enable the **Brightness** and **Brightness/Contrast** radio buttons. Drag the **Brightness** and **Contrast** controls to adjust the brightness and contrast in the image.

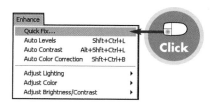

③ Quick Fix the Hue, Saturation, and Lightness

Enable the **Color Correction** and the **Hue/Saturation** radio buttons. Drag the **Hue** slider control to change the colors in the image. Drag the **Saturation** and **Lightness** sliders to adjust those settings as desired.

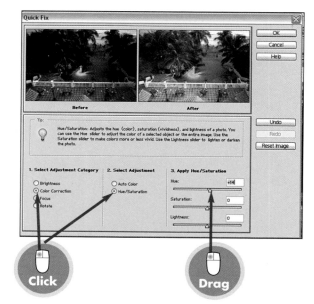

④ Quick Fix Focus

Click the **Focus** and the **Auto Focus** radio buttons. Click the **Apply** button to sharpen the focus of the image. Click the **Apply** button again to reapply the **Sharpen** filter to the image. Each click continues to modify the image with the **Sharpen** filter.

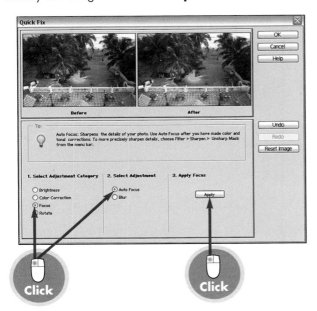

⑤ Quick Fix Blur

Click the **Blur** radio button in the middle column and click the **Apply** button. The image gets a little out of focus. Click the **Apply** button more than once to cumulatively apply the **Blur** filter to the image.

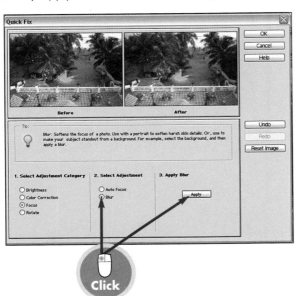

⑥ Rotate the Image

Click the **Rotate** radio button from the **Adjustment** column. Click one of the radio buttons in the middle column such as **Flip Vertical**. Click **Apply**.

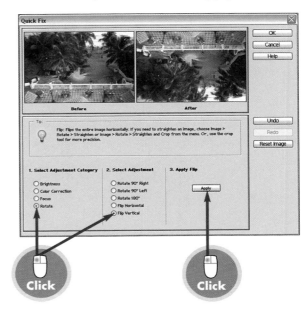

⑦ Undo or Redo a Change

Click **Undo** to delete the previous change. Click the **Undo** button more than once to delete multiple changes. After you've undone a change, you can reapply it by clicking the **Redo** button. Click the **OK** button to save your changes.

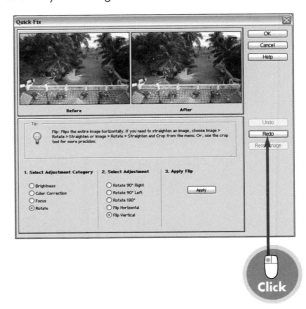

Task

(1) How to Salvage a Portion of an Image 82

(2) How to Remove Glare from Glass 84

(3) How to Warm Up Lighting 86

(4) How to Repair Torn Areas 88

(5) How to Remove Scratches, Mold, and Stains 90

(6) How to Replace Missing Areas 92

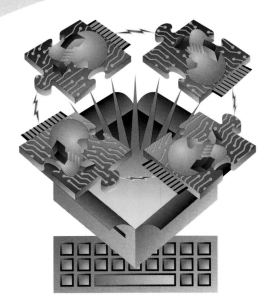

Fine-Tuning and Repairing Images

A digital photo created by a digital camera or scanner can contain millions of pixels. More pixels enable you to work with more colors and image data. If you're working with two to five megapixel images (the size of the image file produced by most current digital cameras), you'll probably have to fine-tune a few pixels after performing full-scale color correction, contrast, or level changes. Some photos, such as a scanned or photographed image of a torn photo, might require a bigger time investment and involve experimenting with one or more sophisticated digital restoration techniques.

In addition to the automatic and manual color correction commands you learned about in Part 4, "Image and Color Correction Techniques," there are several tools that enable you to add, replace, modify, move, or remove pixels from a photo. The **Clone Stamp** tool is the most effective tool for all these tasks. The **Liquify** command comes in a close second. The **Smudge**, **Dodge**, and **Burn** tools are a few more handy pixel-massaging tools.

You can use these tools to make minor tweaks to an image, restore a portion of an image, or fabricate missing portions of a photo. The tasks in this part show you how to clean up, touch up, remove, and brighten pixels primarily using the **Clone Stamp** tool and the **Liquify** command. You'll also learn how to repair torn, damaged, and missing areas of a photo with these tools.

How to Salvage a Portion of an Image

Indoor photos can bring out some of the weaknesses of a digital camera's capabilities. Sometimes cameras do not capture color accurately under low or artificial light. This can result in photos with a limited range of colors. You can use Photoshop Elements to salvage the subject of one image and move it to another to create a more vibrant image.

1 Open an Image

Click the **Open** button in the shortcuts bar. Select an image and open the file.

2 Select a Subject

Select the **Magnetic Lasso** tool from the toolbox. Click and drag in the image window to select the pixels of the subject you want to salvage.

3 Add to the Selection

Click the **Zoom** tool and click in the image to magnify the area you want to add to the selection. Select the **Magic Wand** tool. Hold down the **Shift** key and click on the color you want to add to the selection (here I click brown to select the rest of the bow). Hold down the **Alt** key (**Option** key for Mac users) and click to remove a color from the selection.

④ Apply the Selection Brush

Choose the **Selection Brush**. Hold down the **Shift** key and click any other color you want to add to the selection. Hold down the **Alt** key (**Option** key for Mac users) and click to remove a color from the selection. Here I deselect the brown area over the door. Choose **Edit**, **Copy** to copy the selection to the Clipboard.

⑤ Paste Into Another Image

Open an image file that you want to use as the background for the image you just salvaged. Choose **Edit**, **Paste** to paste the copied selection (the salvaged image) into the new photo. You might have to drag a corner of the selection to resize it to match the scale of the background image.

⑥ Feather the Selection

Choose the **Select**, **Feather** command. Type a number into the **Feather Radius** text box to indicate the number of pixels to blur along the edge of the selection to better integrate the pasted selection into the background. In this example, I typed **7**. Click **OK**. Choose **Select**, **Deselect** to deselect the salvaged image.

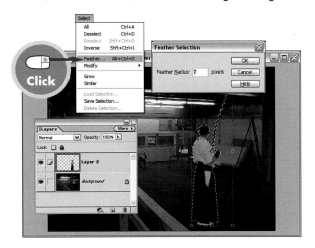

How-to Hint

What's a Composite?

When you take an image from one image file and paste it into another image window, you create a composite. A composite image can consist of two or more layers of color images that overlap each other. Find out more about composites in Part 7, "Combining Images and Creating Panoramas."

Color Correction and Partial Images

Sometimes an image in one photo has different lighting and color hues than an image in another photo. If you want to create a composite image containing elements from both photos, apply color correction commands and tools *after combining the images* into one. Because each image will be stored in its own layer in the composite, you can apply color correction to each image layer separately before merging them all together.

How to Remove Glare from Glass

Glass and mirrors pose unique problems for photographers. Not only can these elements reveal the presence of the photographer, they can reflect glare, add unwanted light sources, and prevent the camera from capturing the intended subject.

① Open an Image

Click the **Open** button in the shortcuts bar. Choose a photo that contains glass and glare or unwanted reflections. Open the file.

② Magnify the Glare

Select the **Zoom** tool from the toolbox. Click in the image window to magnify the area of the image that contains the glare.

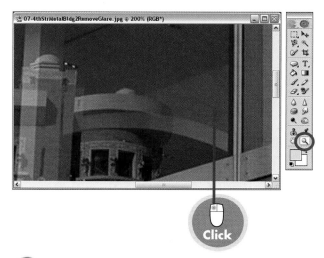

③ Add a New Layer

In the **Layers palette**, click the **Create a new layer button**. When the new layer appears in the list in the palette, click the new layer.

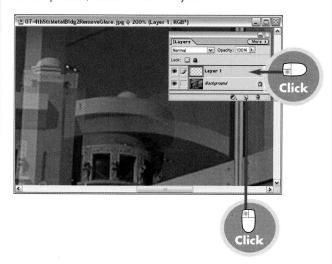

4️⃣ Select the Clone Stamp Tool

Select the **Clone Stamp** tool from the toolbox. Select a soft, round brush. Enable the **Use All Layers** and **Aligned** check boxes in the options bar. Choose the **Normal** blending mode, and set the **Opacity** to 100%.

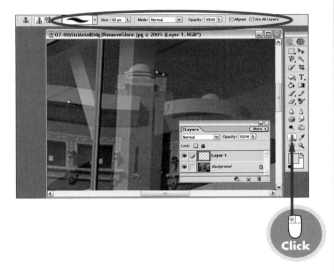

6️⃣ Remove Glare

Drag the **Clone Stamp** tool over the edge of the glare (place the center of the brush over the pixels you want to replace). Repeat step 5, sampling different areas around the glare and replacing the glare with the sampled pixels until the glare is removed from the image.

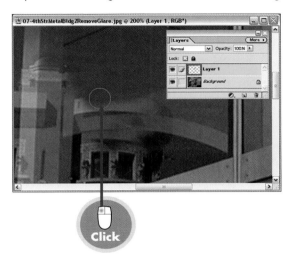

5️⃣ Sample Pixels

Adjust the size of the brush to cover part of the glare (choose a brush size that approximates one third to one half of the glare area you want to cover). Hold down the **Alt** key (the **Option** key for Mac users) and click to set the sample point in the image (place the center of the brush over the pixels outside of the glare area).

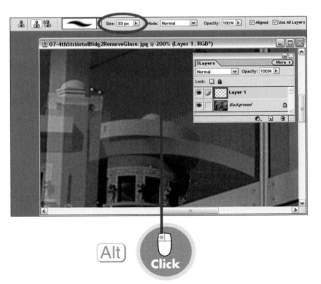

How-to Hint

Magic Eraser Tool

You can use the **Magic Eraser** tool to remove pixels, including glare from an image. Select the **Magic Eraser** tool from the toolbox and then customize its tool options. Specify a low **Tolerance** value if you do not want to select a wide range of colors in addition to the color you sample. Enable the **Anti-aliased** check box in the options bar to smooth the edges of the selected area; enable **Contiguous** to select any pixel touching the one you click. Choose **Use all layers** to apply the tool to all layers of the image. Set the **Opacity** to 100%. Finally, drag the tool on the pixels you want to remove from the image. Use the **Clone Stamp** tool to fill in the missing portions of the image.

How to Warm Up Lighting

Too much sun in outdoor shots can sometimes wash out the subject of a photo. Adding an orange hue to a photo can make an outdoor photo look sunnier or an indoor shot look warmer. Choose a yellow or orange foreground color before performing this task.

① Open an Image

Click the **Open** button in the shortcuts bar. Choose a photo that lacks color or looks washed out because it has been overexposed. Open the file.

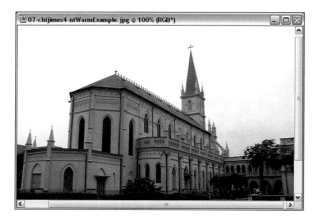

② Choose Gradient Command

Choose **Gradient** from the **Layer**, **New Fill Layer** menu. The **New Layer** dialog box opens.

③ Name the Gradient

Type a name for the gradient you are creating into the **Name** text box and click **OK**. The **Gradient Fill** dialog box opens.

④ Adjust the Gradient

Enable the **Reverse** check box (reversing the direction of the colors in the gradient). Click **OK**. Recall that the color of the gradient is determined by the foreground color you selected at the beginning of this task.

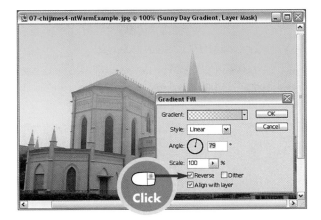

⑥ Lower the Opacity Setting

In the **Layers** palette, select the gradient layer you just created. At the top of the **Layers** palette, drag the **Opacity** slider control to the left to decrease the intensity of the colored gradient.

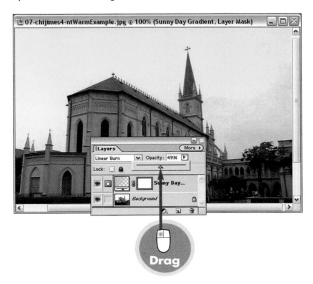

⑤ Change the Blending Mode

Choose a blending mode from the drop-down menu in the **Layers** palette. Experiment with the **Darken**, **Multiply**, **Color Burn**, and **Linear Burn** blending modes to darken the overall color in the image. Adjust the **Opacity** setting; lighter blending modes produce a more subtle coloring effect.

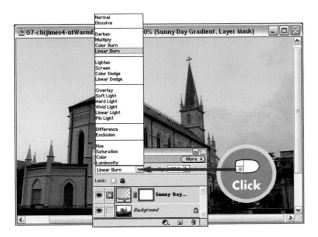

How-to Hint

Modifying Gradient Colors

Click the **Gradient** field in step 4 to open the **Gradient Editor** dialog box. Click below the gradient bar to add a new color to the gradient. Select a sliding color stop (the box slider control) below the gradient and then click the **Color** box located at the bottom of the dialog box to view or change a color in the gradient. Double-click the color stop above the gradient to set the opacity of that area of the gradient. Click **OK** to save your changes and view the gradient.

Adjusting Hue and Saturation

You can use the **Enhance**, **Adjust Color**, **Hue/Saturation** command to adjust the colors of a photo to have more yellow or orange. Select the image layer you want to work with. Apply a selection tool if you want to modify part of a photo. Open the **Hue/Saturation** dialog box. Drag the **Hue** slider control until the selected pixels show more yellow or orange. Move the **Saturation** slider to the right to intensify the yellow or orange color.

How to Repair Torn Areas

A tear in a physical photo creates a ripple in the image and exposes some of the paper behind the photo. A simple approach to removing the tear is to sample the pixels immediately to the left or right of the torn area of the image and then fill in the tear with the cloned pixels.

❶ Open an Image

Click the **Open** button on the shortcuts bar. Choose a photo that contains torn paper. Open the file. This example uses a scanned photo that has two tears: one in the sky and one that left a hole in the beach area of the image.

❷ Create a New Layer

Open the **Layers** palette and click the **Create a new layer** button. When the new layer appears in the list, select the empty layer from the palette list.

❸ Select the Clone Stamp Tool

Select the **Clone Stamp** tool from the toolbox. Specify a soft, round brush, set the blending mode to **Normal**, and set the **Opacity** to 100%. Enable the **Use All Layers** check box.

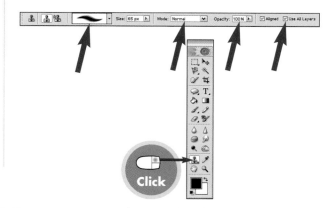

④ Apply the Clone Stamp Tool

Hold down the **Alt** key (the **Option** key for Mac users) and click to sample the pixels immediately above the tear. Release the **Alt** or **Option** key and drag the **Clone Stamp** tool over the top half of the torn area to repair part of the tear.

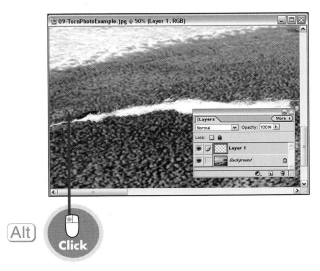

⑥ Shrink Torn Paper

Select the **Pucker** tool from the left side of the **Liquify** window. Drag the tool over the remaining torn edges in the image to shrink the tear. Click **OK**.

⑤ Choose the Liquify Command

In the **Layers** palette, click to select the **Background** layer. Choose the **Liquify** command from the **Filter**, **Distort** menu. The **Liquify** window opens, containing several tools capable of stretching, shrinking, or growing pixels. In this example, we'll use the **Pucker** tool to reduce the seam of the torn paper.

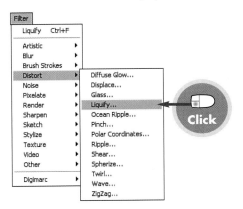

How-to Hint

Can't Match What's Missing?

It might be very difficult to clone appropriate pixels to use to fill in the missing portion of an image. If you don't have another photo of the same scene from which you can sample the missing elements, you might want to crop out the missing area from the original image or take part of the image and create a partial portrait in a new image file.

Layers and Image Reconstruction

The key to effectively repairing damaged photos is to experiment with more than one repair method. One way to keep all the different kinds of image repairs organized is to create a separate layer for each element you want to work on. Name the layers based on the correction it provides. For example, you can create a layer for removing stains or spots in an image, and a second or third layer for reconstructing a missing area or repairing a torn area of the image.

How to Remove Scratches, Mold, and Stains

Photos, like any paper, are susceptible to scratches and moisture damage. Water or changes in temperature that create moisture can result in stains or encourage mold to grow on a photo. You can scan the scratched or stained photo into a computer and use the **Clone Stamp** tool to remove damaged areas of the image.

1 Open an Image

Click the **Open** button in the shortcuts bar. Choose a photo that has a stain or other type of damage. Open the file. This example uses a scan of a photo that was damaged by mold.

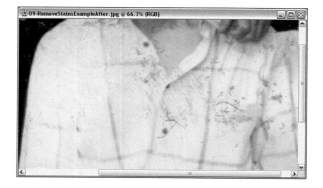

2 Create a New Layer

Open the **Layers** palette from the palette well. Click the **Create a new layer** button at the bottom of the palette. A new, empty layer appears in the **Layers** palette.

3 Select the Clone Stamp Tool

Select the **Clone Stamp** tool from the toolbox. Choose a soft, round brush. In the **Layers** palette, select the repair layer you created in step 2.

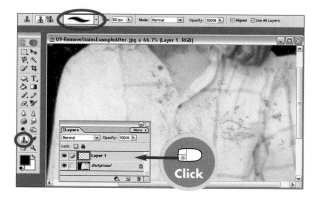

④ Apply the Clone Stamp Tool

Hold down the **Alt** key (the **Option** key for Mac users) and click the **Clone Stamp** tool to set the sample point in the image. Now drag the mouse over a damaged area of the image to apply the sampled pixels.

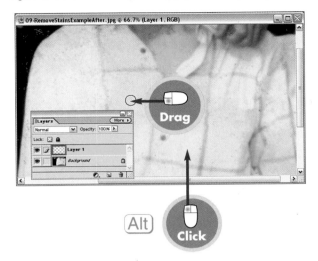

⑥ Apply the Blur Tool

Drag the **Blur** tool over the area where you applied the **Clone Stamp** tool in step 4. The **Blur** tool blends the cloned pixels with surrounding pixels, creating a more seamless patch.

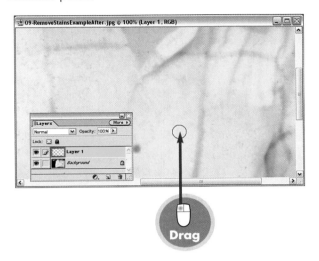

⑤ Select the Blur Tool

Select the **Blur** tool from the toolbox. In the options bar, adjust the size of the brush to roughly match the area where you applied the **Clone Stamp** tool.

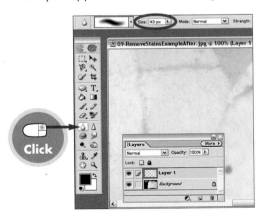

How-to Hint

Finding the Right Brush Size

The secret to using most of the toolbox tools in Photoshop Elements is choosing the best brush type and brush size for the job. A soft, round brush that has feathered edges works great for most image editing. The soft edge helps blend the surrounding pixels into the edit. If you're planning on making precise changes, a smaller brush works better than a large one. A large brush is better for modifying large portions of an image.

Blending Repaired Image Areas

Each time you apply a brush to an image, a stroke is added to the image. If you want to see exactly how a particular brushstroke affects an image, create a new, empty layer. Select the **Paintbrush** or **Clone Stamp** tool and customize the brush type and size. Select the new, empty layer and apply the brush to the image window. You might have to hide the image layer to see how the brush appears in the image window. You can use this test layer to adjust the brush type and size to find the right combination of settings for the work you want to do.

How to Replace Missing Areas

There are a few different ways to reconstruct a missing area of a photo. One way is to use areas of the existing photo to extend and fill in the missing areas. This task shows you how you can rebuild a missing area using the **Clone Stamp** tool.

1 Open an Image

Open an image file. Choose a photo that contains a subject that is missing a portion of the face or head. In this example, the top of the girl's head is missing. In the status bar at the bottom of the screen, note the width and height in pixels of the image.

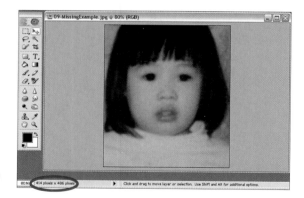

2 Create a New Document

Select the **File**, **New** command. In the **New** dialog box, type values in the width and height fields that are larger than the size of the original image. Click **OK** to create the new window. Copy the image from the first window and paste it into the new document.

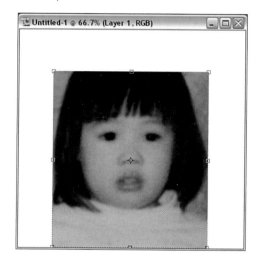

3 Create a New Layer

In the **Layers** palette, click the **Create a new layer** icon. A new, empty layer appears in the **Layers** palette list. Click to select the new layer.

4 Select the Clone Stamp Tool

Select the **Clone Stamp** tool from the toolbox. Select a soft, round brush, and set its size to approximate the area you want to clone (in this example, it's set to 81 pixels).

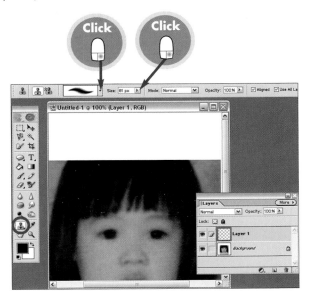

5 Apply the Clone Stamp Tool

Hold down the **Alt** key (the **Option** key for Mac users) and click near the edge of the missing area of the image to set the sample point. Drag the tool across the top of the head to clone the sampled pixels.

6 Complete the Missing Area

Continue sampling and applying cloned pixels to the image with the **Clone Stamp** tool until you have reconstructed the missing portion of the image.

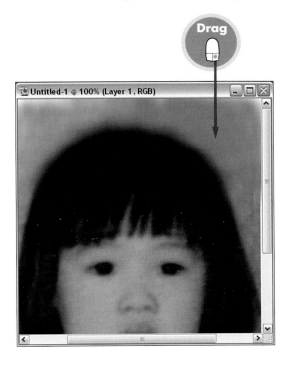

How-to Hint

Moving Around with the Hand Tool

You can use the **Hand** tool to move the image around in the image window. Moving the image around is especially handy if you've magnified the image and don't want to zoom out to go to another area.

① How to Fix a Smile 96

② How to Remove Red Eye 98

③ How to Change a Hair Style 100

④ How to Remove Blemishes 102

⑤ How to Counteract Aging in a Subject 104

⑥ How to Change Facial Expressions 106

⑦ How to Modify Eyes, Nose, and Mouth 108

⑧ How to Reshape a Physique 110

⑨ How to Construct a Portrait 112

Task

6

Correcting Images of People

Photos can make us look our best or our worst. Although lots of folks are camera shy, people who see their own photo expect to see their best smile and their eyes, nose, hair, and face to best effect. Others like to see healthy faces and bodies with shiny hair and a smile, regardless of whether the photo is for a photo album, newspaper, Web site, or television. You can use Photoshop Elements to improve the appearance of any photo subject.

Many of the tools and commands that can improve photos of people have already been introduced in previous tasks. In addition to the color correction, tonal range, and **Clone Stamp** tools described in previous tasks, you can use the **Liquify** command to distort, straighten, or twirl pixels as you like.

How to Fix a Smile

Smiles are unique. Digitally editing a smile can involve whitening teeth, removing wrinkles, or rotating the mouth, depending on what you want to fix. This task shows you how to touch up a photographic smile.

① Open an Image

Click the **Open** button on the shortcuts bar. Choose a file that contains a subject with a big smile. Open the file.

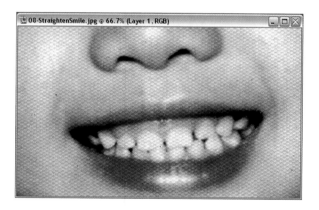

② Select the Smile

Choose the **Magnetic Lasso** tool from the toolbox and select the mouth in the image window.

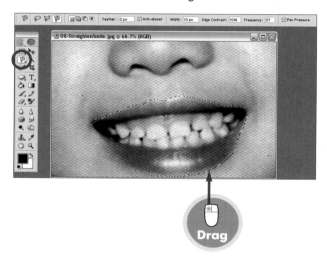

③ Copy and Paste Selection

Choose the **Edit**, **Copy** command to copy the selection. Then choose **Edit**, **Paste** command to paste the selected smile back into the image on a new layer. (Open the **Layers** palette to see the smile on its own layer.)

④ Rotate the Smile

Select the **Move** tool in the toolbox and click the smile (the one on its own layer). Click just outside the corner of the selected area and drag the mouse up or down to rotate the smile. Click the **Check** button in the options bar to save your changes.

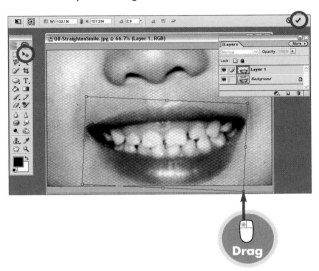

⑥ Straighten Teeth

Hold down the **Alt** key (the **Option** key for Mac users) and click the center part of the tooth to set the sample point. Drag the tool along the edges of the tooth, straightening the bottom, filling in gaps between teeth, and removing gum from the top and sides. Repeat this step for each tooth.

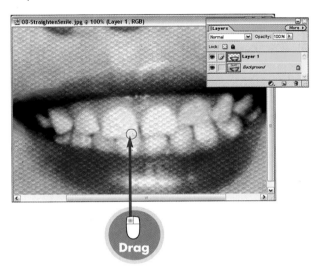

⑤ Select the Clone Stamp Tool

Select the **Clone Stamp** tool and customize the brush type and size so that it approximates one third the area of a tooth.

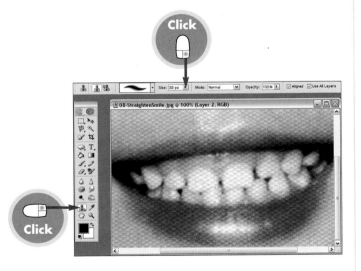

How-to Hint

Straighten with the Smudge Tool

The **Smudge** tool might be able to help repair a crooked tooth because it stretches pixels instead of cloning them. The key to applying this tool is to use short strokes. Choose a brush size that is one quarter to one third the area of a tooth. Click just above the part of the tooth that's crooked and drag the mouse to create a straightened line for the tooth.

Whiten with the Dodge Tool

After straightening the teeth, you can use the **Dodge** tool to brighten and whiten them. For the picture in this example, I applied the **Auto Color Correction**, **Contrast**, and **Levels** commands first. Then I chose a 50-pixel soft, round brush for the **Dodge** tool and applied it to teeth that I wanted to lighten.

How to Remove Red Eye

The red-eye effect can occur in low-light situations when a camera captures the flash bouncing off the subject's retina before the subject's eyes can adjust to the change in light. You can use the Red Eye Brush tool to replace the red with a natural eye color. You can also use the tool to remove glare from glasses, whiten teeth, remove tan lines, color hair, and so on.

1 Open an Image File

Click the **Open** button in the shortcuts bar. Select an image file that is in need of red-eye repair. Open the file.

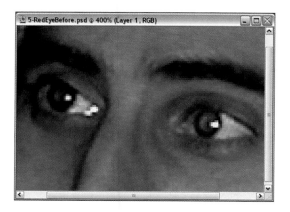

2 Select the Red Eye Brush Tool

Choose the **Red Eye Brush** tool from the toolbox. Type a brush size into the **Size** field in the options bar. For this example, I chose a soft, round 13-pixel brush. I specified a **Tolerance** of 30%. The **Tolerance** value widens the sample range of the tool, replacing the range of color with an adjusted range of replacement color.

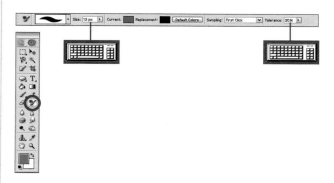

3 Select the Sampling Setting

In the options bar, choose **First Click** from the **Sampling** drop-down menu. This setting enables you to select the color you want to change in the image window (in this example, the red eye color) with the first mouse click. The **Current Color** option shows the color that will be replaced with the replacement color you specify in step 4.

④ Choose the Replacement Color

Click the **Replacement** color square. The **Color Picker** dialog box opens. Click the color you want to replace the color you will sample (in this example, click the subject's eye in the image window) and then click **OK**.

⑤ Apply the Red Eye Brush Tool

Drag the **Red Eye Brush** tool over the colors in the eye area that you want to replace. As you move the brush over the image, the red pixels change to the replacement color.

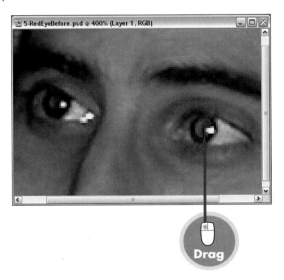

⑥ Correct the Left Eye

Drag the **Red Eye Brush** tool over the other eye to replace the first sample color with the replacement color. View the changed colors. If you want to change the eye color, click the **Replacement** color square in the options bar and select a different color from the image window.

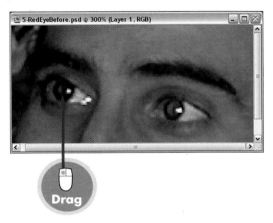

How-to Hint

Making Brown Eyes Blue

You can use the **Red Eye Brush** tool to change brown eyes to blue ones. Simply change the replacement color to any color you like. Using the **Current Click** sampling method, click the **Current** eye color and then click the eye. Drag the **Red Eye Brush** tool over each eye to change the eye color.

As a matter of fact, you can use the **Red Eye Brush** tool to change any color in an image to any other color. Want a red balloon to be green? Adjust the **Tolerance** setting so that all the variety of red pixels in the balloon are replaced with a similar variety of green pixels to provide a realistic result. Choose a lower **Tolerance** value to limit the range of colors that change. Conversely, increase the tolerance value if you want to change a wider range of colors.

How to Change a Hair Style

After smiles, hair is the next most-difficult element to modify in an image. You can use the tools in the **Liquify** window to move, stretch, or twirl hair or to experiment with more dramatic effects. This task shows you how to make subtle hair style changes.

1 Open an Image File

Click the **Open** button in the shortcuts bar. Choose a photo that contains a subject with plenty of hair—or one who was having a bad hair day. Open the file.

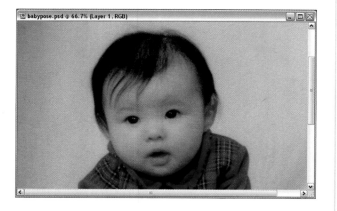

2 Choose the Liquify Command

Select **Filter**, **Distort**, **Liquify** or select the **Liquify** filter from the **Filters** palette. The **Liquify** window opens.

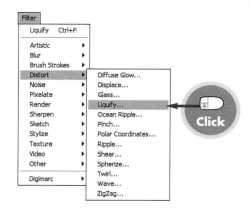

3 Zoom Into Hair

Select the **Zoom** tool from the left edge of the **Liquify** window. Click on the portion of the subject's hair that you want to modify to zoom into that area of the image. Click the **Hand** tool and center the area you want to work on.

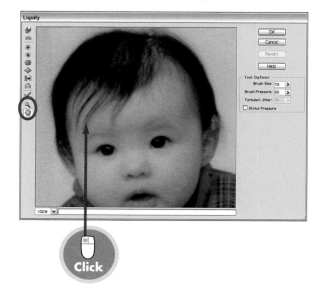

4 Adjust Brush Size

Select the **Warp** tool from the left edge of the **Liquify** window. In the **Brush Size** field, type a pixel value for a brush size that covers roughly half the area of hair in the image.

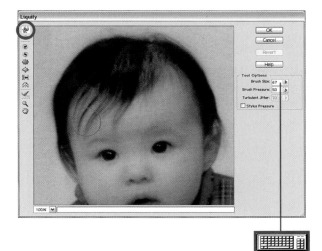

5 Change Hair Shape

Place the center of the brush over the subject's hair. Drag the tool upward to raise the hair pixels. Drag downward to lengthen or shorten the subject's hair.

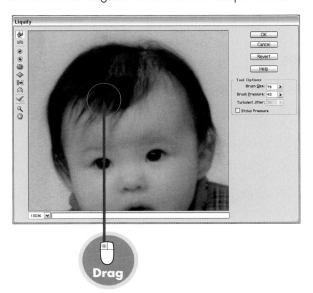

6 Twirl Hair

Select the **Twirl Clockwise** tool from the left edge of the **Liquify** window. Click and hold the mouse button on the image. Release the mouse to stop applying this tool. Notice how the hair pixels have been twirled to create a new hairstyle. Click **OK** to accept your changes and close the window.

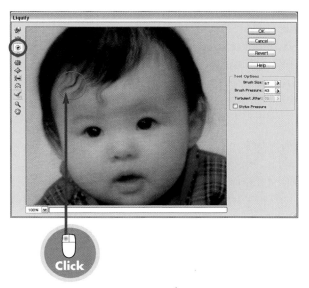

How-to Hint

Hair and the Pucker Tool

You can use the **Pucker** tool in the **Liquify** window to reduce the thickness of the strands of hair. Conversely, you can use the **Bloat** tool to thicken hair strands (or to widen a forehead or the surface area of a head of hair).

Lightening and Darkening Hair Color

Use the **Burn** tool in the toolbox to darken light, white, or graying hair. Use the **Dodge** tool to lighten dark-colored or shadow-covered hair.

How to Remove Blemishes

The subject of a photo may need some retouching even if the photo itself is perfect. Blemishes, moles, and other minor disfigurations can be easily corrected with the **Clone Stamp** tool. This task shows you how to remove blemishes from a subject's face using the **Clone Stamp** tool.

1 Open an Image

Click the **Open** button in the shortcuts bar. Choose a photo of a subject who has some minor facial imperfections. Open the file.

2 Zoom Into Blemishes

Select the **Zoom** tool from the toolbox and click the image to magnify a particular area. Use the **Hand** tool to center the area you want to work on in the image window.

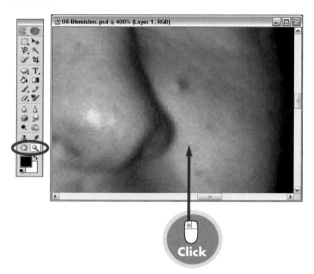

3 Create a New Layer

In the **Layers** palette, click the **Create a new layer** button. Click to select the new layer in the **Layers** palette or right-click (**Ctrl**+click for Mac users) in the image window and choose the new layer from the pop-up menu.

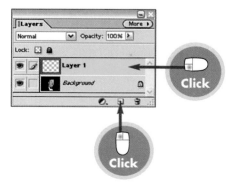

4 Select the Clone Stamp Tool

Select the **Clone Stamp** tool from the toolbox. Choose a soft, round brush and adjust the size of the brush to match the size of the blemish.

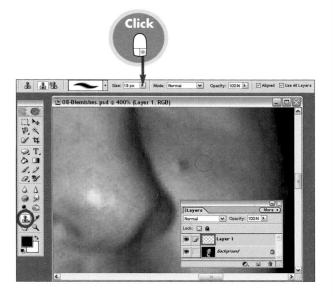

5 Apply the Clone Stamp Tool

Hold down the **Alt** key (the **Option** key for Mac users) and click to the left or right of the blemish to sample an unblemished area. Click once on the blemish to cover it with the sampled pixels.

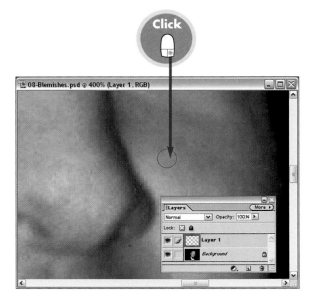

6 View Changes

Click the **Zoom** tool in the toolbox. Hold down the **Alt** key (the **Option** key for Mac users) and click in the image window to zoom out from the image. View the image.

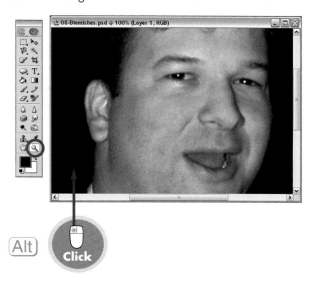

How-to Hint

Some Blemishes Add Character

After you apply the **Clone Stamp** tool, zoom out of the image and take a look at it. What might look like a blemish may be a mole or a birthmark. You can use the **Eraser** tool on the image's correction layer to restore any cloned areas of the image; alternatively, use the **Undo History** palette to undo any blemish removal you might want to modify.

How to Counteract Aging in a Subject

You might want to reduce or remove wrinkles around the eyes and mouth of a subject to improve the overall appearance of the person. This task shows you how to remove wrinkles and other age-related visuals using the **Clone Stamp** and **Smudge** tools.

1 Open an Image

Click the **Open** button in the shortcuts bar. Choose an image containing a subject that you want to make digitally younger. Open the file.

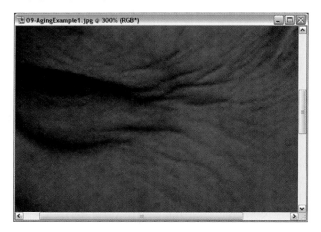

2 Choose the Liquify Command

Open the **Layers** palette and make sure that the background layer is selected. Choose the **Liquify** command from the **Filter**, **Distort** menu.

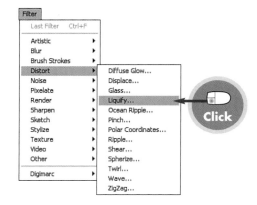

3 Zoom into the Image

Select the **Zoom** tool from the left side of the **Liquify** window. Click the portion of the image you want to magnify to zoom into that portion of the image. Click the **Hand** tool and drag the image to center the area you want to work on.

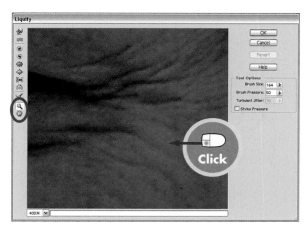

④ Reshape the Face

Select the **Warp** tool from the left edge of the **Liquify** window and click so that the center of the tool is to the immediate left or right of the edge of the face. Drag the tool toward the center of the face to straighten the jaw line.

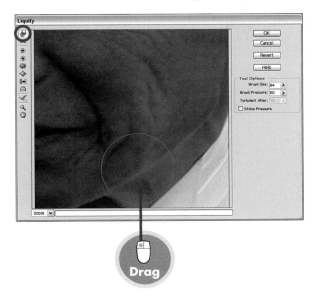

⑤ Enlarge an Eye

Select the **Bloat** tool from the left edge of the **Liquify** window. Place the center of the tool over the center of the subject's eye. Click and release the mouse to apply this tool to enlarge the eye. When you're satisfied with your modifications, click **OK** to close the **Liquify** window.

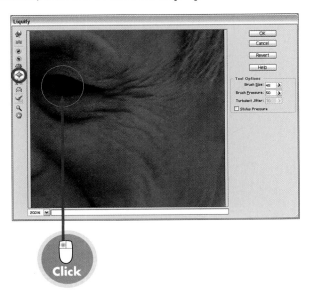

⑥ Remove Wrinkles

Select the **Smudge** tool from the toolbox. Drag the tool over any wrinkles on the subject's face to blend them into the rest of the face.

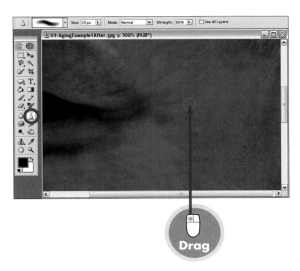

How-to Hint

The Neck and Aging

As you remove wrinkles from the eyes and mouth, take a look at the subject's neck. You might want to use the **Bloat** tool in the **Liquify** dialog box combined with the **Clone Stamp** tool from the toolbox to adjust the size of the neck and remove wrinkles from that area.

Hands Show Aging, Too

Look at the hands of an aging subject. You might want to apply the **Clone Stamp** tool and perform some wrinkle removal on the skin in these areas. The **Dodge** tool in the toolbox can be useful for lightening the color of the fingernails or of any prominent age spots on the hands.

How to Change Facial Expressions

If you've taken a series of photos, you might find the expression in one photo would look great with a pose from another photo. This task shows you how to move a face from one photo to another photo and then adjust the selection to scale it to the rest of the photo.

❶ Open Two Images

Click the **Open** button in the shortcuts bar. Choose two photos that contain a subject with different facial expressions. Open the files.

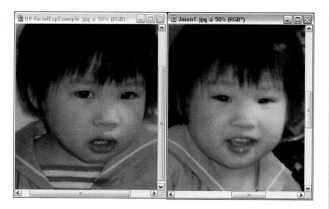

❷ View the Second Photo

Select the **Zoom** tool from the toolbox. Click the image window (the one that contains the source image) and zoom into the face.

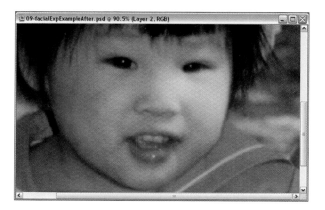

❸ Select the Image Area

Choose the **Magnetic Lasso** tool from the toolbox. Drag the tool around the part of the face you want to move to the other image window (the destination image).

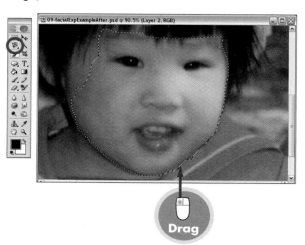

4 Copy and Paste the Selection

Choose **Edit**, **Copy** to copy the selection to the Clipboard. Select the image window for the destination image and choose **Edit**, **Paste** to paste the selection into a separate layer in the destination image.

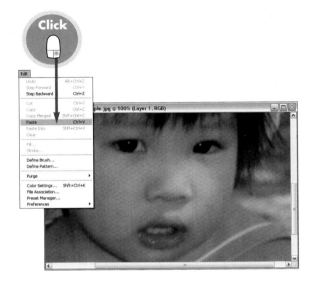

5 Adjust the Orientation

Drag the sides of the pasted selection (in the destination image) to scale it to fit with the rest of the photo. Click the **Check** button in the options bar to save your changes.

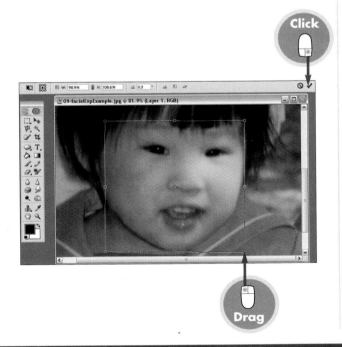

6 Merge Layers

In the **Layers** palette (with the destination image as the active image window), select the layer that contains the new facial expression. Click the **More** button in the **Layers** palette and choose **Merge Down** from the menu list. The two layers are merged into one.

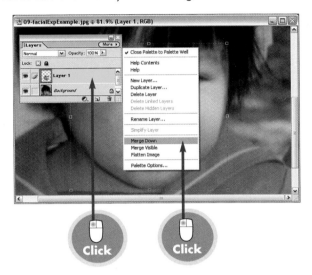

How-to Hint

Scaling an Image to Fit

Sometimes it's difficult to replace part of a photo with a face that exactly matches the area you're working on. With the **Move** tool, you can drag the corner of the pasted selection to grow or shrink its size. If perspective is the problem, you might want to select a smaller part of the replacement image to more precisely replace an eye or nose so that you avoid scaling parts of the face that are close in size to the one you're replacing.

Flipping a Frown into a Smile

A possible shortcut to creating a smiling face is to copy and paste a frown. Use the **Flip Layer Vertical** command from the **Image**, **Rotate** menu to turn the frown upside-down. The **Whirl** tools in the **Liquify** dialog box might also be able to change a straight-lipped mouth into a smiling one.

How to Modify Eyes, Nose, and Mouth

The **Liquify** window provides a nice set of tools that enable you to repair and distort an image. This task shows you how to reshape the eyes and nose of a photo subject using the **Pucker** tool from the **Liquify** window.

① Open an Image

Click the **Open** button in the shortcuts **bar**. Select a photo that contains a face. Open the file.

② Select the Liquify Command

Choose **Liquify** from the **Filter**, **Distort** menu. The **Liquify** window opens.

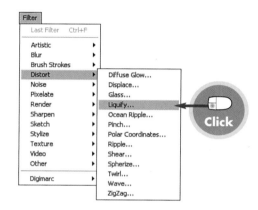

③ Shrink the Eyes

Choose the **Pucker** tool from the **Liquify** window. Type a value into the **Brush Size** text box to create a brush that encircles the subject's eye area. Place the center of the brush over the eye. Click and hold the mouse button until the eye shrinks to the size you want.

4 Shrink the Nose

Still using the **Pucker** tool, click and hold the mouse over the subject's nose to shrink the size of the nose.

5 Reshape the Nose

Still using the **Pucker** tool, click and hold the mouse over the bridge of the nose to make it narrower.

6 Stretch a Smile

Click the **Warp** tool, slowly drag the mouse over each corner of the mouth to curve the mouth into a smile. Click **OK** to close the window and accept your changes.

How-to Hint

When to Use the Revert Button

Click the **Revert** button in the **Liquify** window to return the photo to its first-opened state. Use this feature if you experiment with several tools and don't want to close and reopen the **Liquify** window. If you change any of the brush settings in the **Liquify** window, hold down the **Alt** key (the **Option** key for Mac users) and click the **Reset** button (the **Revert** button changes to the **Reset** button when you press the **Alt** or **Option** key) to return the settings in the **Liquify** window to the settings that were selected when you first opened the **Liquify** window.

Brush Size and the Liquify Tools

Experiment using different brush sizes and try each of the tools in the **Liquify** window. Try applying a tool using a big brush size (100 pixels or larger). Choose a smaller brush size and zoom into the image if you want to fine-tune a particular part of an image.

How to Reshape a Physique

The **Warp** and **Bloat** tools located in the **Liquify** window are both very powerful. The **Warp** tool enables you to move and push image pixels. The **Bloat** tool expands pixels. This task shows you how to reshape the physique of a photo subject.

1 Open an Image

Click the **Open** button in the shortcuts bar. Select a photo that contains a subject showing arms, body, and legs. Open the file.

2 Arrange the Image

Choose **Liquify** from the **Filter**, **Distort** menu. The **Liquify** window opens. Select the **Hand** tool from the **Liquify** window and drag the image until the subject is centered in the viewing area.

3 Massage the Tummy

Click the **Warp** tool in the **Liquify** window and place it over the edge of the subject's belly. Drag the mouse downward to adjust the belt line. Drag the mouse upward or downward to straighten the belt line. Here, I also stretched the tie to make the boy's stomach look smaller.

4 Reshape Legs and Waist

Select the **Bloat** tool from the **Liquify** window and place it over the top of the subject's thigh. Hold down the mouse to apply the tool. Select the **Warp** tool and drag to align the feet (here I moved the right foot up to line up with the left foot).

6 Reduce Tummy and Waist

Click the **Pucker** tool and apply it to the tie, tummy, and belt line. If only real weight loss was this easy! Click **OK** to save your changes and close the window.

5 Enlarge Shoulders and Chest

Choose the **Bloat** tool from the **Liquify** window and apply it to the chest area of the subject. Apply it to the upper arms of the subject to instantly shape and tone those areas as well.

How-to Hint

Tools in the Liquify Window

You can choose from eleven tools in the **Liquify** window. The **Warp** tool enables you to push pixels. The **Turbulence** tool roughly mixes pixels together. The **Twirl Clockwise** and **Counter Clockwise** tools enable you to rotate pixels in a specific direction (which is great for working with hair). The **Pucker** and **Bloat** tools enable you to shrink or enlarge pixels. The **Shift Pixels** tool applies distortion to pixels. The **Reflection** tool creates a copy of the pixels below it. The **Reconstruct** tool can undo the other tools applied to the image. Finally, the **Hand** tool enables you to move the image around in the viewing area, and the **Zoom** tool enables you to magnify and zoom out of the pixels in the viewing area.

Adjusting Brush Pressure

The number in the **Brush Pressure** text box in the **Liquify** window affects how quickly the tools interact with the pixels in an image. Choose a lower value to slow down the application of the tool. Increase the value to intensify the effect of each tool.

How to Construct a Portrait

Some photos capture the subject with a great expression, but have a lackluster background. Photoshop Elements enables you to select a subject from one photo and create a totally new photo. This task shows you how to use layers, adjustment layers, and layer styles to create a portrait from another photo.

① Open an Image

Click the **Open** button in the **shortcuts bar**. Select a photo that contains the head and shoulders of a subject. Open the file.

② Select the Liquify Command

Choose **Liquify** from the **Filter**, **Distort** menu. The **Liquify** window opens.

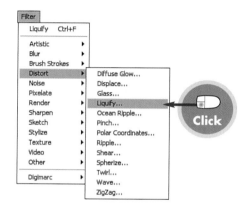

③ Touch Up the Face

Click the **Warp** tool and adjust the **Brush Size** to match an area of the image you want to work with. Drag the mouse to stretch the pixels on the subject. In this example, the stretch marks are reduced along the face of the baby.

4 Add a Smile to the Subject

Select the **Twirl Clockwise** tool. Adjust the **Brush Size** to match the ends of the mouth. Click and hold the mouse to twirl the pixels there, creating a slight smile. Release the mouse to stop applying the tool. Select the **Twirl Counter Clockwise** tool and apply it to the other end of the mouth. Click **OK** to save your changes.

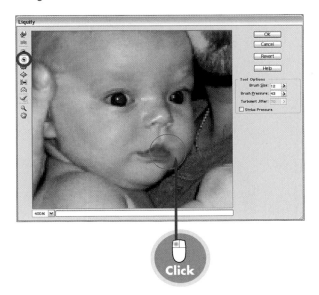

5 Remove Red Eye

Zoom in to the subject and select the **Red Eye Brush** tool. Choose **First Click** from the **Sampling** drop-down menu in the options bar. Click the **Replacement** color box and drag the tool on the subject's eye to change its color.

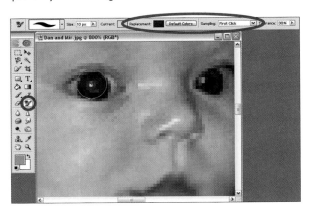

6 Select and Copy the Image

Choose a selection tool such as the **Magnetic Lasso** tool from the toolbox. Select the subject in the image window. After you have selected the portion of the image you want to use in the final portrait, choose the **Select**, **Feather** command to blur the edges of the selection. Choose **Edit**, **Copy** to copy the selection to the Clipboard.

7 Open a Background Image

Click on the **Browse** button on the shortcuts bar. Navigate your hard drive to locate a background image for the portrait you are creating and open it.

⑧ Paste the Image

Choose **Edit**, **Paste**. The copied image appears in the destination image window (the background image).

⑨ Identify Color Mismatches

Zoom into an edge of the pasted subject and look for mismatched colors between the background and the selection.

⑩ Magnify Selection

In the **Layers** palette, click the eye icon of the background layer to hide it. **Ctrl**+click (⌘+click for Mac users) the layer containing the subject in the **Layers** palette. Choose the **Selection Brush** tool and drag to tighten the outline to exclude the mismatched color from the selection.

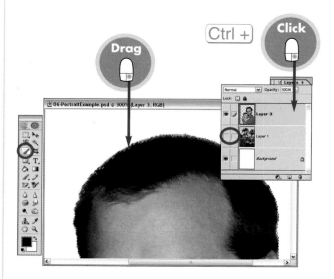

⑪ Remove Mismatched Colors

Choose **Select**, **Inverse** to reverse the selection (so that only the mismatched pixels are selected) and press **Backspace** (**Delete** for Mac users) to remove the selected pixels.

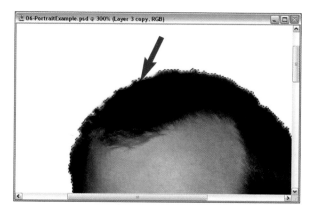

12 Add a Drop Shadow

Select the layer that contains the subject. Open the **Layer Styles** palette and select the **Drop Shadows** option from the drop-down list at the top. Click the **High** tile to apply a drop shadow to the subject.

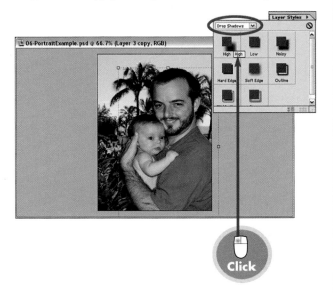

13 Open the Style Settings

In the **Layers** palette, double-click the **f** icon next to the image layer. The **Style Settings** dialog box opens. Drag the **Shadow Distance** slider control to adjust the size of the drop shadow. Adjust the **Lighting Angle** to change the direction in which the drop shadow falls. Click **OK** to apply the effect.

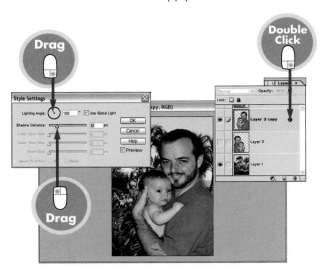

How-to Hint

Note the Light Source

When you choose the subject for the portrait you want to create, determine the light source in the photo. Keep this in mind as you work with the photo subject to construct a custom portrait. If you add additional light sources, you might have to create or eliminate shadows to add realism to all elements in the photo.

When to Clean Up the Image

After you select and clean up the image you want to use to create the portrait, apply **Quick Fix** or adjustment layers to correct colors, adjust brightness or contrast, and correct tonal range distribution. Performing these corrections before you clean up the image with the **Clone Stamp** tool might remove some color information from the image and make the **Clone Stamp** tool less effective.

Reducing Distortion

You might have to adjust the **Brush Size**, **Brush Pressure**, and **Turbulent Jitter** settings in the **Tool Options** area of the **Liquify** window before you are comfortable with the tools. Try to use short stroke lengths to minimize the number of pixels changed as you apply each tool. Choose a large brush size that matches the entire area of the image where you want to make major changes. To apply changes with more precision, decrease the brush size and increase the magnification (zoom) level of the image. Unless your intention is to *create* distortion, applying a tool should not visibly distort the image you're working on.

Adding Depth to a Portrait

Copying and pasting a subject from one photo onto a solid color background can make the photographed subject look two-dimensional, or flat. Although adding a drop shadow or an inner shadow can help add some depth to the image, you might also want to experiment with the **Image**, **Transform**, **Skew** and **Distort** commands. Reducing or growing the top or side of the photo subject might help give a flat image more depth.

① How to Create a Composite 118

② How to Organize Layers 120

③ How to Transform Selections 122

④ How to Fine Tune Composites 124

⑤ How to Create a Reflection 126

⑥ How to Select Photos for Panoramas 128

⑦ How to Create an Outdoor Panorama 130

⑧ How to Create an Indoor Panorama 132

⑨ How to Manually Arrange Photos 134

7

Combining Images and Creating Panoramas

Photoshop Elements enables you to combine two or more images and create composites or panoramas. A *composite* is the result of combining two or more image layers in a single image window. Composites enable you to combine portraits of different people taken at the same or different times. Composites also enable you to compose completely fictitious digital photos. A *panorama* consists of two or more images aligned vertically or horizontally, overlapping areas to create a larger image.

The selection tools, combined with the **Copy** and **Paste** commands, enable you to quickly create composites. You can modify the selection to blend it in with the rest of the photo. The **Photomerge** command enables you to arrange two or more overlapping photos into a panorama. A typical panorama consists of three to six photos.

Working with composites also requires you to work with layers. Layers enable you to view and modify each composite element and work on a separate image until you're ready to merge it with another layer. The tasks in this part show you how to create composites, organize layers, rotate and resize selections, and blend and correct color to create all kinds of composites. You will also learn how to create indoor and outdoor panoramas using the **Photomerge** command.

How to Create a Composite

When you select, copy, and paste one set of image pixels over another image layer, the result is a composite. You can use composites to create special effects by placing an image from one photo into another photo.

1 Open Two Images

Choose **Open** from the shortcuts bar. Select two photo files that you want to combine into a single image. The images can be in any supported file format, such as JPG, TIF, or PSD and can be in any color mode. For example, you can choose a background image in RGB color mode and add RGB, grayscale, indexed color, or black and white selections to the background image. Open the files.

2 Choose a Selection Tool

Decide which image you want to use as the source and which you want to use as the destination. In this example, I use the chicken as the source image and the tree stump as the destination. Choose the selection tool that is appropriate for the subject you want to outline in the source image. For the chicken, I chose the **Magnetic Lasso** tool.

3 Define the Selection

Drag the selection tool around the subject in the source image.

4 Choose the Feather Command

Because the selection tool might crop the subject out of the source image too tightly, you can blur the selection line slightly to better blend the subject into the destination (background) image. Choose **Select**, **Feather** to open the **Feather Selection** dialog box.

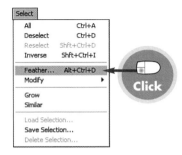

5 Feather the Selection

Type a number into the **Feather Radius** text box. Click **OK**. In this example, I typed **2** to blur two pixels from the edge of the selection.

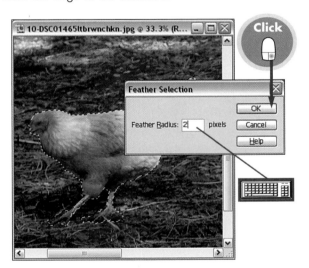

6 Copy and Paste the Selection

Choose **Edit**, **Copy** to copy the feathered selection to the Clipboard. Click the window for the destination image (the image into which you want to paste the selection) and choose **Edit**, **Paste**. The selection appears on a new layer in the destination image.

How-to Hint

Scale and Resolution

It's better to reduce the size of a photo than it is to make it bigger. Growing a graphic introduces pixelation—chunky blocks of colors that degrade the quality of the photo selection. For best results, create a selection using the original, high-resolution image. After adding the selection to another photo, scale it down.

Color Correction and Composites

Each selection you paste into the destination image introduces unique color and tonal ranges that you'll probably want to correct. Because you won't know how to blend the selection until you paste it into another photo, you'll have to add a fill or adjustment layer to blend the newly pasted selection into the background and any other photo selections in the composite.

How to Organize Layers

You can copy and paste multiple selections into a single image window. Only the amount of memory available to Photoshop Elements will limit the size of the composite file. The **Layers** palette enables you to organize selections and compose a complex composite.

❶ Open an Image

Click **Open** from the shortcuts bar. Select a photo that can be used as the background for a composite image. Open the file.

❷ Copy and Paste Images

Open the **Layers** palette. Open additional image files and select, copy, and paste parts of those photos into the image window that contains the background photo. Notice that each selection is added to the background image on a separate layer.

❸ Select a Layer

Select a layer that contains a fairly large photo selection. In this example, I opened the **Layers** palette and selected the layer containing the image of the squirrel.

④ Move to the Foreground

In the **Layers** palette, drag the selected layer to the top of the list of layers. In this example, notice that the squirrel is now in front of all the other animals in the image window.

Drag

⑥ Move a Selection Back

In the **Layers** palette, drag a layer located above the layer you selected in step 5 so that it is located below the selected layer in the list. In this example, notice that the cow has moved behind the goat image.

Drag

⑤ Overlap Images

Select a layer located near the top of the **Layers** palette, such as the layer that contains the goat. Click the **Move** tool and move the goat so that it overlaps the cow. Overlapping image layers enables you to see the layer order change in the next step.

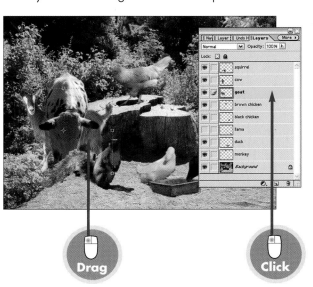

Drag   **Click**

How-to Hint

Renaming a Layer

In the **Layers** palette, double-click the name of the layer you want to rename. The text becomes highlighted. Type a new name for the layer and press **Enter** or **Return**.

Blending Modes and Composites

Blending modes combine color elements from a selected layer with the layer directly below it in the **Layers** palette. Blending modes can help blend an image selection on one layer with a photo or graphic on another layer. Select a layer in the **Layers** palette and click the drop-down menu at the top-left of the palette to change the blending mode from **Normal** to one of the 21 other available blending modes.

How to Transform Selections

Although there's a good chance that you can paste a selection that fits perfectly into another photo, you'll more likely find yourself resizing and rotating a selection until it scales to the background photo. This task shows you how to use the **Move** tool to rotate and resize a selection.

1 Open Two Images

Click the **Open** button in the shortcuts bar. Select two photos that you want to combine into a composite image. Open the files.

2 Copy and Paste a Selection

Select and copy the subject of one photo and paste it into the other image window. Select the image window that contains the composite.

3 Select the Move Tool

From the toolbox, select the **Move** tool. Click the portion of the composite in the image window that you want to resize and reposition (in this example, the horse). Drag the selection to reposition it. Drag one of the corner handles to resize the selection.

Click

4 Rotate the Selection

Click a few pixels outside the corner handle of the selection rectangle. The mouse pointer changes to a rotate icon (a curved line with an arrow at both ends). Drag the mouse up or down to rotate the selection. Click the check mark in the options bar to save this change.

5 Resize the Selection

Click one of the corner handles of the selection. Drag the corner inward to reduce the size of the selection. Drag the corner outward to grow the selection. Hold down the **Shift** key and drag to preserve the proportions of the image while resizing it.

6 Save Changes

Click the check mark in the options bar to save the changes you've made to the composite.

How-to Hint

Rulers and Grids

Having problems aligning pasted-in selection to a background photo? Choose **View**, **Rulers** or press **Ctrl+R** (Mac users press ⌘**+R**) to display the rulers in an image window. If you need more precise alignment guidelines, choose **View**, **Grid**. You can use the grid to align composite selections to a vertical or horizontal axis.

Flipping Selections

Choose the **Image**, **Rotate**, **Flip Layer Horizontal** or **Vertical** command to experiment with different orientations of a selection. The composite might be more exciting if a subject is upside down or facing the other way. You can also rotate a selected layer freely to see whether it blends better with the rest of the composite. After you've composed your subject, consider opening the **Layer Styles** palette and adding a drop shadow to the selection to add realism to the composite.

How to Fine Tune Composites

After you've created a basic composite, it's time to look more closely at what needs to be removed or enhanced in each image layer. This task shows you how to blend and adjust colors in a selection to create a more realistic-looking composite.

❶ Open Three Images

Click the **Open** button in the shortcuts bar. Select three images, open the files, and combine them into a composite. Open the **Layers** palette.

❷ Apply a Blending Mode

Click a layer in the **Layers** palette. Click the drop-down menu at the top of the palette and select a blending mode. Lighter blending modes combine colors from one layer with the colors in the layer directly below, creating a brighter result. Darker blending modes create a darker result color. See Part 4, Task 7, "How to Use Adjustment Layers," for more about color and blending modes.

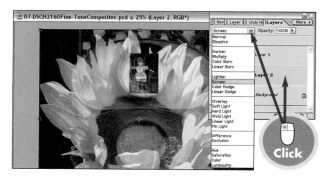

❸ Apply a Filter to a Selection

Click a layer in the **Layers** palette and apply a filter to the layer. Here, I applied the **Diffuse Glow** filter to the image of the girl to blend it with the metal background image. Choose **Filter**, **Distort**, **Diffuse Glow** and lower the values for the **Graininess** and **Glow Amount** sliders. Set the **Clear Amount** to a medium value. Click **OK**. Part 9, "Adding Filters and Effects," provides more information about filters.

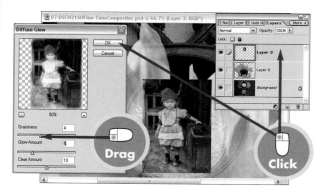

④ Scale Selections

Resize each selection so that it scales to the content in the background photo layer. Refer to Part 3, Task 7, "How to Change the Scale of an Image," for information about how to scale a selection.

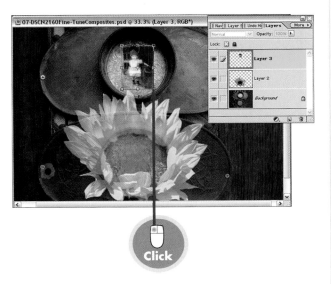

⑤ Choose the Quick Fix Command

In the **Layers** palette, click the eye icon next to all the layers except the one you want to work on (the eye icon should appear only next to the layer you want to work on). Choose the **Enhance**, **Quick Fix** command. The **Quick Fix** window opens. See Part 4, Task 8, "How to Quick Fix Images."

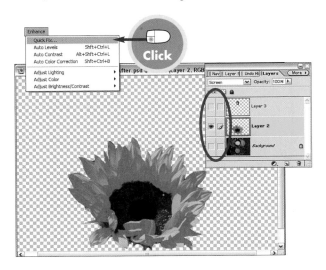

⑥ Modify Colors

Click the **Color Correction** and **Hue/Saturation** radio buttons to adjust those aspects of the selected layer. Drag the **Hue** slider to change the color. Drag the **Saturation** slider to the right to intensify the color. Click **OK** to apply the changes. To find out more about color correction, go to Part 4, "Image and Color Correction Techniques."

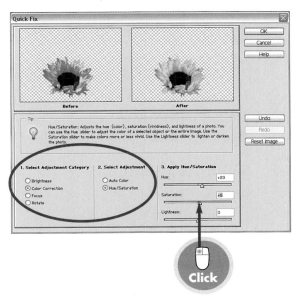

⑦ Blend Image Layers

In the **Layers** palette, click to display the eye icons for all the layers. Select a layer. Drag the **Opacity** slider control to the left to make the selection more transparent (useful if you want to blend a selection with the background image). Refer to Part 3, Task 5, "How to Work with Layers," for more about working with layers and opacity.

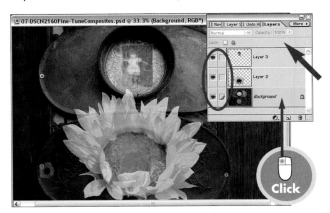

How to Create a Reflection

Composites enable you to add a reflection to a shiny or reflective surface, such as glass or water. Although reflections can add unwanted elements to an image, they can also add depth and realism. Consider the light source and on which surfaces the reflections will be as a result of how the light hits the subject. This task shows you how to copy, paste, and duplicate a selection to create a reflection in a glass surface.

① Open Two Images

Click **Open** from the shortcuts bar. Select an image that contains a window, glass, or shiny tiled surface; select a second image to be reflected in the glass. Open the files.

② Create the Composite

Apply a selection tool to the part of the image you want to be reflected (in this example, the chicken). Copy and paste the selection into the image window containing the glass.

③ Duplicate the Image

Click the selection and choose **Layer**, **Duplicate Layer** to create a second copy of the image you want to reflect. Type a name for the layer and click **OK**.

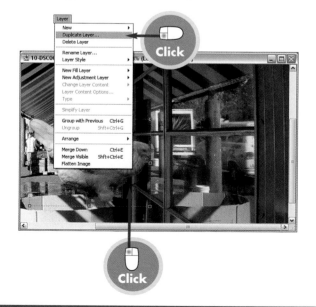

④ Flip the Image

Make sure that the copy of the image you created in step 3 is selected. Choose **Flip Layer Horizontal** from the **Image, Rotate** menu. The copy of the image flips to begin the reflection. Flip an image horizontally to create a mirror effect; flip the image 180 degrees for a rearview mirror effect.

⑤ Resize the Reflection

From the toolbox, select the **Move** tool. Drag a corner handle of the selection box and move it toward the center of the selection to make the image smaller; drag the corner box outward to grow the selection. Make sure that both the original image and its mirrored copy are sized appropriately in the background image. Click the check mark in the options bar to save the changes.

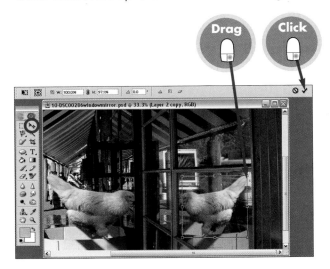

⑥ Lighten the Reflection

Open the **Layers** palette and select the layer containing the reflection. Drag the **Opacity** slider at the top of the palette to the left to make the reflection less opaque.

How-to Hint

One Image, Many Reflections

Consider the light source and the surface on which the reflection appears as a result of how the light hits the subject. You might have to create more than one copy of the image to reflect in the composite. Examine the composite for any materials, such as clothes, glasses, and painted surfaces that are exposed to the image, and consider adding a full or partial reflection of the image to these surfaces, as well as the surface located directly in front of the image.

Enhancing Reflections

A reflection may look a little different from its original. For instance, the texture of a surface or a variation in lighting might create a reflection that has a unique visual effect. You can apply a distortion filter, such as the **Liquify** command, to ripple or warp a reflection. Try applying a filter or effect to add texture to a reflection.

How to Select Photos for Panoramas

The **Photomerge** command tries to arrange any combination of photos you choose into a panorama. Overlapping areas of the photos are blended together into a composite. The first step in creating a wide composite is to select the photos for the panorama. This task shows you how to pick the series of photos for the panorama; the following two tasks detail how to actually combine the photos.

① Open Files

Click **Open** in the shortcuts bar. Select several photos of the same locale. Choose three or four images that share the same dimensions and share the same angle and subject. Open the files.

② Overlap Photos

Place two image windows side by side and see how much of the photos overlap. The best candidates for a panorama are photos that share common elements, such as a landmark. Use the common object (such as a building) in two photos to overlap one with the other.

③ Compare Images

Place two image windows next to each other. Identify any color or lighting differences between the photos. Consider using images that have matching exposures and colors. Exclude blurry images or overexposed images from consideration in the panorama.

④ View Image Size

Choose **Image**, **Resize**, **Image Size** or click the status bar in the work area for each image. All photos should have the same height and width. Resizing one photo (and not others) is not recommended.

⑤ Adjust Color

Select an image window and choose **Enhance**, **Automatic Color Correction** to automatically improve the color for the image. Repeat this step for each photo you plan to use in the panorama.

⑥ Select Photos for the Panorama

Select three to six photos you want to use in the panorama. You might want to place the selected files in a separate folder on your hard drive to keep them handy when you use the **Photomerge** command.

How-to Hint

Photo Overlap

When you're shooting photos that you plan to combine into a panorama, allow approximately one third of the photo to overlap with the next photo. Most photos will overlap in a diagonal pattern, not vertically or horizontally. Photoshop Elements tries to blend any overlapping elements into a seamless panorama.

As you shoot photos for a panorama, take a series of photos from one spot. Then experiment and shoot another series of photos from a different angle, at a different time of day, or with different camera settings. If you're shooting a skyline panorama, for example, you might be able to construct a panorama that shifts lighting from mid-day to sunset.

How to Create an Outdoor Panorama

There are two phases involved in creating a panorama. In the first phase, you select the images for the panorama. In the second phase, the **Photomerge** command automatically arranges them. This task walks you through these two phases to create a panorama.

1 Open Image Files

Click **Open** on the shortcuts bar. Select the image files you want to use to create a panorama. Open the files in any order.

2 Choose Photomerge Command

Select **File**, **Create Photomerge** to open the **Photomerge** dialog box.

3 Select Files

The files you have already opened appear in the **Photomerge** dialog box. Click the **Browse** button and navigate the hard drive to select any additional files you want to include in the panorama. Click **OK**.

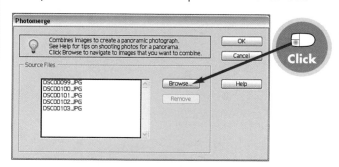

④ Generate the Panorama

The panorama appears in the **Photomerge** window. The **Photomerge** command excludes photos that do not overlap with approximately one third of another photo. Enable the **Advanced Blending** check box and then click **Preview**. The **Advanced Blending** option blends lighting exposure differences between photos in the composite.

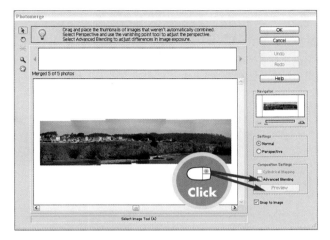

⑤ Blend Photos

View the panorama with the **Advanced Blending** setting applied to each photo. Click **Exit Preview** to return to the **Photomerge** window. Click **OK**.

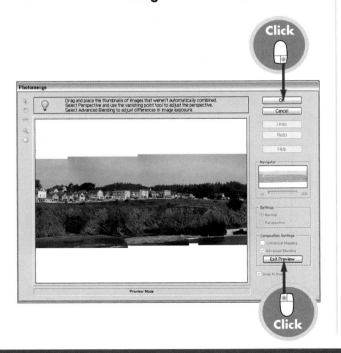

⑥ Create the Panorama

The panorama appears in a new image window. Consider applying the **Crop** tool to remove the uneven edges of the overlapping photos from the panoramic image. Resizing a panorama in this way lets you scale the image to fit a desktop, Web site, or print media.

How-to Hint

Shooting Photos for Panoramas

The key to creating a fluid panorama is to shoot each photo from the same perspective. The **Photomerge** command arranges photos horizontally or vertically, or combines horizontal and vertical axis of photos. The number of photos you can work with is limited only by the amount of memory available on your computer.

Resizing a Panorama

The **Photomerge** command doesn't alter the size of any photos to create a panorama. However, you can resize each file before you select the **Photomerge** command, or resize any portion of the panorama after it's been created in the work area. Save a copy of the original panorama to preserve all the color and pixel data. This high-resolution photo will create great-looking prints. To resize the panorama, select the **Image**, **Resize**, **Image Size** command. Enable the **Constrain Proportions** check box and type a smaller number into the width or height text box to resize the panorama.

How to Create an Indoor Panorama

You can take several photos of any room and arrange them into a panorama. Creating an indoor panorama is very similar to creating an outdoor panorama, except that perspectives and angles can be a little more challenging. This task shows you how to manually arrange photos in a panorama after **Photomerge** tries to automatically arrange them.

1 Open Image Files

Click the **Open** button on the shortcuts bar. Select several indoor photos and open the files in any order.

2 Choose the Photomerge Command

Choose **File**, **Create Photomerge**. When the **Photomerge** dialog box opens to list the images to be included in the composite, click **OK**. The **Photomerge** window opens.

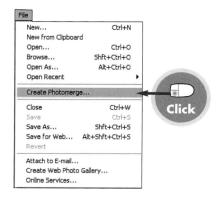

3 Preview Panorama

Wait for the panorama to appear in the **Photomerge** window. Unmatched photos (those that Photoshop Elements couldn't place in the composite) appear at the top of the window.

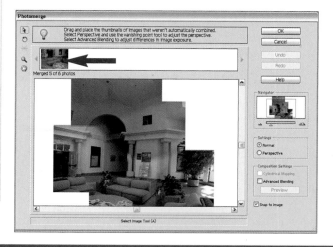

④ Add a Photo to the Panorama

The tools located on the upper-left corner of the **Photomerge** window enable you to add or rearrange the photos. Choose the **Select Image** tool and drag an unmatched photo from the top of the window down to the composite area to position it in the desired location in the panorama.

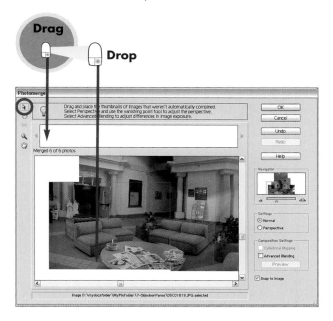

⑤ Create the Panorama

Look for any other misaligned photos and rearrange them to blend into the panorama. When you are ready to create the panorama, click **OK** in the **Photomerge** window. The panorama appears in a new image window. Apply the **Clone Stamp**, **Smudge**, **Dodge**, or **Burn** tool to blend any areas of the image.

⑥ Crop the Panorama

Select the **Crop** tool and drag to exclude the uneven edges of the panorama. Press **Enter** (**Return** for Mac users) to crop the panorama.

How-to Hint

Fixing Mismatched Photos

If some objects in the photo don't line up, choose a central subject across two photos and use that subject to arrange the photos in the panorama. If an area of the composite, such as the window in step 3, doesn't align with the same area in the adjacent image, use the **Smudge** or **Clone Stamp** tool to fix it.

Running Out of Memory?

If you open several images before you select the **Photomerge** command, Photoshop Elements might not have enough memory to process the advanced blending, perspective, and Cylindrical Mapping effects for the final panorama. Close all open image windows before choosing the **Photomerge** command to free up as much memory as possible before creating a panorama.

How to Manually Arrange Photos

After the **Photomerge** command has auto-arranged images into a composite, you might want to manually arrange any image in the panorama. Add, remove, or use the arrow keys to move a photo up, down, left or right. This task shows you how to manually arrange the elements of a panorama composite.

1 Open Image Files

Click the **Open** button in the shortcuts bar. Choose several images taken at the same location that you want to compile into a panorama composite. Open the files.

2 Choose Photomerge Command

Choose **File**, **Photomerge**. The **Photomerge** window opens, listing any open image files.

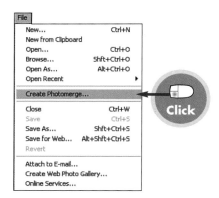

3 Add Images to Composite List

Click the **Browse** button and navigate the computer's hard disk to add any photos you want to use in the panorama. If necessary, **Shift+**click to select multiple files from the **Open** dialog box and then click **OK**. Try to select only files for the panorama. Adding files that won't fit into the panorama uses memory and requires more computing time.

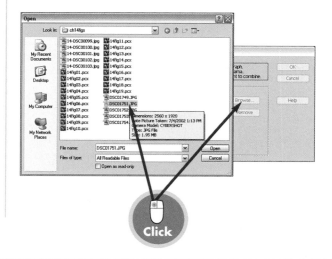

4 Remove Image from Photomerge

To remove an image file from the list of images to be used to create the panorama, select the image file from the window list and click **Remove**. When the image list contains all the images you want to use to create the panorama, click **OK**.

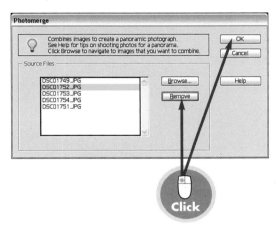

5 Preview Panorama

Wait for Photoshop Elements to assemble the panorama and open the **Photomerge** window. Select the **Hand** tool from the top-left corner of the window and click and drag any portion of the composite to move the panorama in the preview area.

6 Adjust the View

In the **Navigator** area of the window, click the **Mountain** icon on the right to zoom into the panorama. Drag the slider control to adjust the view.

7 Manually Arrange Photos

Choose the **Select Image** tool from the top-left corner of the window. Drag an image from the composite and drop it into the top pane of the window to remove that portion of the composite from the panorama. Drag photos within the composite to rearrange the panorama.

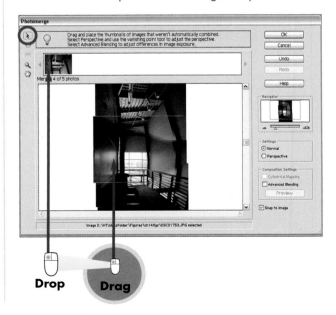

8 Add Perspective

Click in the white area of the preview area with the **Select Image** tool to deselect all the photos in the composite. Enable the **Perspective** radio button to prepare the composite for changes to perspective.

9 Change Center of Perspective

Select the **Set Vanishing Point** tool from the top-left corner of the window. Click an image in the composite to make that image the central photo (the "vanishing point" in terms of perspective). The panorama's perspective redraws each time you click a different photo.

10 Preview Advanced Blending

Enable the **Advanced Blending** check box and click the **Preview** button. The **Advanced Blending** option blends the lighting for overlapping photos in the panorama. Click the **Preview** button to see how **Advanced Blending** affects the panorama.

11 Exit Preview Mode

After viewing the preview, click the **Exit Preview** button. Now you can select any of the tools, radio buttons, or check boxes in the **Photomerge** window to continue to fine-tune the composite.

12 Map the Panorama on a Cylinder

Enable the **Cylindrical Mapping** check box. Be sure that the **Perspective** radio button and the **Advanced Blending** check box are also selected. Click **Preview** to see the Cylindrical Mapping effect.

13 Exit Preview Mode

Click **Exit Preview** to close the **Photomerge** window. The **Photomerge** dialog box reappears. Use the **Select Image**, **Zoom**, and **Hand** tools to arrange each photo in the **Photomerge** dialog box.

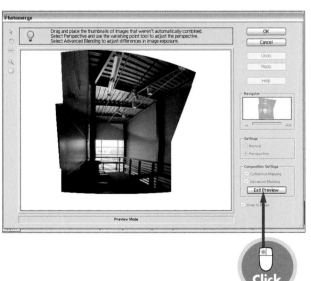

14 Create Final Panorama

After you've finished manually arranging the photos in the panorama, click **OK**. View the final panorama in the new window that opens in the work area.

How-to Hint

How Many Photos to Shoot?

Although you can create a panorama with a minimum of two photos, for best results, shoot an outdoor or indoor set of photos three photos across and three photos tall. Because each photo should overlap about a third, the final panorama will be much shorter and narrower than if the photos were laid out side by side.

Final Touches

For best results, perform color corrections, touch ups, and cover ups after the panorama has been created. The **Color Variations** and **Quick Fix** commands work great with panoramas. If you need to touch up overlapping photos, try lightening the area with the **Dodge** tool; darken areas using the **Burn** tool.

Task

(1) How to Pick Images for Animation 140

(2) How to Create Animation Frames 142

(3) How to Preview Animation 144

(4) How to Animate People 146

(5) How to Animate Shapes 150

8

Creating Animation

Animation is a process that involves frame-by-frame creation of motion. Each frame usually consists of a background and any number of subjects, or animated characters. Bugs Bunny and Mickey Mouse are two very popular animated characters. An animation can play through once or loop continuously.

Photoshop Elements enables you to store an animation in a special file format called *Animated GIF*. You can use layers to animate one or more subjects, and then merge the layers together with the background to create each final frame of animation. The **Save for Web** command enables you to preview and create the Animated GIF file. You can play the Animated GIF in a browser application, such as Internet Explorer or Netscape Navigator.

The tasks in this part introduce you to a few simple animation techniques. Start by picking images, then create a simple four-frame animation and continue on to animating people and graphics.

How to Pick Images for Animation

Choosing the right photos before beginning your animation can save you a lot of time in the long run. Pick photos that contain a captivating or interesting subject. Try to pick a series of photos that show the same subject in several different positions (or use Photoshop Elements to modify a single photo). Finally, choose a background photo that compliments your subject.

① Open Several Images

Click the **Open** button in the shortcuts bar. Open several image files that contain potential subjects for your animation.

② Select Images

Click each image window to view each subject. Select two or more photos of the same subject. In this example, I've selected two cow images: one with the cow's mouth open, the other with the cow's mouth closed.

③ Compare Images

The subject in the second image should be the same size as it is in the first image, with a different pose (here the cow's mouth is open in the second image). The lighting for the two images should be consistent for best animation results.

④ Choose a Background Image

Keeping the subject you want to animate in mind, open, view, and select a background image. The background can be a flat backdrop, a photo with a subject, or a generic landscape like the one shown here. Pick a background image that complements the colors and position of the subject.

⑤ Select Subjects

Click the **Magnetic Lasso** tool in the toolbox. Drag the tool to select the subject in the first image window (the cow with its mouth closed).

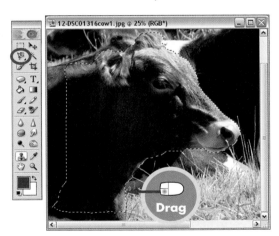

⑥ Combine Photos

Copy and paste the selection into the background image window. Repeat steps 5 and 6 for each image (the cow with its mouth open). Each pasted selection appears in its own layer.

How-to Hint

Using Video to Create Animation

Video is great for capturing motion. You can use the **File**, **Import**, **Frame from Video** command to bring selected frames of video into the work area. Then pick the images you want to use to create your animation.

Analyzing Tonal Range Across Layers

Use the **Histogram** command to analyze the tonal range distribution across the layers of each frame of animation. Hide all layers except the layers you want to use in a particular frame. Choose **Image**, **Histogram** to view the tonal range information for the visible layers. Choose **Layer**, **New Adjustment Layer**, **Levels** to open the **Levels** dialog box and use the controls to change the tonal range in the image layer so that it more closely matches the other images in the animation. For more about the **Levels** dialog box, see Part 4, Task 1, "How to Correct Tonal Range."

How to Create Animation Frames

Each layer in the **Layers** palette represents a frame of animation in a finished Animated GIF file. As you create, fine-tune, and assemble each component of a frame, you will work with a group of several different layers that contain similar images. Only the layers that correspond to a particular frame appear in the image window. All other layers are hidden until you're ready to move on to the next frame.

❶ Open a Photo

Open a file that contains a background image and at least two subject layers (such as the pasture scene with the two different cow poses created in the preceding task). Open the **Layers** palette.

❷ Duplicate the Background

Drag the **Background** layer onto the **Create a new layer** icon at the bottom of the **Layers** palette. A **Background copy** layer appears in the **Layers** palette list. Review the photos selected for the animation and decide on the duration of the animation and how the subject will move.

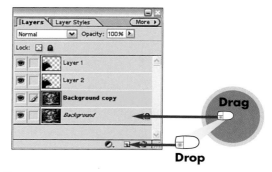

❸ Duplicate Layers

Count each subject pose (key frame) as a required frame in the animation. Add at least one or two in-between frames. Add up all the key and in-between frames to get a total frame count. Drag each subject layer over the **Create a new layer** button to create key frames and in-betweens.

4 Organize Layers

Arrange the layers that belong in the same frame so that they are grouped together, one layer above the other with the background layers below the subject layers. Rename the layers so that the frame number and content are clearly labeled. Renaming layers helps identify which layers belong to a particular frame.

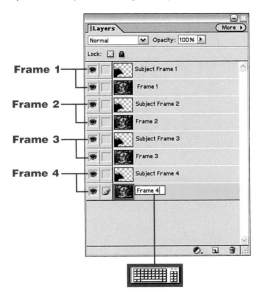

5 Customize Layers

In the **Layers** palette, click the eye icons to hide all layers except the ones that comprise the first frame of animation (in this example, the second cow pose and its background layer). Select **Filter**, **Distort**, **Liquify**, and use the Liquify tools to modify the subject's expression (here, I turned the closed mouth into a smile). Click **OK** to save your changes and exit the **Liquify** window.

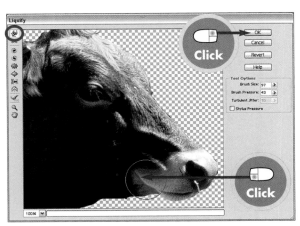

6 Merge Layers

Select the topmost cow layer and choose **Merge Down** from the **More** drop-down menu in the **Layers** palette. Congratulations! You've created frame one of the animation. View the layers that will comprise one frame of animation.

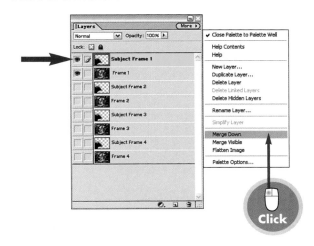

How-to Hint

Photos and Animation

An animation can consist of a minimum of two frames. The flow of the playback of the animation depends largely on how fast your computer is, and how large the photos and resulting animation file are. In this example, each photo of the cow is a five megapixel image. Combined with the background, each frame of animation may be up to 1MB in size. Depending on how slow the computer is, the resulting animation may look more like a yawning cow than a talking cow. For best results, merge each animation frame together, and then resize each layer (the smaller the image size, the faster the playback is likely to be) when creating the Animated GIF.

Key Frames and In-betweens

If you want to use three photos for your animation, the first and last photos are key frames, and the middle photo is the in-between frame. Key frames can help you create an animation consisting of four or more frames of animation. A key frame defines each key position of the animated subject. You can have from one to more than thirty in-between frames. The more in-between frames, the smoother the animated motion.

How to Preview Animation

After each animation frame has been created in the **Layers** palette, you can preview each frame in the **Save For Web**. Before you create the final animation file, you might want to reduce the image size of the animation, save it as an Animated GIF, and view it in a browser.

❶ Create All Frames

Open the animation file you worked on in the preceding tasks. Click a subject layer for one of the frames and choose **Merge Down** from the **More** drop-down menu in the **Layers** palette. Repeat this step for each frame of animation. Review each frame to make sure that each is in the proper order in the **Layers** palette.

❷ Resize Image

Choose **Image Size** from the **Image**, **Resize** menu. Type values into the **Width** and **Height** text boxes, such as **800** and **600**. Click **OK** to resize all the animation frames to these specifications. The optimum size of an animation depends on the type of computer you expect your target audience to use to play back your animation. The smaller the file, the faster the playback, and the more machines can view the animation.

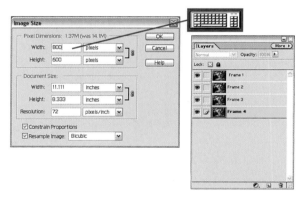

❸ Open Save For Web Window

Select the **File**, **Save for Web** command. The **Save For Web** window opens. Select the **Zoom** tool from the top-left corner of the window. Hold down the **Alt** key (the **Option** key for Mac users) and click to zoom out of the image.

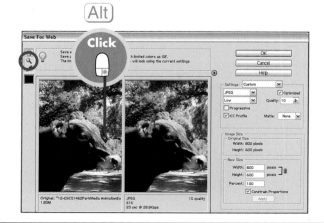

④ Adjust File Settings

Animation files must be saved in the GIF format; choose **GIF** from the drop-down menu in the **Settings** area of the window. Choose **128** from the **Colors** drop-down list to limit the number of colors used (and reduce file size). Enable the **Animate** and **Loop** check boxes to create the animation. Click **OK**; when prompted, type a name for the animation file to save it.

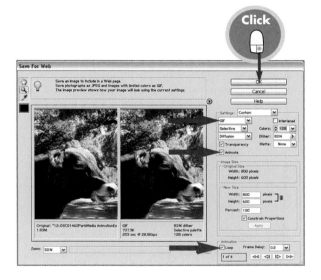

⑤ Start the Browser

Start your browser, such as Internet Explorer. Choose **File**, **Open**. In the **Open** dialog box, click **Browse** and navigate your hard disk to select the GIF file you created in step 4.

⑥ Play Animation

Click **OK** in the **Open** dialog box. The animation file loads, plays, and loops (repeats). To pause the looping animation, right-click (**Option**+click for Mac users) in the browser window. Close the browser window to exit the looping animation. If you want the animation to play through only once, open the **Save For Web** window and disable the **Loop** check box before saving the file again.

How-to Hint

Creating a Cartoon

You can share your animation as a cartoon strip by moving the animation frames into a new document. Choose **File**, **New** and create a new document with the dimensions of the cartoon layout. Copy and paste the animation frames into the new image window. Then resize each image to fit in the cartoon layout. Select the **Custom Shape** tool from the toolbox and choose the cartoon dialog balloon from the Default library in the **Shape** pop-up palette. Drag in the image window to add a thought balloon to any of the animation frames. Then select the **Horizontal** or **Vertical Type** tool and add text to each thought balloon to complete the cartoon.

Not Seeing Animation?

If you don't see the animation play in the browser, make sure that you have a recent browser installed on your computer. Photoshop Elements requires version 5 of Internet Explorer or version 4.7 of Netscape Navigator. If you still aren't seeing more than one frame of animation, check the preference settings for your browser to ensure that Animated GIFs and looping are enabled in the browser.

How to Animate People

Animating a person is similar to creating animations of other objects, such as the cow example in the previous tasks. You can create a simple animation by moving the person across the background in only two or three frames. Animate two subjects in the same set of frames to create a complex animation.

1 Open Photos

Open a background photo for the animation and one or two photos that contain subjects (here a child on a tricycle and a boy standing). Select the subjects and copy and paste them into the image window. Open the **Layers** palette to view the layers in the composite.

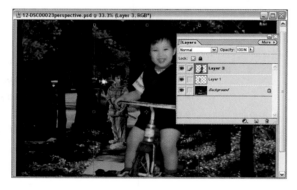

2 Duplicate Layers

Drag each layer and drop it on the **Create a new layer** icon at the bottom of the **Layers** palette. Create three copies of each layer, one for each frame of a three-frame animation. Each frame will contain both subjects, each moving in a different direction. In this example, I group images by frame using the background image to separate the frames of animation. You might want to rename the layers to help identify them.

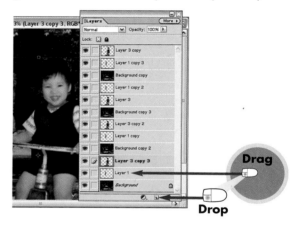

3 Hide and Show Layers

Click the **eye icon** next to each layer you want to hide (the eye icon disappears for hidden layers). Leave at least the background and one subject layer visible in the **Layers** palette. (Later we will apply the **Clone Stamp** tool or **Liquify** command to the subjects to customize each frame.)

④ Lay Out the First Frame

Choose the **Move** tool from the toolbox. In the image window, drag the subject selections around on the background to compose the first frame of animation.

⑤ Create the Last Frame

In the **Layers** palette, click the eye icons to hide the layers you were just working with. Display the layers that will comprise the last frame of the animation by clicking the left boxes to display the eye icons for those layers. Use the **Move** tool to arrange the subjects against the background to compose the last frame.

⑥ Compose In-between Frames

Click the eye icons to hide the layers you were just working with. Display the layers that comprise one of the middle frames of the animation (an in-between frame) by clicking the left boxes to display the eye icons. Use the **Move** tool to arrange the subjects against the background in locations between their first and last positions. Repeat this step for any additional in-between frames.

⑦ Select the Liquify Command

Select a layer that contains a subject of an in-between frame. Choose **Liquify** from the **Filter**, **Distort** menu. The **Liquify** window opens. I'll use the **Liquify** tools to modify this frame so that the eyes of the child on the trike appear to be blinking in the next step.

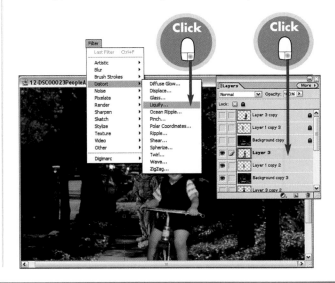

8 Customize a Subject

Use the tools in the **Liquify** window to modify the image so that the subject appears to be in motion. In this example, I used the **Pucker** tool to shrink the pixels around the child's eyes so that he appears to be blinking. Click **OK**.

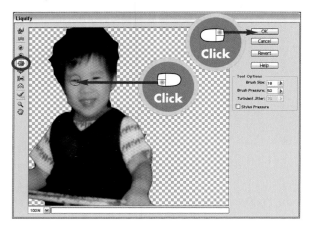

9 Select a Subject

Ctrl+click (⌘+click for Mac users) a layer that contains the subject of an in-between frame. The shortcut keystroke selects the subject (image pixels) in the layer. Choose the **Selection Brush** from the toolbox and drag the tool along the side of the image to which you want to add a blur effect to simulate motion.

10 Blur the Selection

Choose **Motion Blur** from the **Filter**, **Blur** menu. Adjust the **Distance** slider in the **Motion Blur** dialog box until you are satisfied with the amount of blur applied to the subject. Click **OK**.

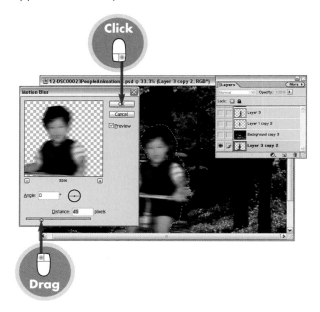

11 Merge Down Layers

After you have modified the layers that comprise each frame, display the eye icons for all the layers to be included in a frame (all other layers should be hidden). Choose the **Merge Down** command from the **More** drop-down list in the **Layers** palette. Continue applying the **Merge Down** command, two layers at a time, to create each separate frame of animation.

12 Select Animation Options

Choose **File**, **Save for Web** to open the **Save For Web** window. Animation files must be saved in the GIF format; choose **GIF** from the drop-down menu in the **Settings** area of the window. Enable the **Animate** and **Loop** check boxes to create the animation.

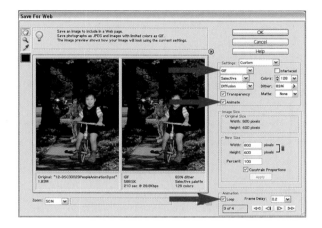

13 Preview the Animation

Click the **Step Forward** and **Step Backward** buttons to preview each frame of animation. Type a higher number in the **Frame Delay** field to increase the delay between each frame; a lower number decreases the delay (the decimal value indicates fractions of a second; whole numbers represent minutes). Click **OK**; when prompted, type a name for the animation file to save it.

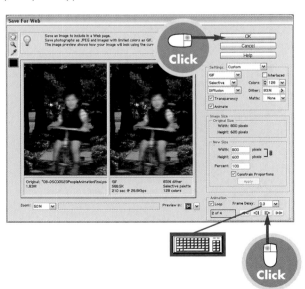

How-to Hint

Creating Smooth Animation

If you're a big fan of five megapixel images, I have bad news for you. The key to smooth animation is keeping each frame small, small, small! For best results, create each frame at a high resolution and save the file as a Photoshop file. Then resize the Photoshop file before creating the smaller Animated GIF.

Focusing on a Character

One way to make an animated character stand out is to apply a subtle blur to the background image before merging down layers to create the frame. Choose the **Blur** filter from the **Filter**, **Blur** menu and apply it more than once if necessary until the background image is slightly out of focus. Keep the animated subject in a separate layer so that the blur filter doesn't affect it.

How to Animate Shapes

You can create animation by designing your own graphics. Use the **Brush** and **Shape** tools to design an abstract art form as the star of your animation. You can use any photo as the background for the animation.

① Open a Background Image

Click **Open** in the shortcuts bar. Select a background photo and open it.

② Compose the First Frame

Select the **Shape** tool from the toolbox and choose a specific shape from the **Shape** drop-down menu in the options bar. Adjust **Style**, **Color**, and other options as desired. Drag to create a shape (the shape appears on a new layer). Add several shapes to the image window. Select the **Move** tool and drag the shapes against the background image to compose the first frame.

③ Duplicate and Arrange Layers

In the **Layers** palette, use the **Move** tool to drag and drop a shape layer on the **Create a new layer** icon. Repeat to create as many copies of the shapes and backgrounds as needed for animation frames. Drag the layers to be included in the first frame to the top of the **Layers** palette. Click the eye icons to hide all the layers not included in the first frame.

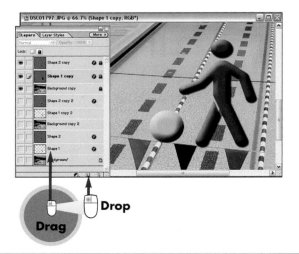

Drag

Drop

④ Compose the Last Frame

Click the eye icons to hide the layers you were just working with; click the left boxes to display the eye icons for the layers in the last frame of the animation. Select the **Move** tool and drag to arrange the shapes to compose the last frame. In this example, I applied the **Brush** and **Eraser** tools to rearrange the front and rear legs of the walking figure.

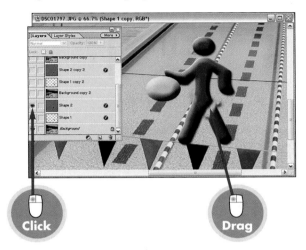

⑥ Merge Visible Layers

In the **Layers** palette, display the eye icons for only those layers you want to merge into a single frame. Choose **Merge Visible** from the **More** drop-down menu. Repeat this step to merge other layers into frames. To view the animation, open the **Save For Web** window and follow the instructions in the preceding task.

⑤ Modify a Shape

Select one of the subject shapes in an in-between frame and choose **Liquify** from the **Filter**, **Distort** menu. A dialog box opens; click **OK** to simplify the shape. Select the **Warp** tool from the upper-left corner of the **Liquify** window and drag the tool over the shape to imply motion (here, I modified the walking-man shape's arms and legs). Click **OK** to accept the changes.

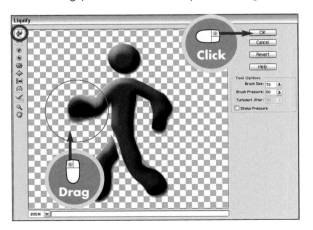

How-to Hint

Bouncing Ball

One way to practice your animation skills is to create a simple animation of a bouncing ball. First start with a simple two-frame animation. Then add more frames between the first two and apply the **Liquify** and **Blur** tools to exaggerate the shape of the ball. The goal of this exercise is to help you create fluid motion with a simple shape. After you've mastered the bouncing ball, try adding a background and more animation elements to the scene.

Motion Graphics and Video Footage

Video plays at approximately 30 frames per second. If you have access to digital video footage, use the **File**, **Import** command to import frames of video into the work area. Then use the **Shape** tool to add a simple TV to your animation. Simply copy, paste, and resize each frame of video and place it in the faux TV. When you play back the animation, each frame of video or motion graphics will also play back to create the illusion of a TV in your animation.

Task

① How to Apply a Filter or Effect 154

② How to Use the Liquify Filter 156

③ How to Add Clouds 158

④ How to Apply Artistic Filters 160

⑤ How to Apply Destructive Filters 162

⑥ How to Add Lighting Effects 164

Adding Filters and Effects

Filters and effects can be used to make an image more interesting. Photoshop Elements comes with dozens of filters and effects, and you can apply any number of them to an image.

A *filter* can do something as simple as sharpen or blur a photo, or apply an artistic brush stroke to a photo. Some filters enable you to adjust coloring in a photo or dramatically warp pixels in a photo. Most filters open a dialog box that enables you to customize one or more filter settings. Each filter is stored as a plug-in file in the Photoshop Elements folder. You can install third-party (non-Adobe) plug-in files if you like, but the tasks in this part of the book stick with the plug-ins that come with Photoshop Elements.

Effects are combinations of filters that can be applied to text or bitmap images. Unlike filters, effects cannot be customized. Some effects add a layer that you can blend with a photo. Because it's difficult to predict exactly how a filter or effect can change a photo, experimentation is required. The tasks in this part show you how to apply filters and effects and explore a few basic concepts so that you feel confident experimenting with filters and other effects.

How to Apply a Filter or Effect

You access filters from the **Filter** menu and the **Filters** palette. Effects are stored in the **Effects** palette. Apply one or several filters and effects to an image to experiment with digital visual effects.

① Open an Image

Click the **Open** button in the shortcuts bar. Select an image file and open it.

② Open the Filters Palette

Choose **Filters** from the **Window** menu. The **Filters** palette opens. Click and drag it away from the palette well so that it is open onscreen. Choose **Window**, **Effects** if you want to work with effects.

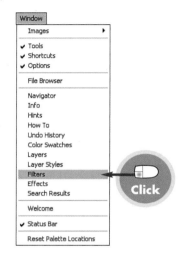

③ Select a Filter

Choose **All** from the drop-down menu at the top of the **Filters** palette. Double-click a filter to open its associated dialog box. For example, double-click the **Wave** filter to open the **Wave** dialog box.

④ Customize the Filter

Adjust settings for the selected filter. For example, in the **Wave** dialog box, click the **Sine** radio button to select that type of waveform. Type a number between 1 and 999 into the **Number of Generators** text box to specify the number of waves.

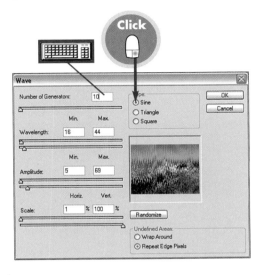

⑤ Adjust Wavelength Settings

Click and drag the **Wavelength** slider controls. Notice the effect your adjustments have on the preview image in the dialog box.

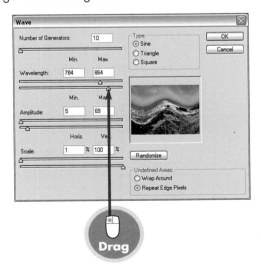

⑥ Adjust Other Filter Options

Type a number into the **Amplitude** text box or drag the slider controls. Drag the **Scale** slider controls. Enable the **Repeat Edge Pixels** radio button. When you are satisfied with the effect you have created, click **OK**.

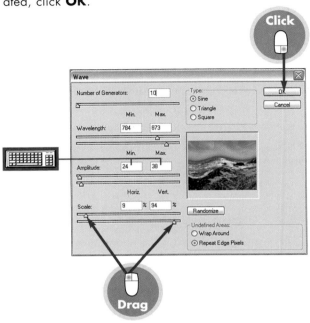

Types of Filters

How-to Hint

The fourteen sets of filters located in the **Filters** palette might overwhelm you at first. All these filters actually fit into five basic groups: artistic, destructive, video, miscellaneous, and watermark detection. The **Artistic**, **Brush Stroke**, **Sketch**, and **Stylize** filters are all artistic filters. The **Blur**, **Distort**, **Noise**, **Pixelate**, **Render**, **Texture**, and **Sharpen** filters are all capable of removing pixels from a photo and so are considered destructive filters. The **Video** filters convert the image so that it uses **NTSC** or **De-Interlaced** colors. The **Other** filters (**Custom**, **High Pass**, **Maximum**, **Minimum**, and **Offset**), especially the **Custom** filter, can be used to apply unique effects. **The Digimarc** filter enables you to view the Digimarc ID for image files that contain Digimarc copyright or author information. You can also view copyright and author information from the **File**, **File Info** dialog box.

How to Use the Liquify Filter

Hidden in the **Filter** menu is the powerful **Liquify** command. The **Liquify** window is home to eleven magical tools: **Warp**, **Turbulence**, **Pucker**, **Bloat**, **Twirl Clockwise** and **Counterclockwise**, **Shift**, **Reflect**, **Reconstruct**, **Zoom**, and the simple but necessary **Hand** tool. The key to using these tools is to select a brush size that roughly matches the area of the image you want to modify.

1 Open an Image

Click the **Open** button in the shortcuts bar. Select an image file you want to modify and open it.

2 Choose the Liquify Command

Choose **Liquify** from the **Filter**, **Distort** menu. The **Liquify** window opens. Select the **Zoom** tool from the **Liquify** window and click the image to magnify it.

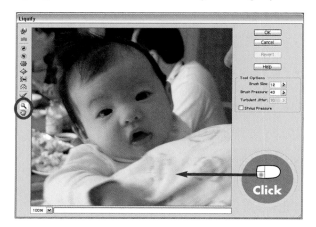

3 Select the Bloat Tool

Select the **Bloat** tool from the left side of the **Liquify** window. Type a value into the **Brush Size** text box, specifying a brush size that roughly matches the area you want to modify. Here, we want to modify the size of the child's eye, so the brush size is appropriately large.

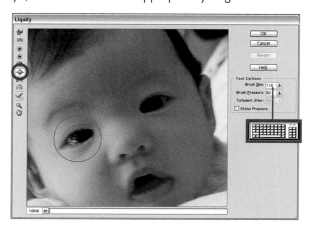

4 Apply the Bloat Tool

Click, drag, and release the mouse on the image. The longer you hold the mouse button, the more the **Bloat** tool affects the pixels.

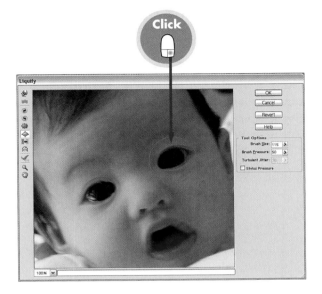

5 Apply the Warp Tool

Select the **Warp** tool. Drag to push pixels around in the image. Here, I drag the Warp tool above the subject's left eye.

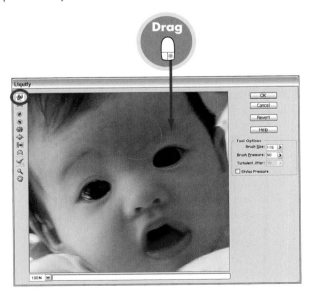

6 Reconstruct Pixels

Select the **Reconstruct** tool. Drag the tool over the image to undo any Liquify effects you applied earlier. Here, I return the child's eyes to their original size. Click **OK** when you're satisfied with the changes you've made to the image.

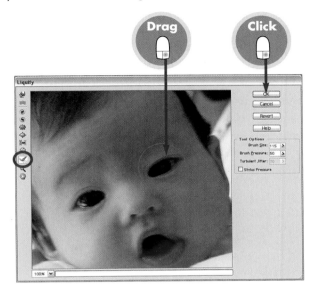

How-to Hint

Brush Size Makes a Difference

In the **Liquify** window, brush size matters. If you're working with a five megapixel image file, larger brush sizes create more gradual, subtle distortions. For starters, choose a 50–70 pixel brush size and apply the **Pucker** or **Bloat** tool by clicking in one spot and holding down the mouse button. The longer you hold the mouse button, the more the selected tool twists and turns the area of the image. Try to apply each tool in small doses. Too much distortion can ruin a great photo.

Undo at Any Time

As you apply different tools in the **Liquify** window, evaluate each change. If you don't like what you see, press **Ctrl+Z** (Mac users press ⌘**+Z**) to undo the previous change.

How to Add Clouds

The **Cloud** filter enables you to add a cloudy sky to a photo. Use the **Magic Wand** tool to select the sky an image file and then choose a foreground color to set the color of the sky behind the clouds. Clouds are rendered in white, and the foreground color defines the color of the sky.

❶ Open an Image

Click the **Open** button in the shortcuts bar. Select an image file that shows a blue sky taken at an upward angle. Open the file.

❷ Select the Magic Wand Tool

Select the **Magic Wand** tool. In the options bar, the **Tolerance** value defines the range of selected colors: a lower value selects a limited range of color, a larger value selects a wider range of color. Enable the **Anti-aliased** and **Contiguous** check boxes. In the image window, click the largest area in the sky to select it.

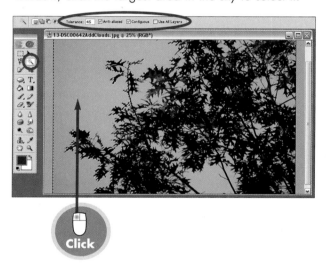

❸ Expand the Selection

Choose the **Similar** command from the **Select** menu. The selection area expands to include all the blue areas in the image window.

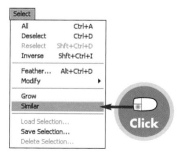

④ Set the Foreground Color

Click the **Foreground** color swatch. The **Color Picker** dialog box opens. Drag the color slider (the vertical rainbow) to the color you want to use, such as blue. Then click in the color field on the left side of the dialog box to choose a color, such as a dark or light blue. Click **OK**.

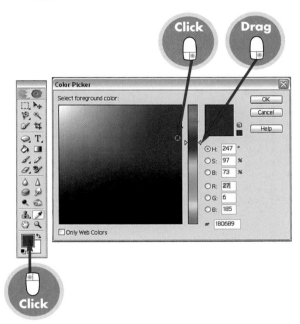

⑤ Choose the Clouds Command

Choose **Clouds** from the **Filter**, **Render** menu. The colors you selected in step 4 is used to show clouds and sky.

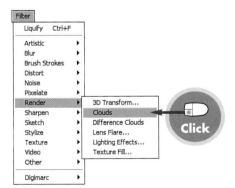

⑥ View the Image

Clouds appear in the sky. You can increase the amount of clouds in the sky by pressing **Ctrl+F** (⌘**+F** for Mac users) in the image window. This shortcut command reapplies the **Clouds** filter.

How-to Hint

Layer Styles

If you like instant gratification, consider applying layer styles to an image to enhance a filter or effect. Drag the **Layer Styles** palette from the palette well or choose **Window**, **Layer Styles**. Select a group of layer styles from the drop-down menu in the **Layer Styles** palette. In the **Layers** palette, select the layer to which you want to apply the style (most likely the layer to which the filter was applied). Double-click a layer style to apply it to the selected layer.

How to Apply Artistic Filters

Artistic filters enable you to redraw a photo using one or several filter options. Each artistic filter enables you to customize a range of options, such as the type, length, and intensity of each brush stroke or style. Experiment with artistic filters on different photos or apply several filters to a single image to create unique, artsy-looking photos!

1 Open an Image

Click the **Open** button in the shortcuts bar. Choose an image file and open it.

2 Choose the Sponge Filter

Choose the **Filter**, **Artistic** menu. Notice the long list of artistic filters from which you can choose. For this example, choose the **Sponge** command to open the **Sponge** dialog box.

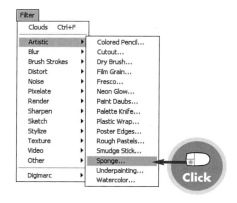

3 Adjust the View

Click the **Minus** button in the dialog box to zoom out of the thumbnail. Drag in the thumbnail to reposition the image until the view is adjusted to your satisfaction.

④ Adjust Settings

In the dialog box, drag the **Brush Size**, **Definition**, and **Smoothness** slider controls. Preview your changes in the thumbnail image in the dialog box.

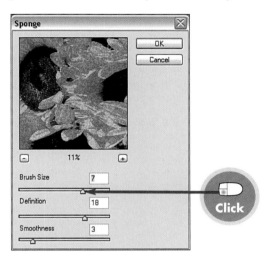

⑤ Apply the Filter

Click **OK** to apply the filter to the image. View the modified image in the image window.

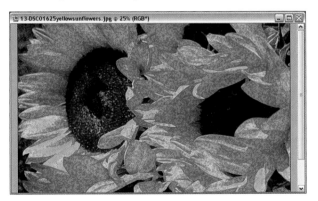

How-to Hint

Using the Smudge Stick Filter

You can apply the **Smudge Stick** filter to add a subtle impressionist effect to a photo. Open the image file and choose **Filter**, **Artistic**, **Smudge Stick**. Start experimenting with the filter by specifying a **Stroke Length** of 2, a **Highlight Area** of 0, and an **Intensity** of 10, and then click **OK**.

Rinsing and Repeating

Some artistic filters might not create a noticeable change to a four or five megapixel image, no matter what settings you choose. If this is the case, press **Ctrl+F** (⌘**+F** for Mac users) to reapply the filter to the selected layer. For example, if you apply the **Twirl** filter (located in the **Filter**, **Distort** menu), successive applications of the filter eventually create a cool-looking circular shape out of the image layer.

How to Apply Destructive Filters

The not-so-good news about filters is that there's a price for such magic: the loss of pixels. In a way, all filters are destructive. The filters in the destructive category are even more so because their sole intent is to distort or destroy the pixels in the image. Destructive filters end up creating new photos despite themselves.

1 Open an Image

Click the **Open** button from the shortcuts bar. Choose an image that has fairly large areas of solid color. Open the file.

2 Choose a Filter

Choose **Filter**, **Distort**. Notice the list of options in the destructive filters category from which you can choose. For this example, choose the **Twirl** filter to open the **Twirl** dialog box.

3 Change the View

Click the **Minus** button in the dialog box to zoom out of the thumbnail. Click and drag in the thumbnail to reposition the image until the view is adjusted to your satisfaction.

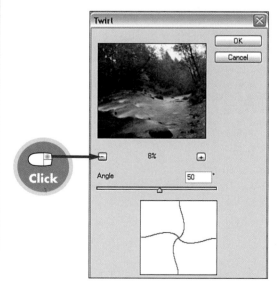

④ **Adjust Filter Settings**

Drag the **Angle** slider control to the left or right to change the direction of the twirl. Preview the effect of the filter in the dialog box.

⑤ **Apply the Filter**

Click **OK** to apply the filter to the image window. View the effect of the filter in the image window.

How-to Hint

Twirling All or Part of an Image

You can apply the **Twirl** filter to all or part of an image. Apply a selection tool if you want to twirl only part of an image. Select the entire image if you want to apply the **Twirl** filter to the entire image.

When to Use Noise Filters

Add a creative reflection to windows or sunglasses. Select, copy, and paste part of a photo and resize it to fit in a window or eyeglass frame. You might want to flip the layer that contains the selection horizontally to better simulate a reflected image. Choose **Filter**, **Noise**, **Add Noise**. In the dialog box, move the slider control to the right to add more noise to the photo. Click **OK** to apply the filter to the layer.

How to Add Lighting Effects

Depending on the size and shape of a flower, tree, orchard, or landscape, it might be fairly simple to light the subject, or it might be difficult to make a particular element stand out in a photo. One way to bring out the water trickling down a stream or a particular flower in a field is to lighten the colors in just that area of the image.

1 Open an Image

Click the **Open** button in the shortcuts bar. Choose a photo that contains a subject that you want to bring out with lighting effects. Open the file.

2 Choose the Lighting Effects Command

Choose **Filter**, **Render**, **Lighting Effects**. The **Lighting Effects** dialog box opens.

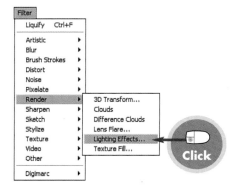

3 Select a Style

Choose **Flashlight** from the **Style** drop-down list. Choose **Omni** from the **Light Type** drop-down list and enable the **On** check box. There are seventeen light styles to choose from. Experiment with the **Soft Spotlight**, **Flood Light**, and **Soft Direct Lights** to create different light effects.

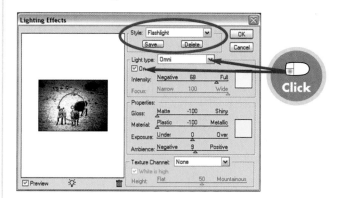

4 Adjust Lighting Effects

In the preview area of the dialog box, drag the center of the outline over the object you want to highlight in the photo. In this example, I want to spotlight the calf on the left side of the image.

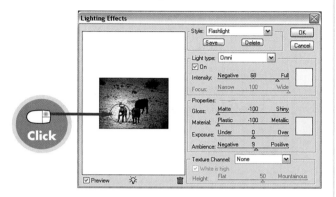

6 Apply the Filter

Drag the **Ambience** slider to lighten or darken the entire image. Drag the **Gloss** and **Material** sliders to adjust the reflective qualities of the light. Click **OK** to apply the settings to the image.

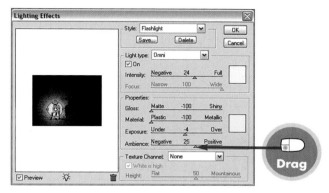

5 Adjust Intensity and Exposure

Move the **Intensity** slider to adjust the brightness of the light. Drag the **Exposure** slider to adjust the properties of the light so that the light you're adding to the image appears realistic.

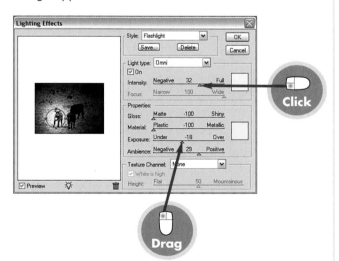

How-to Hint

Creating Shadows

After adding a light source to a photo, consider adding shadows to some of the lightened subjects to add depth and realism to the image. An easy way to create a shadow is to select the object with a selection tool and then choose **Remove Color** from the **Enhance**, **Adjust Color** menu. Flip the image vertically or horizontally, and use the transform tools to grow or shrink the shadow. Reduce the **Opacity** setting for the shadow so that it matches the rest of the lighting in the photo.

Light and Texture

The **Lighting Effects** filter enables you to add texture to an image in addition to adding a light source. If you think adding a texture will enhance the look of your image, choose the red, green, or blue setting from the **Texture Channel** drop-down list located at the bottom of the **Lighting Effects** dialog box. Increase the **Height** value to increase the contrast of the texture.

Task

1. How to Add Text to an Image 168

2. How to Create a Type Mask 170

3. How to Modify Text 172

4. How to Combine an Image with Text 174

5. How to Warp Text 176

6. How to Create Text Effects 180

10

Typing Text and Adding Text Effects

The Type tools enable you to add text to any document. You can create horizontally or vertically aligned text or text masks.

Type tools work best with images in RGB or Grayscale image modes. Photoshop Elements creates text using vector graphics. Vector graphics enable you to dynamically resize a graphic, such as text or shapes, retaining the crisp clarity of the original. The drawback is that vector graphics take more memory and generate a larger file size than do bitmaps, such as photos or graphics created with the Brush tools. If you want to convert vector text into bitmap (raster image) text so that you can apply a filter to the text, for example, first use the **Layer**, **Simplify Layer** command on the text layer.

Photoshop Elements has a total of four Type tools. All share the same set of tool options. You can format one or all the characters in a text layer with a font family, font size, style, and color. You can also change the orientation or warp text.

How to Add Text to an Image

The Type tools enable you to add text to a document. Each time you click a Type tool and type in the image window, a new text layer is added to the document. You can customize the font family, style, or size of any character and change the text's orientation, too.

1 Open an Image

Click **Open** in the shortcuts bar. Select a photo to which you'd like to add some text and open it.

2 Select the Horizontal Type Tool

Select the **Horizontal Type** tool from the toolbox. (Other Type tools are **Vertical Type**, **Masked Vertical Type**, and **Masked Horizontal Type**, which you can access from the toolbox flyout menu or the options bar.) The type options appear in the options bar.

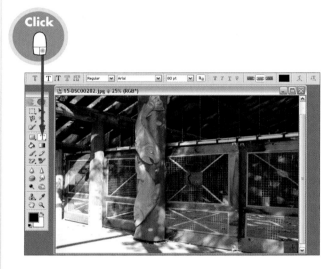

3 Customize Font Settings

From the **Font Family** drop-down list in the options bar, select **Verdana** or your favorite font. Type a point size into the **Font Size** text box. Click the color square to select a font color. Here I specify a huge font size of 200 points (there are 72 points per inch).

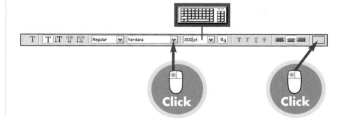

4 Apply the Horizontal Type Tool

Click in the image window and type two or three words. Click the **Check** button in the options bar to accept this addition to the image composite.

5 Change Font Style

Double-click the text in the image window to select a word; triple-click to select a row of text. Drag (or hold down the **Shift** key and click) to select specific text characters. The selected text characters become highlighted. From the **Font Style** list in the options bar, choose **Bold**.

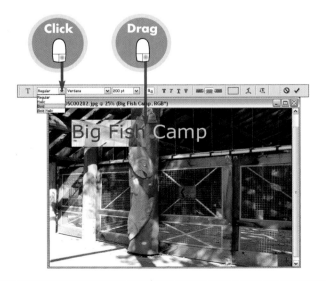

6 Change Orientation

Drag the **Layers** palette from the palette well into the work area. Select the text layer (the layer icon is a big T in a box). Click the **Change the Text Orientation** button in the options bar to change the orientation of all the text on the layer. You might have to change the font size to view the vertical text in the image window.

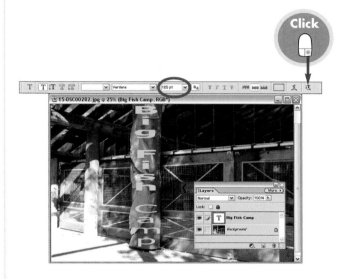

How-to Hint

Resizing Text with the Move Tool

After typing some text into an image window, select the **Move** tool from the toolbox and select the text layer in the **Layers** palette. A box appears around the text in the image window. Drag a corner of the selection to change the font size of the text. After you resize the text with the **Move** tool, you can select the **Type** tool from the toolbox, drag to select text in the image window, and modify any text in the text layer.

How to Create a Type Mask

The **Type Mask** tools enable you to create text-shaped selections. Mask a photo inside a type mask of one or several words to create an unusual effect. You can create horizontal or vertical type masks with the **Horizontal** and **Vertical Type Mask** tools.

① Open an Image

Click the **Open** button in the shortcuts bar. Select a photo to which you want to add some text effects and open it.

② Select the Horizontal Type Mask Tool

Select the **Horizontal Type Mask** tool from the tool-box (or select any Type tool from the toolbox and then click the **Horizontal Type Mask** button in the options bar). Customize the **Font**, **Font Size**, and **Font Style** in the options bar. Choose a big, fat font for best results with a text mask.

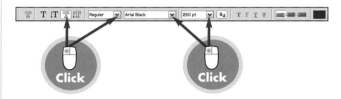

③ Apply the Type Mask Tool

Click in the image window and type one or two words. Notice that the image "grays out" and you have a clear view of the image only through the text you type. Click the **Check** button in the options bar to save your changes.

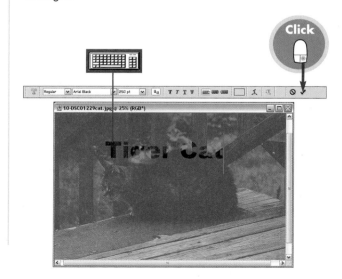

④ Move the Type Mask

Select the **Move** tool from the toolbox. Drag the mask to a new location. Select the **Zoom** tool and click the text mask to increase its size in the image window.

Drag

⑥ Create the Type Mask

Choose **Edit**, **Copy** and then **Edit**, **Paste** to place the text mask in its own layer. Select the **Move** tool and drag the selection to a new location in the image window.

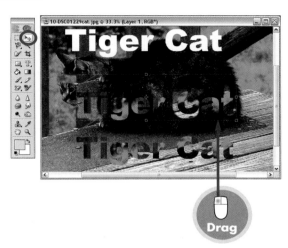

Drag

⑤ Modify the Type Mask

Choose the **Selection Brush** tool from the toolbox. Drag over part of the type mask. The shape of the type mask grows.

Drag

How-to Hint

What's a Type Mask?

A mask is similar to a selection area. Pixels located inside the marching ants or rubylith (outline) color that surrounds the selection areas can be modified by filters, effects, or a tool from the toolbox. Pixels located outside the marching ants or rubylith cannot be modified until the selection is deselected from the image window. A type mask is a selection area that takes the shape of the font and text you type into the image window using the **Horizontal** or **Vertical Type Mask** tool.

How to Modify Text

You can use the settings in the Type tools options bar to format text. In addition to customizing the font size and style, you can also customize the color of the text or add a layer style.

① Open an Image

Click the **Open** button in the shortcuts bar. Select an image file that contains text. Open the file.

② Select Text

Select the **Type** tool from the toolbox. Double-click to select a word, triple-click to select a row of text, or quadruple-click to select all the text in a layer in the image window.

③ Change Font Color

In the options bar, click the **color square** to open the **Color Picker** dialog box. Select a color for the selected text from the **Color Picker** and click **OK**.

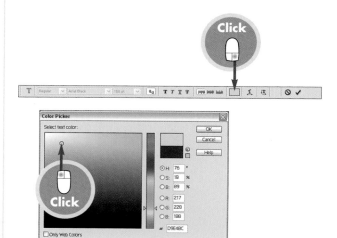

4 Open Layer Styles Palette

Choose the **Move** tool from the toolbox. Use the tool to select some text in the image window. Drag the **Layer Styles** palette from the palette well.

5 Apply a Layer Style

From the drop-down menu at the top of the **Layer Styles** palette, choose **Wow Plastic**. From the list of options, click to apply a layer style to the selected text in the image window.

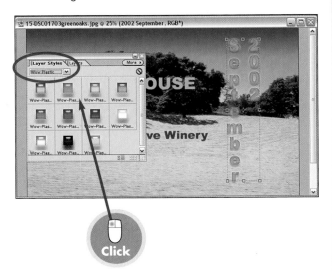

6 Apply Drop Shadow

From the drop-down menu at the top of the **Layer Styles** palette, select **Drop Shadows**. From the list of options, click to apply one to the selected text in the image window. In this example, I selected the **High** option.

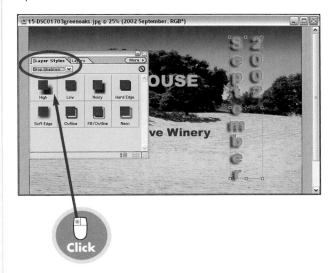

How-to Hint

Changing Type Orientation

Select a text layer in the **Layers** palette and click the **Change the Text Orientation** button in the Type tool options bar to change horizontally oriented text into vertically oriented text. This button is a great way to preview text without typing it into the image window into two separate layers.

Modifying Alignment

You can use one of three alignment buttons in the Type tool options bar to align horizontal text to the left, right, or center of the image window. Use these buttons to align vertical text to the top, bottom, or center of the image window.

How to Combine an Image with Text

The **Type** tool creates text with the color selected in the options bar. If you simplify the vector-graphics text you have added to your image file into a bitmap (technically called "rasterizing the vector graphic"), you can then apply filters, effects, or combine text with an image. The key to combining a photo with text is to use the **Paste Into** command. Pasting a photo into a text selection can come in handy if you want to associate a visual effect or image with a text message.

1 Open an Image

Click the **Open** button in the shortcuts bar. Select a photo to which you want to add some text and open the file.

2 Type Text

Select the **Horizontal Type** tool from the toolbox. Type a few words on the image window. Customize the color, font family, font size, and font style using the settings in the options bar. Open the **Layer Styles** palette and apply these options to the text, if you'd like.

3 Simplify Text

Open the **Layers** palette and select the text layer. Choose **Simplify Layer** from the **More** palette menu. The text has now been rasterized into a bitmap; it is no longer considered a text layer by Photoshop Elements, and you can no longer edit the text with the Type tools.

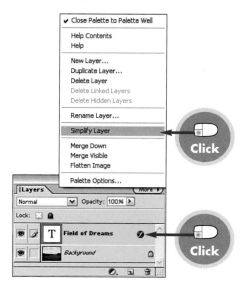

4 Copy Image Selection

In the **Layers** palette, select the **Background** layer. Choose the **Rectangular Marquee** tool from the toolbox and use it to drag a selection area in the image window. The selection area should be roughly the same size as the bitmapped text. Choose **Edit**, **Copy** to copy the selection area to the Clipboard.

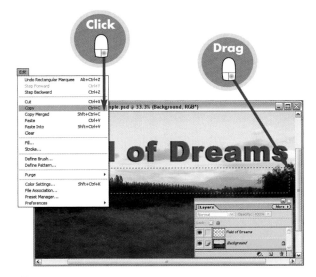

5 Choose the Paste Into Command

In the **Layers** palette, **Ctrl**+click (⌘+click for Mac users) the layer containing the bitmapped text to select the contents of that layer (the text). Choose **Edit**, **Paste Into**. The background selection you copied in step 4 is pasted into the text characters.

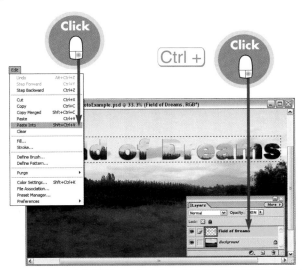

6 Modify the Text Effects

From the **Layers** palette menus, choose a blending mode and decrease the **Opacity** value to fine-tune the look of the text in the image. Select the **Move** tool from the toolbox and drag to resize the image selection.

How-to Hint

An Alternative Method

If you don't want to simplify the vector text, you can use the **Layer**, **Group Previous** command and the **Link** feature in the **Layers** palette to combine a text layer with an image layer. Open an image and use the **Type** tool to add some text to the image window. Open a second image and pick a selection tool from the toolbox. Select part of the image that you want to combine with the text in the first window. Choose **Edit**, **Copy**, return to the first window, and choose **Edit**, **Paste**. The selected image appears in the layer above the text layer in the **Layers** palette. With the selection highlighted in the **Layers** palette, choose the **Layer**, **Group with Previous** command (or **Alt**+click—**Option**+click for Mac users—between the two layers) to group the top layer with the layer directly below it. Click the box immediately to the left of the text layer. The **link** icon (resembling two wedding rings) appears indicating that the pasted graphic and text layers are linked (or "married"). Select the **Move** tool and drag the text around the image window to move the grouped and linked images.

How to Warp Text

Not all text effects require you to simplify the text into a bitmap (raster). You can shape the original vector graphics text you typed in a layer with the options in the **Warp Text** dialog box. Bulge, pinch, or stretch text—or shape the text into a flag or fish. The following steps show you how to warp text.

① Open an Image

Click the **Open** button on the shortcuts bar. Select a file to which you want to add some text effects and open it.

② Add Type

Select the **Horizontal Type** tool from the toolbox, set the font options in the options bar, and type text into the image window. Double-click the text in the image window to select it.

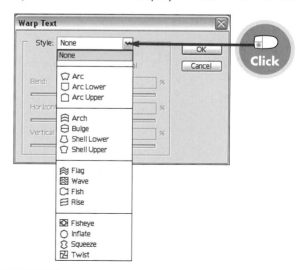

③ Choose the Warp Text Button

Click the **Warp Text** button in the options bar (the letter T with a curved line under it). The **Warp Text** dialog box opens. Click the **Style** drop-down menu and select from the drop-down list the basic shape you want the text to follow.

④ Adjust Warp Settings

Drag the **Bend** slider to adjust the curve in the shape you selected. View the effect this modification has on the text in the image window. When you're satisfied with the shape of the text, click **OK**.

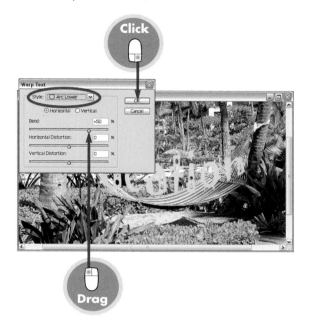

⑤ Duplicate Layers

In the **Layers** palette, drag the text layer and drop it over the **Create a new layer** button to duplicate the text layer. Select the **Move** tool from the toolbox and drag the duplicate text layer in the image window to reposition it.

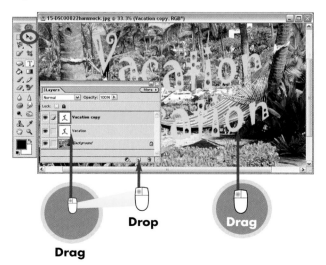

⑥ Choose a Warp Style

In the **Layers** palette, select one of the text layers. From the Type tool options bar, click the **Warp Text** button to open the **Warp Text** dialog box. Choose another warp style from the **Style** drop-down menu and drag the **Bend**, **Horizontal Distortion**, and the **Vertical Distortion** sliders to further distort the text. Click **OK**.

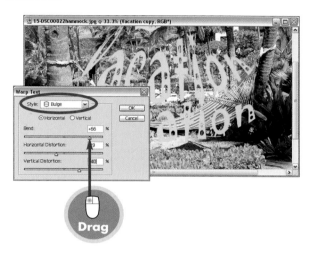

⑦ Open the Layer Style Palette

Drag the **Layer Styles** tab away from the palette well to open the **Layer Styles** palette.

8 Apply Layer Styles

From the drop-down list at the top of the palette, choose the **Bevels** and then click the **Simple Inner** option. For the second layer style, choose **Inner Shadows** from the drop-down list and then click the **Low** option. For the third layer style, choose **Outer Glows** from the drop-down list and click the **Fire** option. The text now shows all three style options.

9 Copy and Paste Layer Styles

Make sure that the text layer you've just been working with is selected. Choose **Layer Style**, **Copy Layer Style**. Select the other text layer (the plainer text layer) and choose **Layer**, **Layer Style**, **Paste Layer Style**. The second text layer now has the same styles as the first text layer.

10 Choose the Gradient Command

We will add a gradient to the text and image layers: In the **Layers** palette, click the **Create fill or adjustment layer** icon and choose **Gradient** from the pop-up list. The **Gradient Fill** dialog box opens.

11 Define Gradient Colors

Click the **Gradient** field. The **Gradient Editor** dialog box opens. Double-click a color stop to define gradient color and click **OK**.

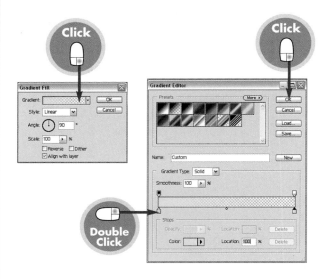

⑫ Apply the Gradient

Back in the **Gradient Fill** dialog box, enable the **Reverse** check box to reverse the direction of the gradient. Click **OK**.

⑬ Finalize the Layout

Select the **Move** tool and drag to arrange the location and scale of the text. In the **Layers** palette, click the eye icon to hide any layers. Doubleclick the **f** icon in a text layer. Drag the slider controls for **Shadow Distance**, **Outer Glow Size**, **Inner Glow Size**, or **Bevel Size** to customize **Style Settings** for that layer. Click **OK**.

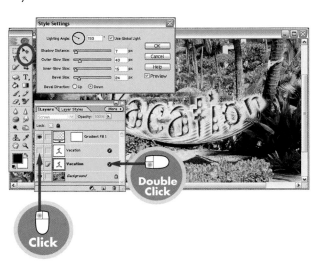

⑭ Flatten Layers

Make any last changes to the text or the image. Choose **File**, **Save As** and save the file as a Photoshop file. Choose **Flatten Image** from the **Layers** palette **More** menu to merge all visible layers. Flattening the image removes any hidden layers from the final single-layer image.

How-to Hint

Removing the Warp Effect

Choose the **Type** tool from the toolbox and select the text layer in the **Layers** palette. Click the **Warp Text** button in the options bar and choose **None** from the **Style** menu to remove the warp effect from the text layer. In the **Layers** palette, the icon for the text layer changes from the **Warp Text** icon to the **Type** icon.

Merging Down Warped Text

Move the layer that contains the warped text effect above a layer that contains a photo. Choose **Merge Down** from the **More** menu in the **Layers** palette. The warped text layer is converted to a raster (bitmap) and merged with the layer below it.

How to Create Text Effects

Text effects is a special group of effects you can access from the **Effects** palette. Eleven text effects are installed with Photoshop Elements. Apply text styles and textures to text by double-clicking a text effect.

1 Open an Image

Click the **Open** button in the shortcuts bar. Select an image to which you want to add some text and open it.

2 Type Some Text

Choose the **Horizontal Type** tool from the toolbox, adjust the font settings in the options bar, and type some text into the image window.

3 Apply a Layer Style

Drag the **Layer Styles** palette from the palette well to the work area. From the drop-down menu at the top of the palette, choose **Wow Plastic** and then click the **Orange** option to apply this layer style to the text.

Click

④ Duplicate Text Layers

In the **Layers** palette, drag the text layer over the **Create a new layer** button to duplicate the layer. Here I've made two duplicates for a total of three text layers.

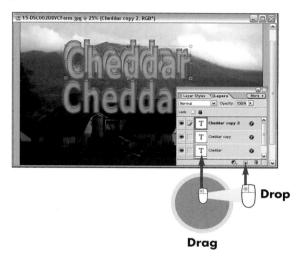

Drop

Drag

⑤ Create Ghost Text

Select a text layer and drag the **Opacity** slider control to the left to make the text nearly transparent. Choose the **Move** tool and drag the ghosted text layer so that it accentuates one of the other text layers.

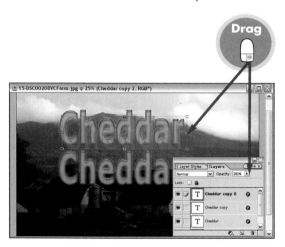

Drag

⑥ Apply a Text Effect

Select a text layer. Open the **Effects** palette and select **Text** from the drop-down list at the top. Double-click the **Water Reflection** effect to apply this effect to the selected text layer. Note that the text effect rasterizes the vector text into a bitmap.

Double Click

How-to Hint

Modifying the Welcome Screen

Each button and text element you see in the Photoshop Elements Welcome screen can be modified by replacing one of the JPEG files stored in the **HTML Palette**, **Welcome**, **Images** folder. If you feel adventurous, use the **File Browser** dialog box to view each element in the Welcome screen. Open and modify each element to create your own custom Welcome screen.

Text and Layer Styles

In addition to using all the cool text settings available in the Type tool options bar, you can also customize text by applying one or more layer styles. Experiment with bevels, drop shadows, and glow layer styles, or combine several patterns and Wow styles to dress up a text layer.

① How to Use Brush Tools 184

② How to Apply Shape Tools 188

③ How to Blend Graphics with Images 190

④ How to Create a Web Button 192

⑤ How to Change the Welcome Screen 194

⑥ How to Apply a Pattern 196

⑦ How to Add a Picture Frame Effect 198

⑧ How to Use Layer Style Commands 200

⑨ How to Create Custom Brushes 202

⑩ How to Create a Pattern 204

Task

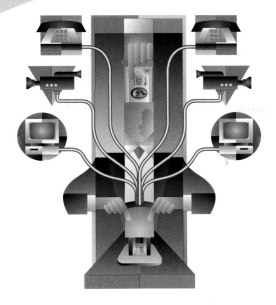

11

Creating Custom Graphics and Using Layers and Brushes

Photoshop Elements enables you to create, modify, and delete bitmap and vector graphics. A *bitmap, or rasterized image,* is a group of pixels. *Vector graphics* are created with a mathematical algorithm and can be resized without loss of image quality. In contrast to vector graphics, bitmaps scale down in size, but pixelate as you enlarge the bitmap.

You can use the Type and Shape tools to create vector graphics that scale without sacrificing image quality. You can use the Brush tool, brush presets, and patterns to work with bitmap graphics. Brush presets enable you to draw raster (bitmap) graphics with a variety of brush styles, such as dry media, wet media, and calligraphic. Patterns are different than brush presets: You apply a pattern by adding a Pattern layer to an image window. Use brush presets and patterns to customize images and create unique effects with all or part of your images.

Layer styles enable you to apply effects, such as a drop shadow or bevel to a vector shape, text, or photo. Layer style commands enable you to hide, scale, copy, and paste layer styles. The tasks in this part show you how to use the Brush and Shape tools to draw graphics freestyle or by working with precise shapes and lines. You will also learn how to work with brush presets, patterns, layer style commands, and how to customize the photo that appears in the Photoshop Elements **Welcome** screen.

How to Use Brush Tools

You can use the **Brush** tool to draw on a canvas or image layer. You can customize the brush, brush size, color, and several other options. You can choose from twelve groups of brush presets, each of which has many brushes. You can also configure the **Brush** tool as an airbrush. This task shows you how to apply the **Brush** and **Airbrush** tools.

1 Choose the New Command

Choose **File**, **New** to open the **New** dialog box. A new canvas enables you to get acquainted with the Brush tools.

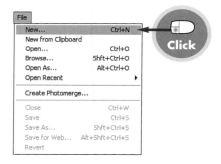

2 Define the Document

From the **Preset Sizes** drop-down menu, choose a document size, such as **800×600**. Specify the color of the document by selecting an option in the **Contents** area (for this example, click the **White** radio button). Click **OK** to create the new document.

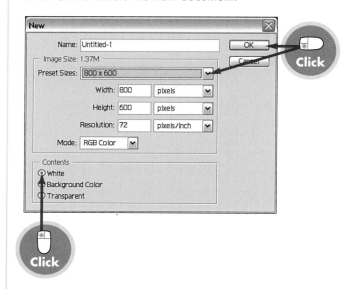

3 Select the Brush Tool

Select the **Brush** tool from the toolbox. View the brush options in the options bar.

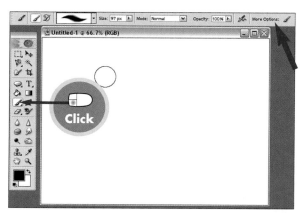

4 Adjust Brush Options

From the **Brush** pop-up palette (click the first arrow next to the brush sample in the options bar), choose a soft-edged brush.

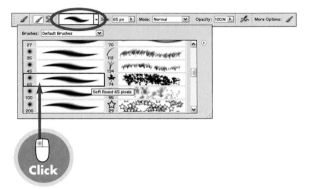

5 Apply the Brush Tool

In the work area, click, drag the mouse in any direction, and release the mouse.

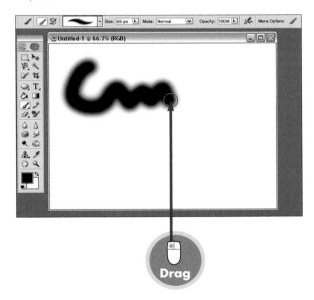

6 Select a Brush Color

Click the **Foreground** color swatch in the toolbox to open the **Color Picker** dialog box. In the left pane of the dialog box, click to select a brush color and click **OK**.

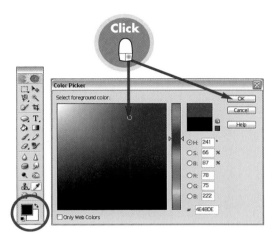

7 Adjust Brush Options

With the brush tool selected, click the **More Options** button in the options bar. In the **Brush** pop-up palette that drops down, drag the **Color Jitter** and **Scatter** slider controls to the right to increase these settings.

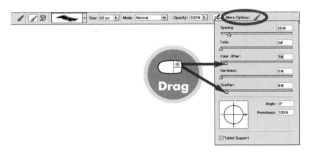

8 Apply the Airbrush

Click the **Airbrush** button in the options bar. Drag and release the newly defined brush in the image window. A brush stroke with the specified color, jitter, and scatter options appears in the image window. The longer you hold down the mouse button, the more color the brush applies.

9 Change Brush Options

From the **Mode** drop-down list in the options bar, choose **Linear Dodge** as the blending mode for the tool. The color of the Brush tool will blend with the original color of the pixels to create a unique resulting color. To add transparency to the resulting color, type a lower value in the **Opacity** text box. Drag the newly defined brush over another brush stroke in the image area.

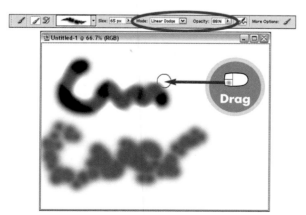

10 Reset the Brush Tool

Click the **Brush** button in the options bar and choose the **Reset Tool** from the flyout menu. The options bar resets to the default settings for the **Brush** tool. You can apply the **Reset Tool** command to any toolbox tool.

11 Change the Brush

In the options bar, click the **Brush Preset** drop-down arrow and choose a hard-edge brush from the list of options. Drag this brush in the image window.

⑫ Create a Straight Line

You can draw a straight line with any brush: Click the mouse button in the image window, press and hold down the **Shift** key, and click in another location in the image window. A straight line connects the two clicked points.

⑬ Show the Grid and Draw a Circle

Choose **View**, **Grid** to display the grid in the image window. Select the **Brush** tool from the toolbox and drag a circle in the image window. Use the grid to help you draw a circle that is as wide as it is tall.

How-to Hint

Layers and Brush Strokes

If you don't want to make a permanent change to a graphics layer, create a new layer and select it before applying a brush stroke to the image window.

Stroke and Fill Settings

You can adjust the size, color, and other options of a brush stroke when you are creating a bitmap graphic. Create a new window with a white or transparent background. Select the **Brush** tool and draw in the image window. Select the **Magic Wand** tool and click the brush stroke to select it. Choose **Edit**, **Stroke** to open the **Stroke** dialog box. You can customize the **Stroke**, **Location**, and **Blending** options to change the thickness of the outer edge of the selected graphic. Note that you can apply the **Stroke** command to photos and graphics.

Customizing Fill Settings

You can modify the fill color for a selection. Define a selection (select a fat line or graphic you have drawn, for example) and then choose **Edit**, **Fill** to open the **Fill** dialog box. Choose an option from the **Contents** and **Blending** drop-down lists to customize the pixels within the selection. Note that you can apply the **Fill** command to photos and graphics.

How to Apply the Shape Tools

Like their cousins the Type tools, the Shape tools are used to create vector graphics. You can grow or shrink the size of a vector-graphic shape, and it retains its original form and image clarity. You can apply Layer Styles to shape layers. You can also convert (simplify or rasterize) vector shapes into bitmap shapes, which enables you to apply filters or effects to shapes.

① Open an Image File

Click the **Open** button in the shortcuts bar. Choose an image to which you'd like to add some graphic shapes and open the file.

② Select the Shape Tool

Select the **Shape** tool from the toolbox. Click the **Color** box in the options bar to open the **Color Picker** dialog box. Click in the image window to pick the color you want the shape you'll draw in the next step to be. You can match a specific color in an image by clicking in the image window instead. Click **OK**.

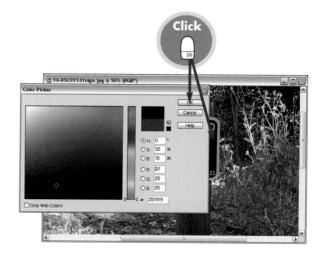

③ Create a Shape

With the **Shape** tool selected, drag to create a shape. Notice that the shape is filled with the color you selected in step 2.

④ Change Shape Options

In the options bar, click the **Style** drop-down arrow. Click the down-arrow next to the **Style** pop-up palette and choose **Bevels** from the drop-down list. Click one of the bevel options (such as **Simple Inner**) to apply it to the shape.

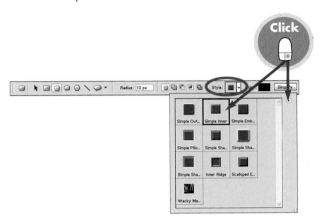

⑤ Change Shapes

In the options bar, select a different shape tool from those presented at the left end of the options bar. In this example, I chose the **Custom Shape** tool and selected **Symbols** from the **Shape** pop-up palette in the options bar. Drag in the image window to create another shape using this new tool.

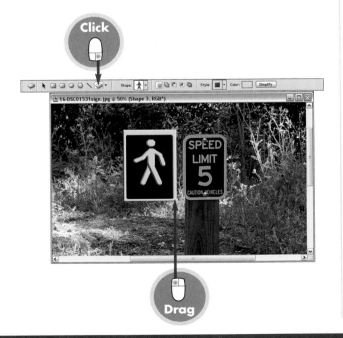

⑥ Simplify Layers

Select the **Move** tool from the toolbox. Click a shape in the image window to select it. Choose **Layer**, **Simplify Layer** (or click **Simplify** in the options bar) to rasterize the vector shape into a bitmap shape.

How-to Hint

Shape Library Files

The **Shape** tool is home to a slew of pre-installed vector graphics that are available through the options bar. Each group of shapes is stored in a file located in the **Photoshop Elements**, **Presets**, **Custom Shapes** folder. However, you cannot modify these files with Photoshop Elements.

Merging Shapes

Shapes lose their vector qualities if you simplify (rasterize) them, merge two shape layers together, or flatten the layers in an image. You can create one shape per layer, so be sure that each shape is exactly the way you want it before merging a shape layer with any other layers.

How to Blend Graphics with Images

Create hand-drawn effects by applying graphics tools to a photo. For instance, you can use the **Brush** tool to write your name on a sidewalk (okay, a photo of a sidewalk), preview a t-shirt graphic design, or hand-draw graffiti on a wall. Adjust the **Blending Mode** and **Opacity** settings to more successfully mix graphics with a photo.

1 Open an Image

Click the **Open** button in the shortcuts bar. Select a photo to which you'd like to add some graphic effects and open it.

2 Select the Brush Tool

Select the **Brush** tool from the toolbox and adjust the brush size in the options bar.

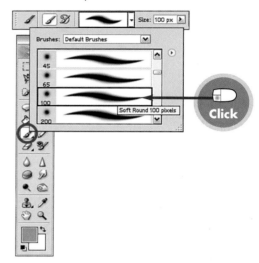

3 Select a Color

Click the **Foreground** color swatch in the toolbox. The **Color Picker** dialog box opens. Click in the image window to choose a foreground color; alternatively, pick a color from the **Color Picker** dialog box. Click **OK**.

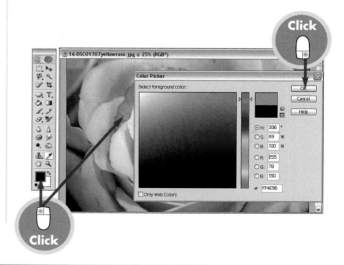

④ Decrease Opacity

In the options bar for the brush tool, drag the **Opacity** slider to a value between 50 and 75. The lower the **Opacity** value, the more transparent the image becomes. An opacity value between 50 and 75 ensures that the color created by the Brush tool remains visible in the background image.

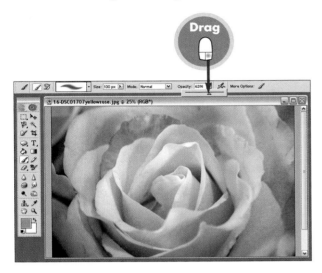

⑤ Change Blending Mode

From the **Mode** drop-down menu in the options bar, choose **Multiply** as the blending mode you want the brush to use as it lays the new color on top of the existing pixels in the image window. Blending modes combine the color of the brush with the original color in the image window in different ways to create a new resulting color.

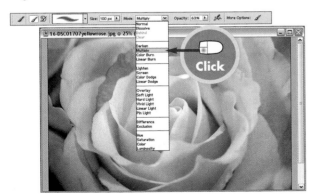

⑥ Apply the Brush Tool

Drag in the image window to apply the brush. Here I use the brush I configured to add some depth of color to the petals of the white rose. Experiment with different blending modes and opacity settings to blend the brush strokes of the graphic with the photo.

How-to Hint

Graphics and Layer Styles

You can apply layer styles to any bitmap selection area, vector graphic, or to all pixels in a layer. Achieve a three-dimensional effect by applying a **Simple Inner** bevel and a **Low** drop shadow to a brush stroke. Make a solid color neon by applying a **Wow Neon** or a **Wow Plastic** layer style. The possibilities are virtually endless! For best results, rasterize the vector graphic into a bitmap graphic before applying the layer style. Otherwise, you should reapply the layer style after resizing the vector graphic or text. Layer styles are raster images and will pixelate if enlarged.

Organizing Graphics Files

If you plan to create lots of reusable graphics files, create a folder and start a graphics library. You can create a master folder to store Photoshop Elements files that contain multiple layers of graphics. Save graphics as GIF or JPEG files if you want to share them on the Web; alternatively, save the graphic at different compression settings or with different numbers of colors.

How to Create a Web Button

Buttons are some of the more common Web graphics. Search pages, for example, usually have a Search or Go button located somewhere at the top of the page. This task shows you how to create different button graphics by applying different combinations of layer styles to a shape.

1 Create a New Window

Click **New** from the shortcuts bar. In the New dialog box, choose a document size such as **800×600** from the **Preset Sizes** drop-down menu. Select the **White** radio button in the **Contents** area and click **OK**. A new window opens in the work area.

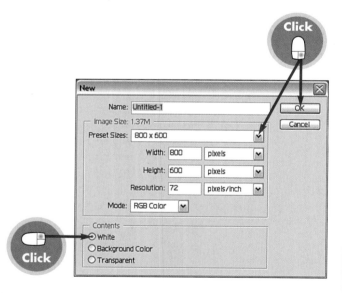

2 Choose the Shape Tool

In the toolbox, click the **Shape** tool. From the flyout menu, select the **Rounded Rectangle** shape.

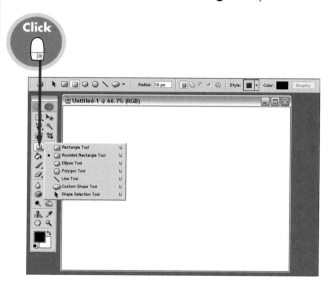

3 Choose Shape Color

In the toolbox, click the **Foreground** color watch to open the **Color Picker** dialog box. Choose a color for the shape you will be drawing and click **OK**.

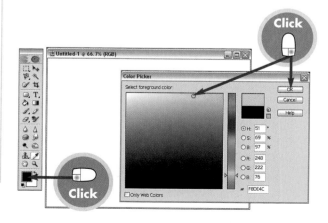

④ Create Shapes

Drag in the image window to create at least one rounded-rectangle shape.

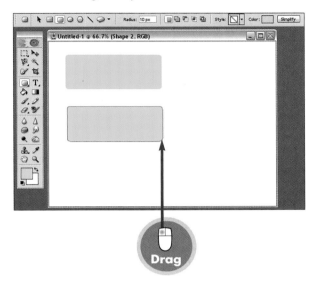

Drag

⑤ Apply Layer Styles

Click the arrow button next to the **Style** field in the options bar and choose **Bevels** from the **Style** drop-down menu. Click the **Simple Inner** option to apply that bevel to the shape you just drew.

Click

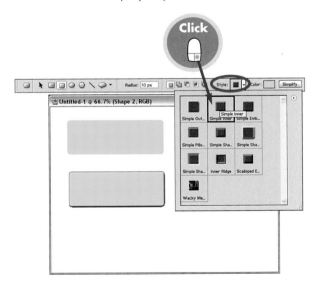

⑥ Customize Layer Style Settings

Choose **Style Settings** from the **Layer, Layer Style** menu to open the **Style Settings** dialog box. Use the options to customize the style you just applied: Drag the **Bevel Size** slider to the right to increase the bevel edge in the shape. Click **OK**.

Click

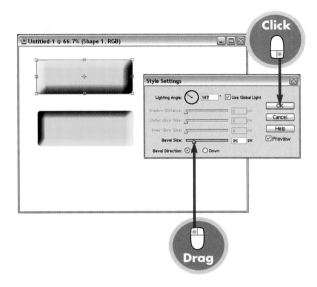

Drag

How-to Hint

Mac OS X Buttons

You can create buttons that look like the blue 3D buttons in Mac OS X. First, draw a rounded rectangle shape. Open the **Layer styles** palette and apply the **Wow Plastic Aqua Blue** layer style to the shape. Apply a **High Drop Shadow** layer style to the shape. Open the **Style Settings** dialog box and change the global light source to 159 and set the **Shadow Distance** of the drop shadow to 7 pixels.

What's a Rollover?

The term *rollover* is used to describe different button states on a Web page. For example, if you hover the mouse pointer over a button, an outer glow can appear around the button shape. If you click the button, the bevel setting can be changed to down instead of up. Although Photoshop Elements can't generate the HTML or JavaScript code to create a rollover effect, you can use the shape tools and layer styles to create the button states for a rollover.

How to Change the Welcome Screen

If you're running Photoshop Elements 2 with Mac OS X, you can customize the photo that appears in the Welcome screen. Adobe installs the **PS_Elemements-Quickstart_06.jpg** file to the **HTML Palettes**, **Welcome**, **Images** folder within the **Photoshop Elements** folder. Customize the Welcome screen to see your favorite photo each time you open Photoshop Elements.

1 Open a Photo

Click the **Open** button in the shortcuts bar. Select the photo you want to see on the Photoshop Elements Welcome screen and open it.

2 Resize the Photo

Choose **Image**, **Resize**, **Image Size** to open the **Image Size** dialog box. Making sure that you are working with dimensions in **pixels**, type **305** into the **Width** text box and **343** into the **Height** text box (this is the maximum size of the image for the Welcome screen). Click **OK**.

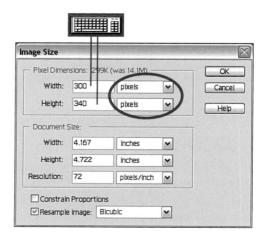

3 Apply a Layer Style

Drag the **Layer Styles** tab from the palette well to open the **Layer Styles** palette in the work area. Choose **Image Effects** from the drop-down menu at the top of the palette and then choose an effect, such as **Circular Vignette**.

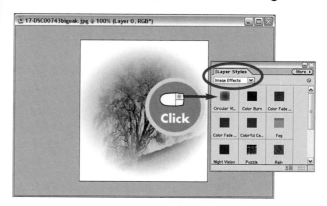

4 Save the File

Click the **Save** button on the shortcuts bar. The **Save** dialog box opens.

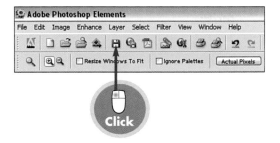

5 Choose File Options

Type **PS_Elemements-QuickStart_06** in the **File name** field (you must use this filename). Choose **JPEG** from the **Format** drop-down list. Click **Save**. When the JPEG options dialog box opens, click **OK**.

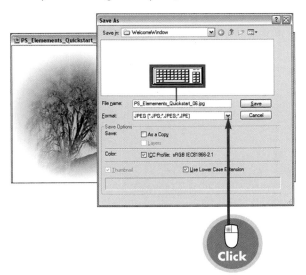

6 Relaunch Photoshop Elements

Choose **File**, **Quit**. Move the **PS_Elemements-QuickStart_06.JPEG** file you just created to the **HTML Palettes**, **Welcome**, **Images** folder. Start Photoshop Elements. The Welcome window now displays your photo.

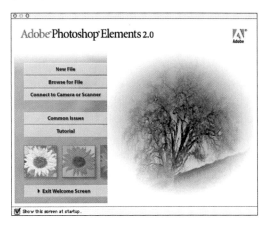

How-to Hint

Windows Customization

Windows folks can't create a custom Welcome screen for Photoshop Elements unless they have Photoshop 7. The Welcome image is sliced into several different files in the Windows version of Photoshop Elements.

Indexed Versus RGB Mode

If you want to reduce the size, amount of memory used by, or number of colors in the new Welcome screen photo, change the image mode of the photo from RGB to Indexed. Indexed photos have a limit of 256 colors. Choose **Indexed** from the **Image**, **Mode** menu and click **OK**. If the photo looks more or less the same as it did in RGB mode, save it.

How to Apply a Pattern

You can create your own patterns or use one of the many installed with Photoshop Elements. A *pattern* is a rectangular-shaped set of pixels that can be applied with a brush or as a layer to an image. You can also apply pattern layers to an image, as described in Task 10, "How to Create a Pattern." A separate set of patterns is located in the **Patterns** group of the **Layer Styles** palette.

① Open an Image

Click the **Open** button on the **shortcuts bar**. Select a photo that you want to modify with patterns and open it.

② Duplicate the Background Layer

Open the **Layers** palette. Drag and drop the **Background** layer on the **Create a new layer** button to duplicate the background layer. Click the **Background copy** layer in the palette list to select it.

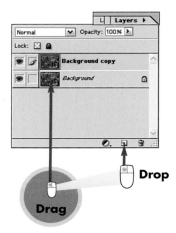

③ Choose Layer Styles Command

Choose **Window**, **Layer Styles** to open the **Layer Styles** palette. Drag it from the palette well into the work area.

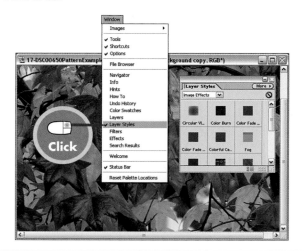

4 Select a Pattern Layer Style

Select **Patterns** from the drop-down list at the top of the **Layer Styles** palette. Click to apply one of the patterns to the image. Here you see the **Stucco** pattern applied.

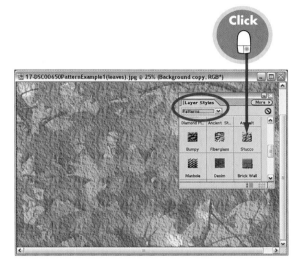

6 Adjust Layer Options

Drag the **Layers** palette from the palette well to the work area. Choose a blending mode, such as **Multiply**, from the drop-down list at the top of the palette. Type a number into the **Opacity** text box to vary the impact the blending mode has on the layer styles you have already applied.

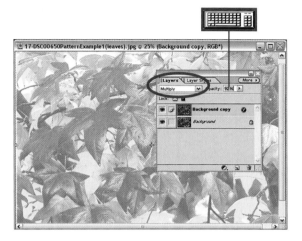

5 Apply Several Patterns

Click several additional pattern options (such as **Bumpy** and **Diamond Plate**). These layer styles are applied on top of the previous ones.

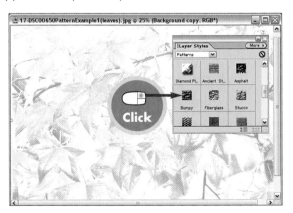

How-to Hint

Unlocking the Background Layer

Unlocked layers are fully editable; locked layers cannot be modified. When you first open a photo or a new window with a colored background, the image is stored in a locked **Background** layer. To apply a pattern to the locked background layer, you must first unlock it. Open the **Layer Styles** palette and select a pattern to apply. Photoshop Elements asks whether you want to unlock the **Background** layer. Click **OK** and type a name for the unlocked layer in the **New Layer** text box (**Layer 0** is the default name). The **Background** layer will be replaced with the unlocked **Layer 0** (unless you named the layer).

How to Add a Picture Frame Effect

Tucked away in the **Effects** palette is a group of picture frame effects. Simply double-click a picture frame effect to surround a photo with a picture frame graphic. This task shows you how.

❶ Open an Image

Click the **Open** button on the shortcuts bar. Choose a photo to which you want to add a frame graphic and open it.

❷ Open Effects Palette

Choose **Window**, **Effects** to open the **Effects** palette.

❸ Choose Frames Option

Choose **Frames** from the drop-down list at the top of the palette. Click the thumbnails to preview each frame in the **Effects** palette.

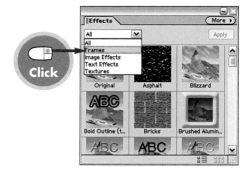

4   Add a Frame to the Photo

Double-click the button for the frame you want to place around the open image. Here, I double-click the **Wild Frame** button.

6   View the Picture Frame

Close the **Effects** palette and view the photo with its new frame graphics.

5   Add Another Frame

Double-click a second frame option, such as **Wood Frame**, to add a second frame around the first frame.

How-to Hint

Creating a Matte Effect

If you don't want a photo to fill the entire space within a picture frame, add a matte. In the analog world, a matte is a separate colored sheet of paper with the center portion cut out to show the photo. You can create a matte with the **Shape** tool. Apply a pattern and bevel from the **Layer Style** palette if you want to add texture and a 3D edge to the matte. Simplify the **Shape** layer into a bitmap.

Circular Frames

If you don't mind a 2D picture frame, you can create a circular-shaped frame for a photo. Drag the **Elliptical Marquee** tool to define a selection area on the photo. Cut and paste the photo into a new document that contains a background color. Feather the edges of the selection and customize the photo as you like.

How to Use Layer Style Commands

Layer styles are stored in the **Layer Styles** palette. Previous tasks have shown you how to apply layer styles from the **Layer Styles** palette. Additional layer style commands are located in the **Layer** menu. This task introduces you to some of the **Layer Style** menu commands.

❶ Open a Photo

Click the **Open** button in the shortcuts bar. Select a photo that you want to modify with some special effects and open it.

❷ Define a Selection

Choose the **Magnetic Lasso** tool from the toolbox. Drag it around the subject in the photo to select that area of the image. Choose **Edit**, **Copy** to copy the selection to the Clipboard. Choose **Edit**, **Paste** to paste the selection back into the image on a new layer.

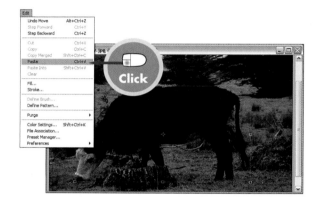

❸ Apply Layer Styles

Open the **Layer Styles** palette from the palette well. Choose **Bevels** from the drop-down list at the top of the palette. Click the arrow next to the **Style** pop-up palette and then choose **Bevel Simple Inner** in the **Layer Styles** palette. Choose **Wow Neon** from the drop-down list and then choose **Wow Neon Orange-Off**.

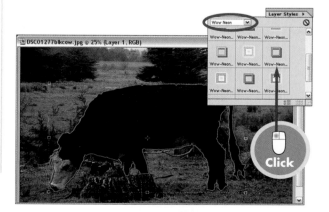

4 Hide Layer Styles

Choose **Hide All Effects** from the **Layer**, **Layer Style** menu to view the original image. Choose **Edit**, **Undo**.

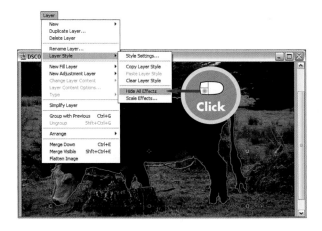

5 Choose Scale Command

You can modify the layer styles effects you added. Choose **Scale Effects** from the **Layer**, **Layer Style** menu. The **Scale Layer Effects** dialog box opens.

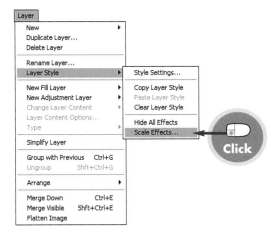

6 Scale Layer Styles

Drag the **Scale** slider control to the right to increase the layer style effect you applied. Watch the layer styles change in the image window as you change the scale value.

How-to Hint

Where Do Layer Styles Live?

Layer styles are stored in the **Photoshop Elements**, **Presets**, **Styles** folder on your hard drive. Each layer style is an **asl** file, a custom format for layer styles. You can't preview these files with the **File Browser** dialog box.

Saving Layer Styles

The best way to preserve a single or combination of layer styles is to save an image file in the Photoshop (PSD) file format. The Photoshop file format preserves layer, vector shape, and text information in addition to layer style custom settings.

How to Create Custom Brushes

You can use the **Define Brush** command to turn all or part of a photo into a brush preset. Each brush preset is stored as a file on your hard drive. Create as many presets as you like, and then save a group of brushes and share your brush presets with others. This task shows you how to create a custom brush.

1 Open an Image

Click the **Open** button on the shortcuts bar. Select a photo that contains elements you'd like to save as a brush preset and open the file.

2 Choose a Selection Tool

From the toolbox, choose a selection tool that's appropriate for the shape of the brush you want to create. For a square-tipped brush, for example, click the **Rectangular Marquee** tool.

3 Define a Selection

Drag the tool in the image window to select the portion of the image you want to use as the brush.

4 Create Custom Brush

Choose **Edit**, **Define Brush**. The **Brush Name** dialog box appears.

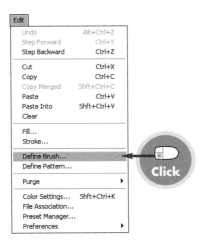

5 Type a Name

Type a name for the brush in the **Name** text box. Click **OK**.

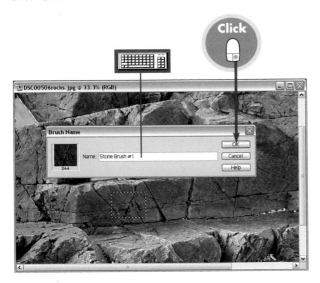

6 Save the Brush Set

Select the **Brush** tool from the toolbox. In the options bar, click the **Brush Preset** drop-down arrow and scroll to view the custom brush you just created. Choose **Save Brushes** from the pop-up menu to save the brush preset to the preset group that appears in the pop-up palette in the options bar.

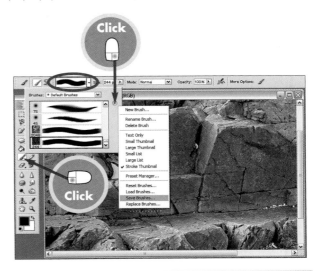

How-to Hint

Saving and Deleting Brushes

If you have heavily modified the settings for a brush and want to save those settings for later use, click the **Brush Presets** drop-down arrow in the options bar and click the right-arrow to display the pop-up menu. Choose **New Brush**, type a name for the brush, and click **OK**. The new brush will appear in the **Brush Presets** drop-down list.

Click the right-arrow in the **Brush Presets** drop-down list, choose **Save Brushes**, and type a name for the file that stores the group of brush presets. Later, you can choose **Load Brushes** from the menu and select the file to access the saved brushes from the **Brush Presets** pop-up menu.

If you create a brush and decide not to keep it, select the brush from the **Brush Presets** drop-down list, click the right-arrow button in the list window and choose **Delete Brush** from the pop-up menu. Brush preset files are stored with the Photoshop Elements files on your hard drive in the **Presets**, **Brushes** folder. If you don't want a brush set to be used with Photoshop Elements, create a backup of the file (just in case) and then delete it from the hard drive.

How to Create a Pattern

The **Define Pattern** command enables you to create a pattern from a photo or a custom graphic. Although there's no size limit for a pattern file, smaller size patterns work best. You can then apply the pattern by adding a pattern layer to an image.

① Open an Image

Click the **Open** button on the shortcuts bar. Select a photo that you'd like to convert to a pattern and open the file.

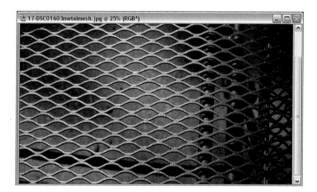

② Create a Selection

Choose a selection tool and drag in the image window to create a selection area that will become the pattern.

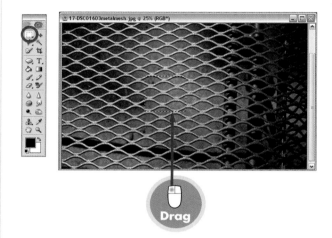

Drag

③ Define the Pattern

Choose **Define Pattern** from the **Edit** menu. The **Pattern Name** dialog box opens. Type a name for the pattern and click **OK**. The pattern is saved to the **Presets** folder in the **Photoshop Elements 2** folder.

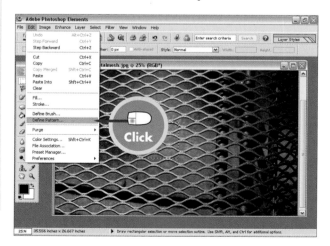

Click

④ Open Another Image

Open another image to which you want to apply the pattern you just saved.

⑤ Apply the Saved Pattern

Choose **Layer**, **New Fill Layer**, **Pattern** to open the **New Layer** dialog box. Type a name for the pattern fill layer and click **OK**. The **Pattern Fill** dialog box appears. Click the drop-down arrow on the left side of the dialog box and select the pattern you created in step 3. Change the **Scale** if desired and then click **OK** to apply the pattern to the new image.

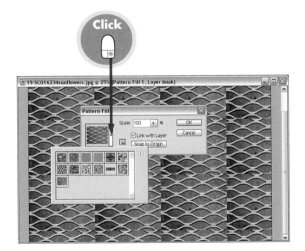

⑥ View the Pattern Effect

Choose **Window**, **Layer** and click the pattern layer in the **Layers** palette. Click the arrow button next to the **Opacity** field and drag the slider to the left to decrease the value. Blend the background image with the pattern. View the effect the pattern you saved has on the second image file.

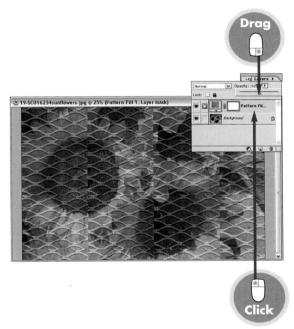

How-to Hint

Pattern Sizes and Photos

As you can see in this task, the size of the pattern is smaller than the photo. If you want each side of a pattern to seamlessly blend together so that a small pattern can automatically tile to fill a larger photo, copy and paste different selection areas of the photo you want to use to create a pattern. You'll have to experiment with the selection tools to see whether the pattern can indeed be selected in such a way that it can be repeated.

Filters and Effects

Don't forget that you can apply filters and effects to a photo after applying one or more patterns to it. Preview a filter or effect in the image window. Use the **Undo History** list to revert the photo if you want to undo filters or effects.

1 How to Send a Photo in Email 208

2 How to Optimize an Image 210

3 How to Choose a File Format 212

4 How to Create a Web Photo Album 214

5 How to Create a Slideshow 218

6 How to Print a Picture Package 220

7 How to Print a Contact Sheet 224

8 How to Resize a Photo to Fit on a Page 226

Task

Publishing to the Web and Printing

12

The easiest way to share your photos with the world is to make them available on the Internet. Send photos to others by email, upload files to a Web server, or use an online service to share your photos online. You can send a photo as is or use Photoshop Elements to fine-tune colors and optimize a photo before you send it to others. For those who are not connected to the Internet, you can share photos the old-fashioned way and print them.

Many online services, such as Yahoo!, MSN, and Apple provide Web-page-hosting services that enable you to upload your photos to a Web server in addition to more traditional photo-printing services. You can also share or print your photos by using one of the many online photo-processing services, such as Ofoto.com or Shutterfly.com. Before you upload photos to the Internet, you can organize photos and create a photo gallery or slide show.

The tasks in this part show you how to send a photo in email, optimize and save a file for sharing on the Web, and create a slide show and photo gallery. You will also learn how to scale a photo to fit on print media and how to print a picture package and contact sheet.

How to Send a Photo in Email

Email is one of the fastest ways you can share a photo. Photoshop Elements enables you to attach a photo to an email message with a click of a button—the **Attach to Email** button in the shortcuts bar.

1 Open a Photo

Click the **Open** button in the shortcuts bar. Select the photo you want to send to a friend and open the file.

2 Click Attach to Email

Click the **Attach to Email** button in the shortcuts bar. The **Attach to E-mail** dialog box opens.

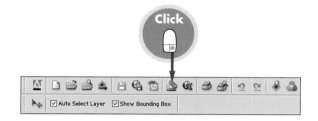

3 Resize the Photo

Because photo files can be larger than some of your friends can receive through their email programs, click the **Auto Convert** button to reduce the photo size (the file is stored in a temporary folder on your hard drive; choose **As Is** if you don't want to resize the photo). The file is copied and converted to a JPEG if it is not already a JPEG file.

④ Choose a Profile

After converting the file, Photoshop Elements opens the **Choose Profile** dialog box if you are using Microsoft Outlook. Choose an email program from the **Profile Name** drop-down menu and click **OK**. If you are using a mail program other than Outlook, such as **Outlook Express** (or **Entourage** for Mac users), Photoshop Elements launches the program.

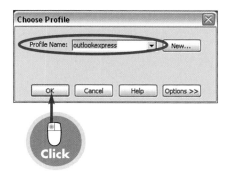

⑤ Type a Message

A blank message window for the email program you specified in step 4 opens. Type a message into the body of the email window.

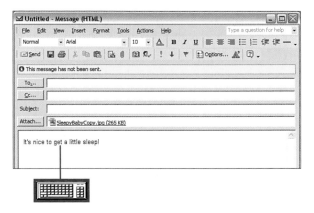

⑥ Send the Message

Type the email addresses of the recipients into the **To** field. Type a **Subject** line if desired. Click the **Send** button to send the message and its photo attachment to the named recipients.

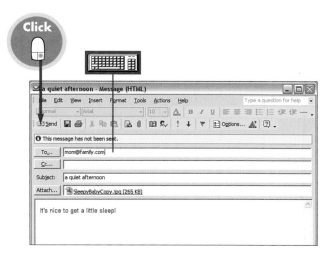

How-to Hint

Dragging and Dropping Email Attachments

Another way to attach a photo to an email message is to drag and drop the image file onto the body of the new email message. Some email programs, such as Outlook Express, enable you to view photo attachments in the preview pane of the email window.

Attach to Email Menu Command

If the shortcuts bar isn't available, choose **File**, **Attach to Email**. This menu command works exactly the same way as the **Attach to Email** button located in the shortcuts bar.

How to Optimize an Image

Keeping the size of your photos down to a minimum is a goal if you're publishing photos to a Web site. The best way to reduce the size of a file is by compressing it or by limiting the number of colors it uses. Different file formats (such as GIF, PNG, and JPEG) have their own way of compressing image data to reduce file size.

1 Open an Image

Click the **Open** button on the shortcuts bar. Select a photo that you want to optimize the size of and open the file. We'll optimize this file as a GIF image by choosing a small color palette and then compare it to a PNG-8 file.

2 Choose the Save for Web Command

Choose **Save for Web** from the **File** menu. The **Save For Web** window opens.

3 Adjust the View

Select the **Zoom** tool from the top-left corner of the window. Press the **Alt** key (the **Option** key for Mac users) and click the image in the **Original** pane on the left to zoom out.

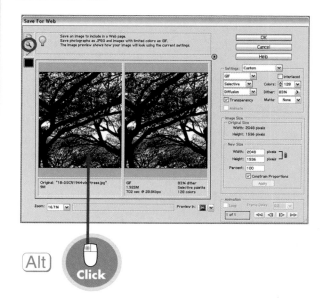

④ Choose a File Format

From the first drop-down menu in the **Settings** area of the window, choose the file format you're considering for this file. For example, choose **GIF**.

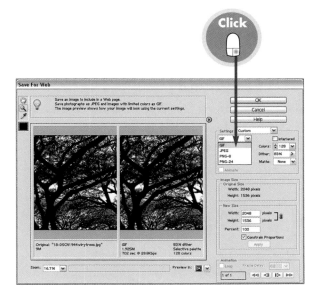

⑥ Compare File Formats

From the first drop-down menu in the **Settings** area of the window, choose **PNG-8**. Compare the quality of the GIF image in step 5 and the PNG image in this step. Compare file size and download times. In this example, the GIF image is smaller than the PNG-8 file when both are set to a 16-color palette.

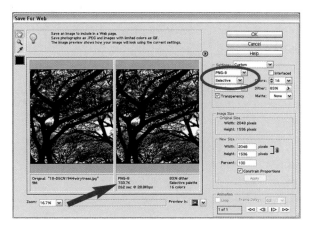

⑤ Choose Colors

From the **Colors** drop-down menu, choose the number of colors you want the optimized image to use. The fewer the colors, the smaller the file size. Here, I chose **16** colors. Compare the file size and image quality of the photo on the right with the original on the left. You can see that the image quality appears to be very similar to the original in this example.

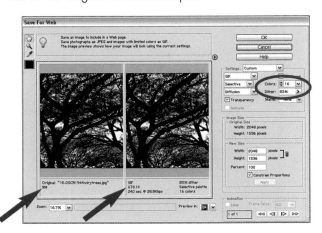

How-to Hint

Matte Color and Transparency

Assign a color to the transparent areas of a GIF image. Choose **GIF** from the drop-down menu in the **Save For Web** window and enable the **Transparency** check box. Click the color square in the **Matte** field and select a color to match a specific background color of the Web page. When you save the GIF file, the **Matte** color appears in place of the gray-and-white checkerboard pattern. You can also save a JPEG file with transparency and a matte color.

JPEG 2000 File Format

An alternative to the JPEG file format is the JPEG 2000 file format (an optional plug-in you can install with Photoshop Elements 2). You can access the JPEG 2000 file options by opening an image file, then choose **File**, **Save As**. Then choose **JPEG 2000** from the **Format** drop-down list. The JPEG 2000 file format enables you to not only preserve compatibility with the JPEG file format, you can customize a detailed set of compression settings, ultimately giving you more control over the resulting quality of the resulting image file.

How to Choose a File Format

JPEG (Joint Photographic Experts Group) and GIF (Graphics Interchange Format) are the most common file formats used for photos on Web pages. For nearly all photos, the JPEG file format is the best file format for preserving image quality and providing the smallest file size. PNG-8 and PNG-24 (Portable Network Graphics) file formats are also supported, although not quite as popular.

1 Open a Photo

Click the **Open** button on the shortcuts bar. Select a photo you want to save for use on the Web and open the file.

2 Choose the Save for Web Command

Choose **File**, **Save for Web**. The **Save For Web** window opens.

3 Choose GIF File Format

From the first drop-down menu in the **Settings** area of the window, choose the **GIF** file format. Note that at 128 colors, the file is 496K in size and takes 178 seconds to download at 28.8Kbps.

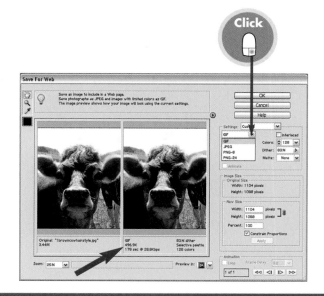

④ Choose Number of Colors

From the **Colors** drop-down menu, choose the number of colors you want the optimized image to use; the fewer the colors, the smaller the file size. Here, I chose **32**. Notice how the image quality degrades after the number of colors decreases. Note the size and download time of the optimized file and compare it with this information for the original file.

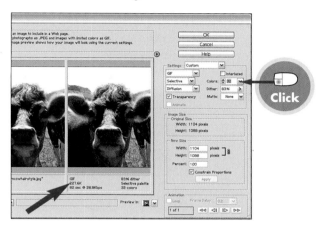

⑤ Choose JPEG File Format

Choose **JPEG High** from the **Settings** drop-down menu. The JPEG file format was designed for photos to create the smallest possible file with the largest possible color palette. The JPEG file options are different than those available with the GIF file format. In particular, note that the file size is 244K—significantly smaller than for the GIF options chosen in step 3.

⑥ Choose PNG-8 File Format

From the first drop-down menu in the **Settings** area of the window, choose **PNG-8**. Compare the quality of the GIF images in steps 3 and 4 with the JPEG image in step 5 and the PNG-8 image in this step. Compare file size and download times.

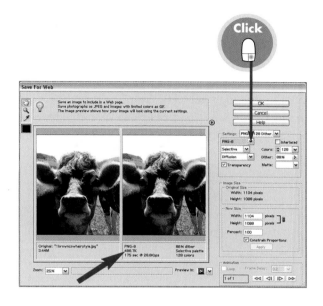

How-to Hint

Photoshop File Format

Make sure that you also save a master copy of each photo, especially if the photo contains layers. Choose the Photoshop (PSD) file format to preserve all layer information. The resulting file is considerably larger than an optimized JPEG or GIF, but you can go back and make changes to the PSD file.

When to Save Files

If you're just playing with different tools and commands in Photoshop Elements, there's no need to save the image window as a file on your hard drive. However, if you're working on a photo, choose **File**, **Save** or press **Ctrl+S** (⌘**+S** for Mac users). Save any changes you want to preserve as a file on your hard drive. You can always undo changes after saving if you change your mind. After you close the image window, however, the Undo History list is permanently discarded.

How to Create a Web Photo Album

The **Create Web Photo Gallery** command enables you to convert a folder full of photo files into a digital photo album. You can choose from a dozen different layouts and customize the size of each photo or its thumbnail. There's even room to add security information to each photo, such as a copyright label.

❶ Choose the Web Gallery Command

Choose **Create Web Photo Gallery** from the **File** menu. The **Web Photo Gallery** dialog box opens.

❷ View Gallery Styles

Click the **Styles** drop-down menu to view a list of fifteen photo gallery styles. Each gallery style is a folder located in the **Presets**, **WebContactsSheet** folder; you can use Photoshop Elements to modify these gallery styles.

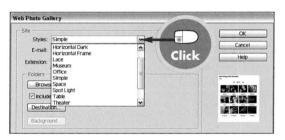

❸ Choose a Gallery Style

Choose a style, such as **Horizontal Dark**, from the **Style** drop-down menu. The style determines the layout of the images selected for the gallery. A preview of the gallery layout appears on the right side of the dialog box.

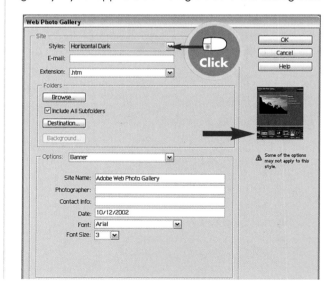

4 Select Photos

Click the **Browse** button (Mac users click **Choose**). Navigate your hard drive to select the folder that contains the photos you want to include in the photo gallery. Click **OK** (Mac users click **Choose**).

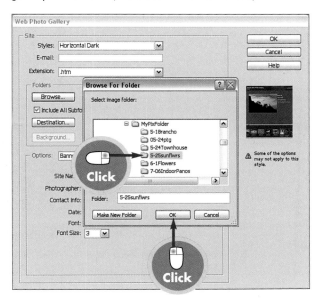

5 Select Output Folder

Click the **Destination** button (Mac users click **Choose**). Choose a folder for the completed gallery files. You might want to put the gallery files you'll create in the same folder as the original photo files; here, I've selected a different folder for the gallery files.

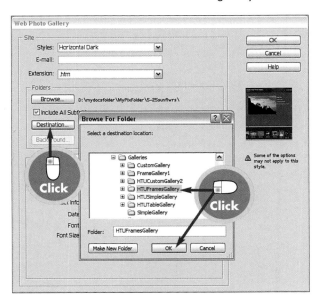

6 Format Photos

Back in the **Web Photo Gallery** dialog box, choose **Large Images** from the **Options** drop-down menu. Type a number, such as 640, into the **pixels** text box to specify how large you want the main images to appear in the gallery. Choose **High** for the **JPEG Quality**.

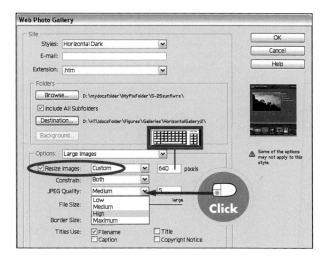

7 Format Thumbnails

Now choose **Thumbnails** from the **Options** drop-down menu. Type a number, such as 100, into the **pixels** text box to specify a size for the thumbnail images. Type a number into the **Columns** and **Rows** text boxes (for galleries that use multiple columns and rows). Select a size option from the **Font Size** drop-down menu.

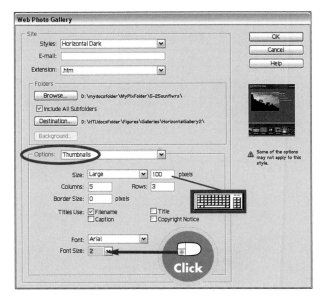

8 Customize Gallery Info

Choose **Banner** from the **Options** drop-down list. Type a name into the **Photographer** text box. Type a name for the gallery into the **Site Name** text box.

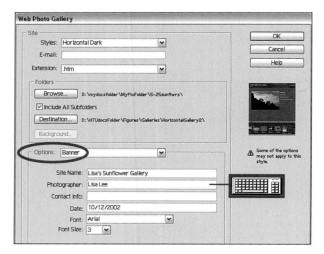

9 Add Copyright Information

Select **Security** from the **Options** drop-down menu. Choose **Copyright Notice** from the **Content** drop-down list. Click on a drop-down item to customize the security settings.

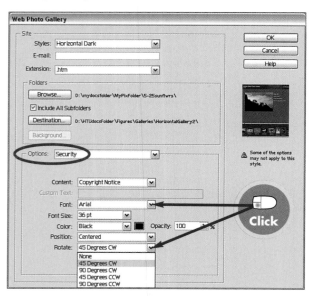

10 Create a Frames Gallery

Click **OK**. Photoshop Elements creates a frames gallery resulting in a directory of Web pages. The finished gallery opens in a browser window. Click a thumbnail at the bottom of the window to open it as a larger image in the top frame. Use the scroll bars to view all the thumbnails. Close the browser window to close the gallery.

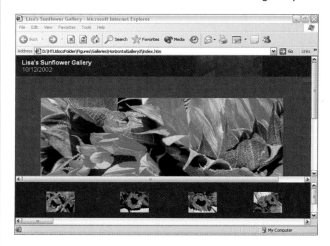

11 Create Other Gallery Styles

Choose **Tables** from the **Style** drop-down menu. Click **Background** if you want to add a photo to the background of the gallery. Select a photo and click **Open**. If you want to use a different set of images for this gallery, click **Browse** (**Choose** for Mac users) to select a different folder on your hard drive. The next steps show different gallery styles available to you.

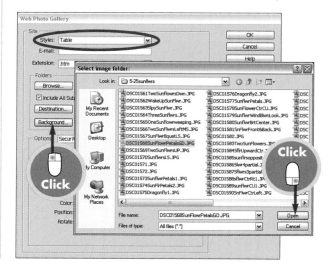

12 View Tables Gallery

View and navigate the tables gallery in the browser window. Note the position of the background photo. You might have to resize it if you want to center it in the browser window.

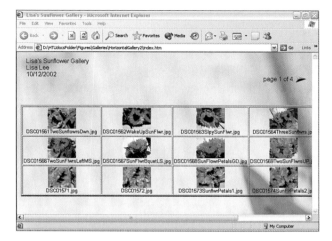

14 Create a Theme Gallery

Choose one of the eight theme gallery designs from the **Style** drop-down menu. Customize the options and folder settings and click **OK**. View and navigate the photos in a browser.

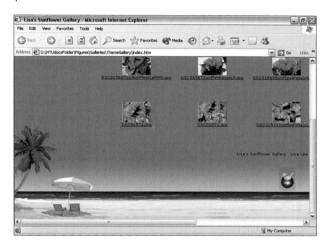

13 Create a Simple Gallery

Choose **Simple** from the **Style** drop-down menu. Personalize the folder and options and then click **OK**. View and navigate the gallery in a browser window.

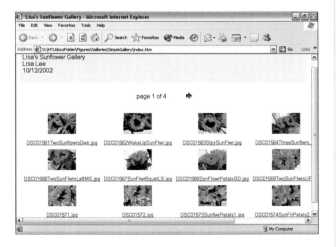

How-to Hint

Processing a Folder of Photos

The name of each photo can be shown in the Web photo gallery. You can use the **File**, **Batch Processing** command to rename a folder full of files and place them in a different output directory.

Editing HTML

Photoshop Elements generates HTML and JavaScript code to create the Web photo gallery. If you're familiar with HTML and JavaScript, you can use a text editor program to view, change, add, or delete HTML or JavaScript to personalize each Web page in the photo gallery.

How to Create a Slideshow

You can view your digital photos as a slideshow. The **PDF Slideshow** command enables you to store a folder of photos in a single PDF file and view them as a slideshow in a browser window. You can customize several options, such as the delay time and transition effect. You can view the slideshow with any browser that supports the Adobe Acrobat Reader version 5.0 plug-in, or you can use the Acrobat Reader 5.0 program.

1 Organize Photos

Organize the photos you want to include in the slideshow and place them into the same folder on your hard drive.

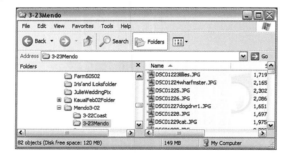

2 Choose PDF Slideshow Command

Choose **PDF Slideshow** from the **File**, **Automation Tools** menu. The **PDF Slideshow** dialog box opens.

3 Select Photos

Click the **Browse** button and navigate your hard drive to select the photos you want to include in the slideshow. Click **Open**.

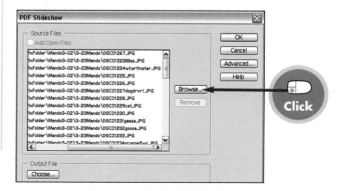

④ Choose Output Folder

Click the **Choose** button in the **Output File** area and navigate your hard drive to select a folder to store the slideshow file. Click **Save**.

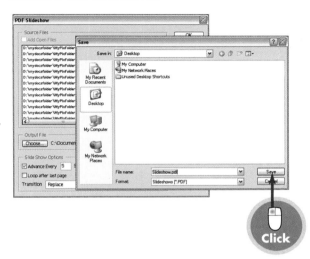

Click

⑤ Create PDF File

If you want the slides to advance automatically, enable the Advance Every check box and type a number of seconds. If you want the slideshow to loop (go back to the first slide after showing the last slide), enable the **Loop after last page** check box. Choose a transition effect such as **Replace** from the **Transition** drop-down list. Click **OK** to create the slideshow.

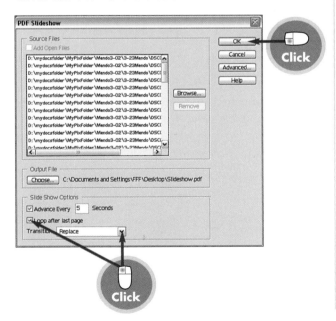

Click

⑥ View Slideshow

Double-click the slideshow file (Mac users drag and drop it on the Acrobat Reader program icon) to view the slideshow full-screen. Watch the slideshow. Each slide displays after pausing for the preset number of seconds. Press the **left arrow key** to see the previous slide or press the **right arrow key** to skip ahead to the next slide. Press the **Escape key** to stop the slideshow.

Advanced Options

How-to Hint

Click the **Advanced** button in the **PDF Slideshow** dialog box to customize settings for TIF or JPEG image compression. Click **OK**.

File Size for Slideshows

It's perfectly acceptable to use different size photos in a slide show. However, transitioning from photo to photo tends to be easier on the eyes if all the photos are the same size. You might want to consider using the **File**, **Batch Processing** command to convert or resize a folder of photos to prepare them for use in a slideshow.

How to Print a Picture Package

You can use the **Picture Package** command to print several different sizes of one or more photos on 8×10, 7.5×10.8, 10×16, or 11×17 inch sheets of paper. This is a great way to optimize paper usage for printing photos. Simply pick the photo and a picture package layout, and Photoshop Elements does the rest of the work.

1 Open a Photo

Click **Open** from the **shortcuts bar**. Choose a portrait photo of which you want to print multiple copies. Open the file.

2 Choose Picture Package Command

Choose **Picture Package** from the **File**, **Print Layouts** menu. The **Picture Package** dialog box opens.

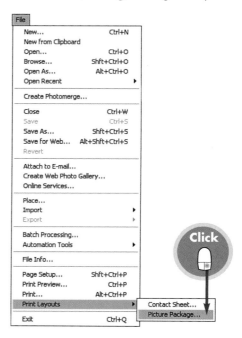

3 Select Source

Choose **Frontmost Document** from the **Use** drop-down menu. This option tells Photoshop Elements to use the image file you just opened. If you select the **File** or **Folder** option, browse to select the file or folder you want to use.

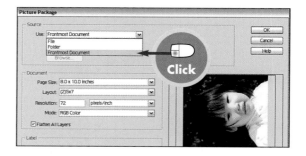

④ Choose a Page Size

Select a paper size, such as **8.0×10.0 inches**, from the **Page Size** drop-down menu. Type **300** (choose a ppi within the capabilities of the printer you're working with) and choose **pixels/inch** from the **Resolution** text box and drop-down menu.

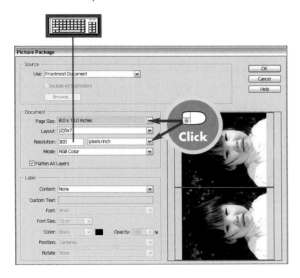

⑤ Pick a Layout

Select a layout arrangement from the **Layout** drop-down menu. Preview the arrangement on the right side of the dialog box.

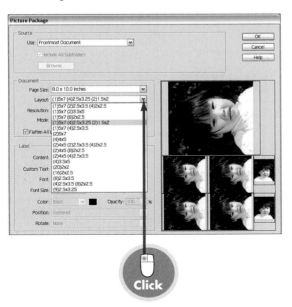

⑥ Add Copyright Info

To add copyright information to each printed photo, choose **Copyright** from the **Content** drop-down menu. If desired, type personalized copyright text in the **Custom Text** box.

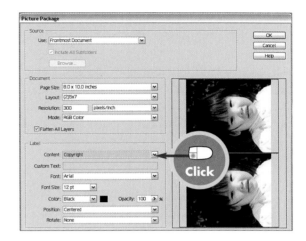

⑦ Customize the Label

Choose a font for the label text from the **Font** drop-down menu. Select a font size from the **Font Size** drop-down menu. Click the color square to open the Color Picker dialog box; select a font color and then click **OK**.

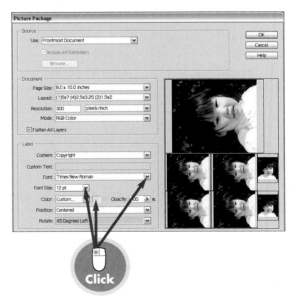

⑧ Create the Picture Package

Connect the printer to your computer or network. Click **OK** to create the picture package. The picture package opens in a new image window. The original image is shown on the left, and the resulting picture package is on the right.

⑨ Print the Picture Package

Click **Print Preview** from the shortcuts bar. In the **Print Preview** dialog box, click **Page Setup** to specify the page orientation. Back in the **Print Preview** dialog box, enable the **Scale to Fit Media** check box and click **Print**. In the **Print** dialog box that opens, click **OK**.

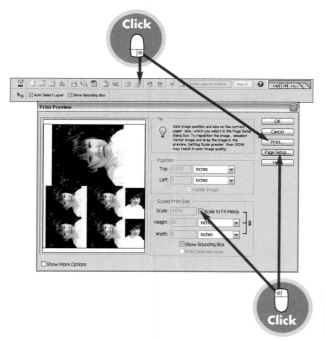

⑩ Create Another Picture Package

Choose **File**, **Print Layouts**, **Picture Package**. Repeat steps 2 through 5. In this example, I selected a different photo than the one shown in step 1.

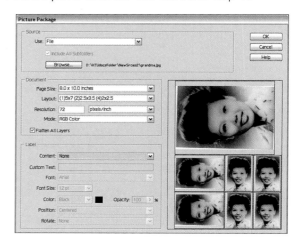

⑪ Change a Photo

Click a photo in the **Picture Package** dialog box. The **Open** dialog box opens. Navigate your hard drive and select a photo you want to add to the picture package layout. Click **Open**. The new photo replaces the previous photo in the **Picture Package** dialog box.

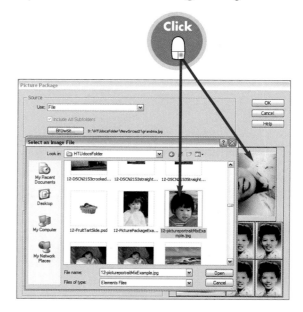

12 Change More Photos

Repeat step 11 for as many photos as you want to change in the layout. If you choose a different layout, all the photos revert to the first photo selected for the picture package. Disable the **Flatten All Layers** check box if you want each image to remain in separate layers in the new image window. Click **OK** to create the picture package window.

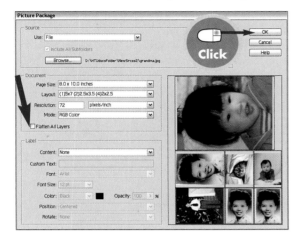

13 View the Picture Package

View the picture package in the new image window. Select the **Move** tool from the toolbox and drag an image to rearrange the layout. When you're ready to print, click **Print Preview** from the shortcuts bar. If you're satisfied with the arrangement, click the **Print** button. In the **Print** dialog box that opens, click **OK**.

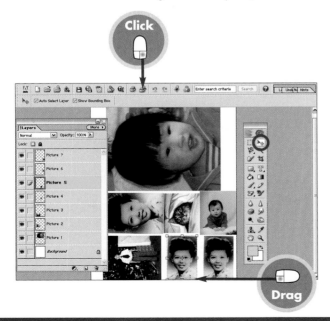

How-to Hint

Picture Package and Image Quality

Photoshop Elements resizes the master photo to match the layout you've selected. Unfortunately, one of the side effects of reducing the size of the original photo is that image and color information are lost as the file size shrinks. You may not notice a difference seeing the printed results of a picture package. However, don't be surprised if you notice some pixelation, or are underwhelmed with the image quality of smaller-sized photos.

Page Settings for Picture Packages

Be sure to select the paper size and page orientation for the printer so that it matches the layout selected in the **Picture Package** dialog box. The printer settings are set up independently of what you select in the **Picture Package** dialog box.

Paper Size and Photo Size

Digital cameras capture images in resolutions from 640×480 to more than 1200×900 pixels. A 640×480 pixel photo printed at 72 ppi prints to a 6×8-inch sheet of paper. 1200×900 pixels map to 12×16 inches, 2560×1920 to 27×36 inches. You can open the **Image Size** dialog box to adjust the pixel and document sizes of a photo, or you can scale a photo to fit a particular paper size in the **Print Preview** dialog box.

Rulers and Print Size

You can adjust the print info in the status bar of the work area by changing the ruler measurement in an image window. Press **Ctrl+R** (⌘**+R** for Mac users) to view rulers in an image window. Right-click (Ctrl-click for Mac users) a ruler and choose **Inches**. Click the arrow button at the bottom of the work area and choose **Document Dimensions**. The printed size of the image appears in inches at the bottom of the work area. Click the printed dimensions to compare the width and height of the image in pixels with the dimensions in inches.

How to Print a Contact Sheet

A *contact sheet* enables you to save and print a folder of photos as thumbnails and filenames. You can customize the page size, the number of thumbnails per page, and the font family and size of the printed filenames. Print as many copies as you like, or share them with others on the Internet. This task shows you how to print a folder of photos onto a contact sheet.

1 Organize Photos

Create a folder and move a group of photos into the folder. The folder can contain subfolders. You can use the **File Browser** dialog box to select and drag photos from one folder to another.

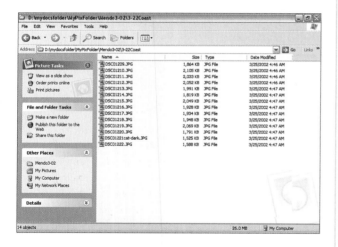

2 Choose Contact Sheet Command

Choose **File, Print Layouts, Contact Sheet**. The **Contact Sheet** dialog box opens.

3 Select a File

Click the **Browse** button (the **Choose** button for Mac users) and navigate your hard drive to select the folder that contains the photos. Click **OK**. Enable the **Include All Subfolders** check box if you want to include subfolders in the contact sheet.

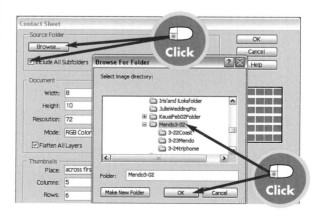

4 Configure the Layout

Choose **inches** from the **Width** and **Height** drop-down list. Type a number into the **Width** and **Height** text boxes, such as **8** and **10**, to match the dimensions of the sheet of paper you're printing to.

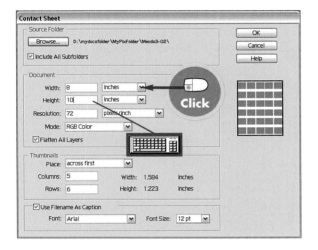

6 Generate a Contact Sheet

A new window opens for each contact sheet page. Select the **Zoom** tool from the toolbox and click in the image window to magnify the contact sheet images. Choose **File**, **Save** to save the file to your hard drive. Choose **File**, **Print** to print the contact sheet.

5 Customize Options

Select **RGB Color** from the **Mode** drop-down menu. Choose a **Font** family and **Size** from the drop-down menus for the filename labels that will be printed under the thumbnails. Click **OK.**

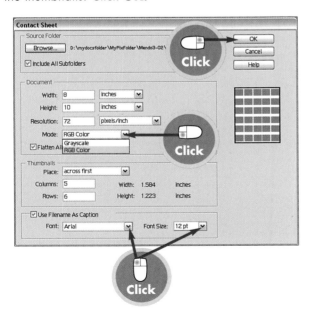

How-to Hint

Modifying Contact Sheets

Deselect the **Flatten All Layers** check box in the **Contact Sheet** dialog box if you want to modify the layout after Photoshop Elements creates the contact sheet.

Sharing Contact Sheets Online

You can optimize each contact sheet and embed the image in an HTML file. You can use a text editor program to write HTML code using the **<image>** tag to embed an image in the Web page. Upload the contact sheets and Web pages to a Web server to share them with the world. To find out how to optimize an image, go to Task 2 of this Part.

How to Resize a Photo to Fit on a Page

The **Scale to Fit Media** check box in the **Print Preview** dialog box is a handy way to scale any image to fit any sheet of paper. This option usually results in a higher quality printed image than if you resize the same photo to fit onto a page manually.

1 Open a Photo

Click the **Open** button on the shortcuts bar. Choose a high-resolution color photo and open the file. High-resolution photos (photos with a large number of pixels, such as a 2 to 5 megapixel image) enable you to print more image information.

2 Choose Print Preview Command

Click the **Print Preview** button on the shortcuts bar. The **Print Preview** dialog box opens.

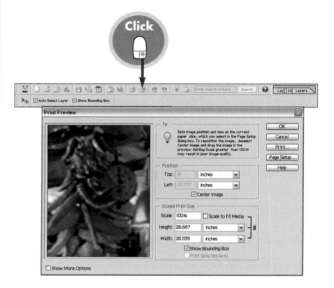

3 Adjust Settings

Enable the **Scale to Fit Media** check box. The thumbnail image is redrawn to fit in the preview area.

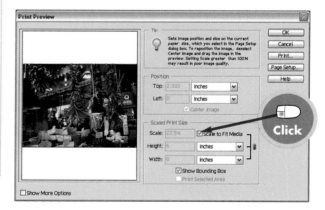

4 Choose Page Setup

Click the **Page Setup** button. The **Page Setup** dialog box opens.

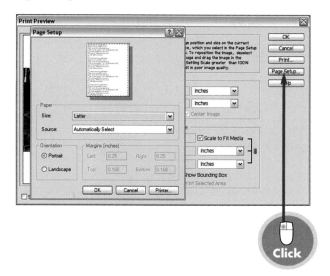

5 Adjust Page Orientation

If your photo is wider than it is tall, click the **Landscape** radio button. If your photo is taller than it is wide, leave the **Portrait** option selected. Make sure that the paper **Size** option is correct and click **OK**.

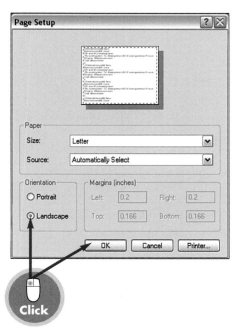

6 Print the Photo

Preview the photo in the thumbnail area in the **Print Preview** dialog box. Click **Print**. The full image should print on the page.

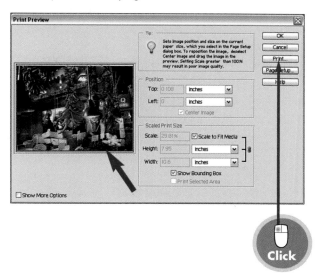

How-to Hint

About the Print Clipping Warning

If the photo is larger than the selected paper size, Photoshop Elements presents you with the **Scale to Fit Media** check box in the **Print Clipping Warning** dialog box (see step 2 of this task). Enable the check box to squeeze a large photo onto the selected sheet of paper.

Printing and Resolution

Photoshop Elements opens most photos at a resolution of 72 ppi (although it may open some at 300 ppi). Printers usually print at 300, 600, or higher dpi (dots per inch). The higher the resolution, the crisper the image appears on paper. Using the **Scale to Fit Media** option in the **Print Preview** dialog box, a 2560x1920 pixel photo at 300 ppi would print on a 6x8-inch sheet of paper instead of a 27x36-inch sheet of paper at 72 ppi.

Appendix A
Installing Photoshop Elements 2

Every program you install on a Windows or Macintosh computer has a set of hardware and software requirements: the minimal and recommended processor, amount of memory, and hard drive space necessary for a program to work properly. I use the term properly to indicate stability, such as few or no crashes, and reasonable performance—hopefully you won't have to constantly wait for Photoshop Elements to draw to a computer screen. The system requirements for Macintosh and Windows computers are similar. Checking each requirement will involve approximately ten minutes of your time if all goes well.

Macintosh System Requirements

Adobe's minimum requirements for running Photoshop Elements 2 on a Macintosh computer are detailed in the following list.

- Power PC processor
- Mac OS 9.1, 9.2 or Mac OS 10.1, 10.1.3–10.1.5
- 350MB of available hard drive space
- Color monitor with at least thousands of colors and a desktop size of 800×600 pixels
- CD-ROM or DVD-ROM drive
- At least 128MB (with virtual memory activated) of available memory

The key to finding out whether your computer matches the system requirements for Photoshop Elements is to open the Apple System Profiler or the About This Computer program. You can find out how much memory and disk space your computer has and determine the monitor settings from the Apple System Profiler. To change your monitor's settings, open the Display control panel in the System Preferences window of Mac OS X, or open the Monitors control panel in Mac OS 9.

Windows System Requirements

Although the hardware requirements for Windows machines are somewhat different than those for Macs, Adobe's system requirements for Windows are very similar to its system requirements for Macs. In addition to the physical memory installed on a computer, virtual memory—one of the memory-related features in Windows and Mac OS—is always on. The memory requirement for Windows is 128MB more than the amount of memory required for running the Windows operating system. Adobe's minimum system requirements for Photoshop Elements 2 for Windows appear in the following list.

- Intel Pentium processor
- Windows 98, Windows 98 Second Edition, Windows Millennium Edition, Windows 2000, or Windows XP Home or Professional
- 150MB of available hard drive space
- Color monitor with at least thousands (16-bit) of colors and a desktop size of 800×600 pixels
- CD-ROM or DVD-ROM drive
- At least 128MB of available memory

You can view your PC's hardware configuration by choosing a software application, Control Panel, or Properties menu command from the Windows 98, Windows 2000, Windows XP Home, or the Windows XP Pro **Start** menu. Right-click the **My Computer** icon on your desktop and then choose **Properties** to view the memory and operating system information for a computer.

Installing Photoshop Elements

The Photoshop Elements 2 CD-ROM contains both the Mac and Windows versions of Photoshop Elements. If you have a Mac *and* a PC that meet or exceed the system requirements for Photoshop Elements, you can use the same Photoshop Elements CD to install Photoshop Elements onto either computer.

Adobe offers a free 30-day trial version of Photoshop Elements that you can install on a Mac or Windows computer. Follow the instructions on Adobe's Web site to install the 30-day trial software onto your computer. If you want to purchase Photoshop Elements, visit Adobe's Web site to find out how to purchase Photoshop Elements and upgrade the 30-day trial version into a non-trial version. The following sections explain how to install Photoshop Elements from the CD-ROM.

Installing on a Macintosh Computer

The Photoshop Elements installer program is similar to many other Macintosh installer applications. The installation process involves following onscreen instructions and navigating from the first screen of the installer to the last. The installer screens introduce you to different installation options for Photoshop Elements 2. The following steps walk you through the installation process.

1. Double-click the **Install Photoshop Elements** icon located on the content list for the Photoshop Elements 2.0 CD-ROM. Click the **Continue** button.

2. The **License Agreement** screen appears. Click the scrollbar arrows to read the complete license agreement. If you agree with the terms of the license agreement, click the **Accept** button. If you disagree, click the **Decline** button to exit the installer application.

3. If you clicked the **Accept** button in the previous step, the **Read Me** window appears. When you have finished reading the Photoshop Elements information, click the **Continue** button. Mac OS X users are prompted to type the administrator's password and click **OK** to proceed.

4. Type the serial number into the dialog box and then click **Next**. Review the registration information. Click **Back** if you want to change the registration information. Click **Continue** to proceed with the installation.

5. The **Install Photoshop Elements** screen appears. **Easy Install** is the default installation option.

6. Click the **Install** button to install Photoshop Elements onto your hard drive.

7. Follow the onscreen instructions and wait for the software to install.

8. When the installation completes, a dialog box appears. Click the **Quit** button to exit the installer application.

If you choose the **Custom Install** option that appears in step 5, you can select a particular folder in which you want to install Photoshop Elements on your hard drive. If you've already installed Photoshop Elements on your Mac, don't worry. You can simply move the Photoshop Elements folder to another folder on your hard drive instead of rerunning the installer application.

Using Custom Installation Options on the Mac

For most folks, the **Easy Install** option puts everything they'll need to run Photoshop Elements on a Mac. However, if you want to re-install part of Photoshop Elements, you can do so with the **Custom Install** option offered by the installer application.

Photoshop Elements 2 consists of several parts. In addition to the application, there are plug-in files, recipes, preferences, help, and tutorial files. You can install many of these components with the **Custom Install** option offered by the Photoshop Elements installer application. The following steps show you how to access the **Custom Install** options:

1. To view **Custom Install** options, choose **Custom Install** from the pop-up menu located in the upper-left corner of the install window.

2. Each **Custom Install** package appears in the install window.

3. Click a check box to select the package you want to install. For example, click the **Plug-Ins** check box to install the Photoshop Elements plug-in files to your hard drive.

4. Click the **I** button to view package information.

5. When you're ready to install the packages you've selected, click the **Install** button.

Removing Photoshop Elements from a Mac

The Photoshop Elements installer application does not have a **Remove** option. Select the **Adobe Photoshop Elements** folder icon on your hard drive and drag it to the **Trash** icon if you want to remove Photoshop Elements from your Macintosh computer.

Installing on a Windows Computer

Installing Photoshop Elements on a Windows machine is similar to installing it on a Macintosh. The installer program walks you through the installation process step by step. To begin the installation process, insert the Photoshop Elements CD-ROM into the computer's CD-ROM drive.

When you first insert the CD-ROM, an Adobe Photoshop Elements splash screen will appear. Click the **Next** button, and select the country where you purchased the software, and then click the **Next** button. You can install Adobe Acrobat in addition to Photoshop Elements from the Windows installation screen of the Photoshop Elements installer program. Click the **Installation** button and then click the **Adobe Photoshop Elements 2.0** button. The following steps walk you through a **Standard** installation of Photoshop Elements 2 on a PC with Windows XP Pro:

1. Click the **Next** button in the **Adobe Photoshop Elements 2.0 Setup** window.

2. Choose the language you want to install from the **Select Language** window and click the **Next** button.

3. The **License Agreement** screen appears. Click the scrollbar arrows to read the entire license agreement. If you agree with the terms of the license agreement, click the **Accept** button. If you disagree, click the **Decline** button; the installer application will terminate.

4. If you clicked the **Accept** button in the previous step, the **User Information** screen appears. Type your user information and enter the product serial number. Click **Next**. Review your registration information and click **Yes;** click **No** if you want to modify your user information.

5. The **Adobe Photoshop Elements Setup** screen appears. The **Standard** option is selected by default.

6. Click the **Browse** button if you want to select a different folder for the installation.

7. Click the **Next** button to begin the installation.

8. A dialog box appears when the installation completes. Click the **Quit** button to exit the installer application.

Using Custom Installation Options for Windows

The **Typical** installation puts everything you'll need to run Photoshop Elements on a Windows computer. However, if you want to re-install part of Photoshop Elements, you can do so with the **Custom** option offered by the installer application.

Photoshop Elements 2 consists of several components. In addition to the program file, there are required program files, recipes, preferences, help, and tutorial files. You can install most of these components with the **Custom** option offered by the Photoshop Elements installer application. The following steps show you how to access the **Custom** options:

1. To view **Custom** options, start the Photoshop Elements installer and then choose the **Custom** radio button from the **Click the type of Setup you prefer** screen.

2. Click the **Next** button. A list of custom installation packages appears in the Components window list of the installer program.

3. Click a check box to select the package you want to install. For example, click the **Adobe Photoshop Elements Program File** check box if you want to install the required files onto your hard drive.

4. Click the **Next** button and follow the installation instructions to complete the custom installation.

Removing Photoshop Elements from Windows

Open the **Add/Remove Programs** application from the Windows Control Panel menu to remove Photoshop Elements 2 from your Windows computer: Click the **Start** button, select **Settings**, choose **Control Panel**, and then choose **Add/Remove Programs**. Select **Photoshop Elements 2** from the **Add/Remove Programs** window and click the **Remove** button. Follow the onscreen instructions and wait for Windows to delete the software from your PC.

Appendix B
Command and Tool Matrix

It's easy to navigate the palettes, menus, shortcut buttons, and tools in the Photoshop Elements work area. Simply click a palette, button, menu command, or tool to select it. As you become familiar with your favorite tools, shortcut buttons, and menu commands, and start learning and repeating workflows, the work area will become increasingly easier to use. Soon you'll find yourself whizzing through color corrections, photo repairs, and animation without having to follow step-by-step instructions. The menu commands, shortcuts bar, and toolbox tools are referenced in this appendix.

The shortcuts bar enables you to quickly access frequently utilized menu commands, such as opening the Quick Fix dialog box, or opening a file. Tools are stored in the toolbox: your one-stop shopping place for editing pixels with the mouse. The following sections provide a brief description of commands in the menu bar, buttons in the shortcuts bar, and tools in the toolbox.

Toolbox Tools

Each tool in the toolbox enables you to customize pixels in the image window. There are a total of forty tools stored in the toolbox. However, only twenty-four are visible. An arrow in the lower-right corner of some of the tool buttons indicates that additional tools are stored in that location in the toolbox. Click the toolbox button or press the shortcut key (such as V for the Move tool) to select a tool. Figure B.1 displays each tool.

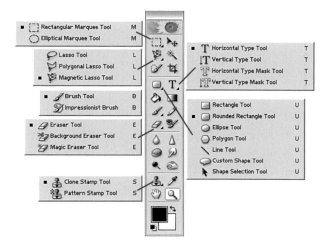

Figure B.1

Forty tools are stored in the toolbox. Click a button to select a tool.

Toolbox Tool	Keyboard Shortcut Key
Move Tool	V
Magic Wand Tool	W
Crop Tool	C
Gradient Tool	G
Pencil Tool	N
Red Eye Brush Tool	Y
Sharpen Tool	P
Smudge Tool	F
Burn Tool	J
Eyedropper Tool	I
Zoom Tool	Z
Selection Brush Tool	A
Paint Bucket Tool	K
Blur Tool	R
Sponge Tool	Q
Dodge Tool	O
Hand Tool	H
Switch Foreground and Background Colors	X
Set Current Colors to Black and White	D

These are effectively four groups of tools in the toolbox:

- **Selection Tools**—Select an area by shape, define a shape with a lasso tool, or select pixels by color using these handy tools. The selection tools are located at the top of the toolbox.

- **Drawing and Painting Tools**—Choose the Brush or Pencil tool and customize the brush settings and other options before you draw or paint on an image. Shape tools enable you to add simple geometric shapes to any image window or photo.

- **Effects Tools**—Remove red eye, blur or sharpen pixels with a custom-sized brush; you can also darken or lighten (burn or dodge) pixels in the image window using the effects tools.

- **Zoom**, **Hand**, **Clone/Pattern Stamp**, **and Set Color Tools**—Magnify or zoom out from the contents in the image window, move an image around in the image window, select a foreground or background color, or clone a pattern of pixels to another part of an image. These multipurpose tools are located at the bottom of the toolbox.

The Shortcuts Bar

Eighteen buttons are located in the shortcuts bar, as is the palette well. Each button in the shortcuts bar is a shortcut to a menu command. For example, the **New** button is the equivalent of the **File**, **New** menu command. Click a button to quickly access a command. Table B.1 describes the function of each button in the shortcuts bar.

Table B.1   The Shortcuts Bar Buttons

Toolbar Icon	Icon Name	Description
	Adobe.com	Click this button to visit Adobe's Web site. Click the links to locate and view the latest information available about Photoshop Elements, including information about software updates and third-party plug-ins.
	New Document	Open the **New Document** window by clicking this shortcut button.
	Open Document	Click this button to navigate your hard drive and select an existing image file to open in the work area.
	Browse	Click this button to open the **File Browser** window so that you can navigate to images on your hard drive or network and select the file you want to open.

Toolbar Icon	Icon Name	Description
	Import	Click this button to open the **Acquire** dialog box so that you can select a device (such as a scanner or camera) to import an image into the work area. You can also import a frame of video from the **Acquire** dialog box.
	Save Document	If you've made any changes to an image file, click this shortcut button to save your changes.
	Save For Web	The **Save For Web** window enables you to customize a file you want to save for the Web. Click this button and select a Web file format and preview settings for the image in the **Save For Web** window.
	Save as PDF	Click this button to save the image in the active window as a PDF file.
	Attach to Email	Click this button to share a photo by attaching it to an email. You can either resize the photo or send it as is.
	Online Services	If your computer is connected to the Internet, you can click this button to connect to Adobe's Web site to get the latest updates and to hang out with the Photoshop Elements community in Adobe's online forum.
	Print Document	When you're ready to print your image, click this shortcut button to send the image file to a color or black-and-white printer.
	Print Preview Document	Preview a document before sending it to the printer by clicking the **Print Preview** shortcut button.
	Step Backward/ Step Forward	Click one of these buttons to move backward or forward through tasks performed on the document (the tasks are logged in the **History** palette).
	Quick Fix	Click this button to open the **Quick Fix** dialog box. Adjust colors, brightness and contrast, foreground or background lighting, focus, and tonal range from the **Quick Fix** dialog box.
	Color Variations	Click this button to open the **Color Variations** dialog box, where you can modify red, green, and blue color intensity, saturation, and lightness. Contrary to its name, you can also use this fabulous dialog box to tweak grayscale photos.
	Search	Type a word or words into the **Search** text box to search the **How to** and **Help** data. Find out how to do virtually anything with Photoshop Elements 2 by using this tool!
	Help Contents	Click the **Help** button to open a browser window and display the HTML-based help contents for Photoshop Elements.
	Palette Well	Click a **tab** to select a palette from the palette well.

Menu Commands

Ten menus fill the Photoshop Elements menu bar. If you're using Mac OS X, you'll find an additional **Apple** and **Photoshop Elements** menu to the left of the **File** menu. Each menu contains a list of commands. Some commands are further organized into submenus. The following sections provide a brief description of each command in the menu bar.

File Menu

Located on the left side of the menu bar, the **File** menu enables you to create, save, and close Photoshop Elements documents. Most applications store similar commands in the **File** menu. In addition to the common **File** menu commands, Photoshop Elements stores some special features, such as the **PhotoMerge** command and the **Create Web Photo Gallery** command. The following list provides a brief description of each command located in the **File** menu.

- **New**—Opens the **New** document window, enabling you to define the exact dimensions, image mode, and resolution.
- **New from Clipboard**—Creates a new image window using the contents of the Clipboard, such as text or an image. Use the **Copy** command in Photoshop Elements or another program to place text or graphics in the Clipboard.
- **Open/Open As**—Opens an image file. The **Open As** command enables you to convert an image file into a supported Photoshop Elements file format. For a complete list of supported file formats, see Appendix C.
- **Browse**—Opens the **File Browser** palette or the **File Browser** window (if the palette is detached from the palette well).
- **Open Recent**—Displays a submenu containing the ten most recently opened image files.
- **Create PhotoMerge**—Opens the PhotoMerge window that enables you to create horizontal or vertical panoramas.
- **Close**—Closes the active window.
- **Close All**—Closes all open windows. This command is available only for Mac OS X computers.
- **Save**—Saves the active image window. If this command is used on a new image window, the Save dialog box appears, enabling you to name the image, navigate to the folder where you want to save the file, and choose a file format.
- **Save/Save As**—Use this command, and use it often, to save a native Photoshop file or any other supported file format. For a complete list of supported file formats, see Appendix C. The **Save As** command enables you to choose a new name and file format for the file you want to save.
- **Save For Web**—Optimizes an image for the Web by opening the **Save For Web** window. You can save a GIF, JPEG, PNG-8, PNG-24, or Animated GIF from this window.
- **Revert**—Removes any changes made to the document, returning it to its original contents (as the image appeared when it was first opened). This command can revert the document only to its last-saved state.
- **Attach to Email**—Opens a dialog box enabling you to resize or send the image as-is to your default email program.
- **Create Web Photo Gallery**—Opens the **Web Photo Gallery** dialog box. Select layout and photos you want to use to create a photo gallery you can view on CD-ROM or on your Web site.
- **Online Services**—Updates Photoshop Elements and gets the latest bug fixes and software updates.
- **Place**—Enables you to place an imported PDF, Illustrator, EPS file, or an image stored in the Clipboard into a specific place in the document window.
- **Import**—Controls a scanner or camera device that works with installed TWAIN software. A list of installed TWAIN plug-ins can be found in the **Import** submenu.
- **Export**—Saves an image file with a particular file format. You can install plug-in files that enable you to export an image file to a custom file format.
- **Batch Processing**—Opens the **Batch** window that enables you to resize or convert one or more image files automatically.

- **Automation Tools**—From the submenu, choose to create an automated PDF slideshow or to convert a multipage PDF into a Photoshop (PSD) file.
- **File Info**—Adds caption, copyright, URL, and EXIF information to a document. EXIF information displays camera, scanner, or other device-specific information related to the image file.
- **Print Preview**, **Print**—Print commands enable you to preview the page layout, configure the way the document will print, and then send the image to the printer as a print job.
- **Page Setup**—Enables you to choose portrait or landscape orientation for the open image file and to select the paper size and scale of the active image window.
- **Print Layouts**—Choose a **Picture Package** if you want to print a photo at different sizes on a single sheet of paper. Select **Contact Sheet** to print thumbnail images of images stored on your hard drive.
- **Quit/Exit**—Terminates the Photoshop Elements 2 program. This command is located in the **Photoshop Elements** menu in Mac OS X.

Edit Menu

Don't be surprised if you feel a sense of déjà vu when you see the commands in the **Edit** menu. Like the **File** menu, many of the commands in the **Edit** menu are commonly found in Windows and Mac programs. Copying, pasting, and deleting selections are just a few of the commands you can choose from the **Edit** menu. The following list provides a brief description for each of the commands in the **Edit** menu.

- **Undo/Undo State Change**—Select this command once to reverse the previous task or command performed on the document window. You can perform multiple Undo commands. Set the number of undo tasks from the **General Preferences** window.
- **Step Forward/Backward**—Choose **Step Forward** to redo the previously undone task. Choose **Step Backward** to undo the previous task.
- **Cut**—Removes the selected area from the document window and puts it on the Clipboard. The

Clipboard is a part of the Windows and Mac operating systems and is used to store temporary data.

- **Copy/Copy Merged**—**Copy** creates a copy of the selected area in the document window and places it in the Clipboard. **Copy Merged** enables you to copy all the layers in the selected area.
- **Paste/Paste Into**—**Paste** places the image stored in the Clipboard into a new layer in the document window. **Paste Into** places the image from the Clipboard into a selected area in the document window.
- **Clear**—Deletes the selected image and its layer from the document window. You can revert the document by opening the **History** palette or by choosing the **Undo** command from the **Edit** menu.
- **Fill/Stroke**—**Fill** enables you to adjust content and blending settings for the fill or color after you've applied a tool to an image. **Stroke** enables you to customize a stroke after it has been applied to an image.
- **Define Brush/Pattern**—These commands enable you to select a customized brush stroke or pattern and save it as a custom brush or pattern.
- **Purge**—Clears the **Undo** list, the **Clipboard** contents, or the **History** list; choose the contents you want to purge from the **Purge** command's submenu.
- **Color Settings/Preset Manager/Preferences**—Use these commands to customize the color management, tools, and your work preferences. To find out more about how to use color setting, go to Part 2, "Getting Started with Color Management." To find out how to use the Preset Manager, go to Part 11, "Creating Custom Graphics and Using Layers and Brushes." To find out how to work with Preferences, go to Part 1, "Getting Around in Photoshop Elements." These commands are located in the **Photoshop Elements** menu in Mac OS X.
- **File Association**—This command is only available for Windows XP machines. Select this command to open the **File Association Manager** window. Click a check box to select the supported file format you want Photoshop Elements 2 to open by default. Click **OK** to save your changes.

Image Menu

The **Image** menu stores commands that enable you to resize, rotate, or transform an image. You can also access the histogram and color modes from this menu. Go to Part 3, "Basic Image Editing Techniques" to find out how to apply the commands in the **Image** menu. The following list provides a brief description for each of the commands in the **Image** menu.

- **Duplicate Image**—Creates a copy of the active image window. You can use a duplicate image window to view your edits at different magnification settings.

- **Rotate**—Flips or turns one layer (or all layers in an image) horizontally, vertically, or anywhere in-between. Choose the desired command from this menu.

- **Transform**—Skews or distorts an image or changes a selected image's perspective. Choose the **Free Transform** command to apply the skew, distort, and perspective effects in combination.

- **Crop**—Defines new boundaries for the active image and reduces its dimensions.

- **Resize**—Choose **Image Size** to adjust the size of the image; choose **Canvas Size** to adjust the size of the canvas. Choose **Scale** to adjust the size of the selected area in the image window. Select a hidden layer and choose **Reveal All** to show the outline of a hidden object or image stored in the **Layers** palette.

- **Adjustments**—Choose one of the commands in this menu to reduce the number of pixels in an image by defining a reduced set of colors to apply to the open image.

- **Histogram**—Enables you to view the tonal range distribution for each or all color channels in the open image.

- **Mode**—Changes the number of colors available to an image. Choose from **RGB**, **Grayscale**, **Bitmap**, and **Indexed Color** modes.

Enhance Menu

The **Enhance** menu stores a wide, powerful range of color correction commands. Automatically or manually correct colors by choosing a command. Find out more about how to correct color in Part 4, "Image and Color Correction Techniques." The following list provides a brief description for each of the commands in the **Enhance** menu.

- **Quick Fix**—Opens the **Quick Fix** dialog box to access the tools like the Brightness/Contrast, Color Correction, Focus, and Rotate tools.

- **Auto Levels**—Automatically corrects the tonal range of colors in an image. This feature can save you time by quickly correcting colors rather than you having to do it manually.

- **Auto Contrast**—Automatically corrects the contrast levels in an image.

- **Auto Color Correction**—Automatically corrects the contrast levels in an image.

- **Adjust Lighting**—Choose the **Fill Flash** or **Adjust Backlighting** menu commands:

  Fill Flash—Use this option to brighten shadowed areas of an image.

  Adjust Backlighting—Use this option to manually adjust washed-out colors in the background of an image.

- **Adjust Color**—Use the **Adjust Color** submenu to adjust the hue, saturation, and lightness of colors in an image or to replace or remove colors. You can use the **Color Variations** command to experiment with color adjustment. You can make changes to Shadows, Midtones, Highlights, and Saturation, and view the results as you manually adjust colors.

- **Adjust Brightness/Contrast**—Manually adjust the brightness and contrast levels of an image with this command. The submenu options open either the **Brightness/Contrast** dialog box or the **Levels** dialog box so that you can make the adjustments.

Layer Menu

Create, modify, and delete layers by choosing one of the many commands stored in the **Layer** menu. To find out more about how to use layers, go to Part 7, "Combining Images and Creating Panoramas." The following list provides a brief description for each of the commands in the **Layer** menu.

- **New**—Choose from four commands: **Layer**, **Layer from Background**, **Layer from Copy**, **Layer from Cut**.
- **Duplicate Layer**—Creates a copy of the selected layer.
- **Delete Layer**—Removes the selected layer from an image window.
- **Rename Layer**—Enables you to give each layer a unique name. You also can double-click a layer to open the **Layer Properties** window and then type a new name for the selected layer.
- **Layer Style**—Applies or modifies a layer style.
- **New Fill Layer**—Adds a solid-color, gradient, or pattern layer to a document.
- **New Adjustment Layer**—Use these commands to experiment with Levels, Brightness/Contrast, Hue/Saturation, Gradient Map, Invert, Threshold, and Posterize settings to adjust the tonal ranges of an image.
- **Layer Content Options**—Use the **Change Layer Content** and **Layer Content** commands to modify adjustment or fill layers that exist in the **Layers** palette.
- **Type**—Choose one of the commands in this submenu to format a text layer in a document. The **Warp Text** command enables you to create some cool-looking text effects.
- **Simplify Layer**—Some layers can contain more than one element. Choose this command to merge complex layers into a simple, single-object layer.
- **Group with Previous/Ungroup**—Keep layers together or apart by choosing one of these two commands.
- **Arrange**—Changes the order of the selected layer in the **Layers** palette. Note that the Background layer cannot be moved, although any other layer can be moved freely.

- **Merge Layers/Merge Down**—When only one layer is present, this menu command appears as **Merge Layers** in the **Layers** menu. If a layer is selected and there is a second layer located directly below it in the **Layers** palette, **Merge Layers** changes to the **Merge Down** command.
- **Merge Visible**—Combines all visible layers (those layers marked with the eye icon) into a single layer. Hidden layers (those layers that don't have the eye icon) remain unchanged.
- **Flatten Image**—Merges all visible layers into a single layer. Hidden layers are discarded.

Select Menu

The selection commands work in conjunction with the selection tools located in the toolbox. The selection tools enable you to pick which pixels you want to modify. The selection commands enable you to customize the selection area. Grow, shrink, blur, invert, or deselect a selection with one of the **Select** menu commands. The following list provides a brief description for each of the commands in the **Select** menu.

- **All**—Selects everything in the active image window.
- **Deselect**—Deselects everything in the active image window.
- **Reselect**—Well, you get the picture by now. This command reselects the previously selected image.
- **Inverse**—Selects all parts of the image except for the currently selected area.
- **Feather**—Blends the edges of the selected image object into the pixels surrounding the selected area.
- **Modify**—Adjusts the border or expands, smoothes, or contracts a selected area of an image.
- **Grow**—Extends the edges of the selected area.
- **Similar**—Selects similarly colored pixels that match pixels in the selection area.
- **Load/Save/Delete Selection**—This combination of commands enables you to save a selected area of pixels and restore or delete the selection independently of what is selected or visible in the image window.

Filter Menu

Adobe installs dozens of plug-in files with Photoshop Elements. These plug-ins are located in the **Filter** menu. You can view and select any installed filters from the **Filter** menu. The following list provides a brief description about each of the commands in the **Filter** menu.

- **Last Filter**—The previously selected filter or effect will appear at the top of the **Filter** menu. Press **Ctrl+F** (⌘**+F** for Mac users) to reapply the filter or effect to the selected area of the document.
- **Artistic**—Applies neon glow, colored pencil, smudge stick, rough pastels, and other artistic stroke effects to an image.
- **Blur**—These filters smooth out pixels by averaging the color of pixels located beside hard edges, lines, or shaded areas.
- **Brush Strokes**—Applies another variation of brush strokes to an image, similar to the artistic effects.
- **Distort**—Each distort effect takes a shape, such as a sphere, and applies a specific effect, such as pinch, ripple, or shear, combined with the shape, to distort an image. The **Liquify** tool is also located in this menu list.
- **Noise**—Adds pixels to an image to reduce the clarity of an image. This filter can be used to minimize sharp color or tonal contrasts in an image.
- **Pixelate**—Groups pixels in a specific shape or size to create a unique effect.
- **Render**—Applies a render effect to add a lens flare, lighting effect, or a 3D effect to an image.
- **Sharpen**—Sharpen filters work in contrast to **Blur** filters, increasing the contrast of nearby pixels to bring out an image.
- **Sketch**—Applies a texture or stroke to an image to enhance the image. Works similarly to the **Artistic** and **Brush Stroke** filters.
- **Stylize**—Applies a painted effect to an image with options such as Emboss, Diffuse, Solarize, Glowing Edges, Trace Contour, and Wind.
- **Texture**—Intensifies the depth or substance of an image by applying effects such as Grain, Patchwork, Stained Glass, and Texturizer to an image.
- **Video**—Changes an image to match colors with video filters.
- **Other**—Choose the Custom, DitherBox, High Pass, Maximum, Minimum, or Offset filter to apply a color adjustment filter to an image.
- **Digimarc**—Image files can be saved with a unique identification, or watermark. This filter enables you to search for a digimarc watermark in an image.

View Menu

The **View** menu commands enable you to customize the zoom level and view options of the image window. The following list provides a brief description for each of the commands in the **View** menu.

- **New View**—Opens a second, duplicate window of the image in the active window.
- **Zoom In**—Magnifies the image in the document window.
- **Zoom Out**—Reduces the size of the image in the document window.
- **Fit on Screen**—Adjusts the size so that the full image fits in the document window.
- **Actual Pixels**—Changes the view to 100%—the unaltered view of the image—in the document window.
- **Print Size**—Defines the printed dimensions of the image file. Changes the image in the document window to the way it will appear if printed.
- **Selection**—Enables you to view or not view a dash-line marquee (also called *marching ants*) when a selection tool is applied to the image window.
- **Rulers**—Shows or hides horizontal and vertical rulers on the document window.
- **Grid**—Adds or removes a grid in the document window.

- **Annotations**—If an image contains annotation data, you can view or hide this information by selecting this command. You must use a program such as Adobe Acrobat to add annotations to a PDF file.
- **Snap to Grid**—Helps align an object being placed in the image to the nearest grid cell.

Window Menu

The **Window** menu consists of a menu command for each palette, plus a few additional commands. To find out more about palettes and the palette well, go to Part 1, Task 7, "How to Use the Work Area." You can also choose a **Window** command to reorganize the open windows in the work area. The following list provides a brief description for each of the commands in the **Window** menu.

- **Images**—A list of any open windows appears in this menu along with the following submenu commands:

  Cascade—Overlaps each window from the left corner of the work area toward the right corner.

  Tile—Resizes each open window so that you can view each open image in the work area.

  Minimize—In Mac OS X, this command moves the active image window to the dock. In Windows, this command reduces the window to the size of the title bar and stashes it in the lower-left corner of the work area.

  Bring All to Front—Shows all open image windows in the work area. Sorry Windows and Mac OS 9 users, this command is available only in Mac OS X.

- **Arrange Icons**—Aligns minimized images in the work area. This menu item is available only in the Windows version of Photoshop Elements.
- **Close All**—Closes all document windows. This menu item is available only in the Windows version of Photoshop Elements.
- **Show/Hide Tools**—Shows or hides the toolbox.
- **Show/Hide Options**—Shows or hides the options bar.

- **Show/Hide Shortcuts**—Shows or hides the shortcuts bar.
- **Show/Hide Palettes**—A check mark appears beside each toolbar and palette open in the work area. Select a window to open or close it in the work area. Shows or hides the **File Browser**, **Navigator**, **Info**, **Hints**, **How To**, **Undo History**, **Color Swatches**, **Layers**, **Layer Styles**, **Filters**, **Effects**, and **Search Results** palettes.
- **Show/Hide Status Bar**—Shows or hides the status bar in the work area. This menu item is available only in the Windows version of Photoshop Elements.
- **Show/Hide Welcome**—Opens or closes the **Quick Start** window.
- **Reset Palette Locations**—Returns the palette windows to their default locations in the work area.

Appendix C
Supported File Formats

Photoshop Elements enables you to open and save images in a number of file formats. Some file formats are better suited for Windows; others work better on Macintosh computers. If you're saving photos or images for Web pages, you can choose one of the formats listed in Table C.1 from the **Save For Web** dialog box or from the **Save As** dialog box.

Image files created on a digital camera are saved in the color management system used by the camera. If you want to preserve this information, create a CD-ROM or DVD-ROM copy of the original images before you open them in Photoshop Elements. After you open any image file in Photoshop Elements, the file adopts the color management system used by Photoshop Elements, regardless of whether or not you save the file.

File Formats for the Web

Table C.1   File Formats for the Web

File Format	Definition
GIF	*Graphics Interchange Format.* This format works best for images that use fewer than 256 colors or for images that have large areas of similar or solid color. This file format supports compression, transparency, and can be edited into an animation if the file is saved as an animated GIF in the **Save For Web** dialog box.
JPEG	*Joint Photographic Experts Group.* This format works best for compressing and preserving images that have thousands or millions of colors. Transparency is also supported from the **Save For Web** dialog box.
JPEG 2000	*Joint Photographic Experts Group 2000.* JPEG 2000 is a new file format available in Photoshop Elements 2. This file format enables you to adjust the amount of compression used in the JPEG file. You can also adjust the quality of the image, as well as its size and the amount of compression applied to it.
PNG	*Portable Network Graphics.* This format is an alternative to GIF or JPEG image files. The latest versions of Internet Explorer and Netscape Navigator are capable of displaying PNG files. This file format supports thousands or millions of colors, transparency, and animation. However, the resulting file might require more disk space than a GIF or JPEG.
TIFF	*Tagged Image File Format.* This file format is most commonly used for publishing images and is equally compatible with Windows and Macintosh computers. Photoshop Elements offers several compression options as well as Macintosh or IBM preferences you can choose from when saving an image to this file format. The compression settings are unique to Adobe's software products, so if you plan to work with an image using various image-editing programs, avoid using the TIFF compression options when you save files. If the file contains layers, the **Layer Compression** options appear in the **TIFF Options** dialog box. Choose from **RLE**, **ZIP Compression**, or **Discard Layers and Save a Copy**.

Supported File Formats

It's difficult not to notice the long list of file formats from which you can choose when you save a file with Photoshop Elements. A couple of file formats to keep in mind are Photoshop's native file format (PSD) and Adobe's Portable Document Format (PDF). The native Photoshop file format enables you to preserve layers and masks, and you can open a PSD file with any version of Photoshop Elements. The PDF file format is one of Adobe's universal file formats. You can use Adobe's free Acrobat Reader program to read any PDF file or use the Acrobat plug-in for Web browsers.

The native image file formats for Windows (BMP and PCX), for Mac OS 9 (PCT or PICT), and for Mac OS X (TIFF) are additional file formats supported by Photoshop Elements. Table C.2 lists all the file formats supported by Photoshop Elements 2.

Table C.2 Photoshop Elements Supported File Formats

File Format	Definition
BMP	*Bitmap, or Device-independent Bitmap.* The bitmap image file format is most frequently used with Windows computers.
PCX	*Paintbrush graphics file format.* This is another graphics file format most commonly used by Windows graphics applications. This file format was originally created for the PC Paintbrush graphics program.
PCT *or* PICT	A file format that supports 32-bit color and relies on QuickDraw. It is the file format used by Mac OS 9 to store captured screenshots. This file format can store object-oriented and bitmap images. Mac OS X captures screenshots in the TIFF file format. A *PICT resource* is a type of image stored in a Mac OS file.
Photo CD	A file format created for image files stored on Kodak's Photo CD-ROM discs. If you shoot a roll of 35mm film, many stores can create a Photo CD of that roll of film so that you can open the images on your computer. The Photo CD contains several sets of the 35mm images. Each set contains the images stored at different resolutions, such as 640×480 pixels or 1024×768 pixels.
CompuServe GIF	*Graphic Interchange Format.* GIF images use LZW compression, combined with a transparency layer and a color table to store an image. Choose CompuServe GIF to save an image as a GIF file.
JPEG	*Joint Photographic Experts Group.* This file format supports the widest range of colors of all image file formats. The JPEG format also offers file compression. Also note that the more compression you apply to a JPEG file, the more image data is lost.
TIFF	*Tagged Image File Format.* This file format is great if you're working with Mac and Windows computers. You can save a TIFF file as a grayscale or color image, using no compression, or as a JPEG, using LZW or ZIP compression. The TIFF file format was created in 1986 by a committee led by Aldus, which is now owned by Adobe, with Microsoft and Hewlett Packard participating. Use this file format for faxing, printing, and publishing.

File Format	Definition
Photoshop EPS	*Encapsulated PostScript.* Sound like some sort of medicine? It's not. This file format was originally created by Adobe to preserve font and line art and vector graphic data in a file. Opening an EPS file converts the vector graphics into pixels. Photoshop Elements can open Generic EPS, EPS PICT Preview, or EPS TIFF Preview file formats. You can use the **Place** command, the **Paste** command, or **drag and drop** to add a PostScript element into an image window.
PDD	The native file format created by Adobe Photo Deluxe.
Photoshop PDF	*Portable Document Format.* This is the standard file format used by Adobe Acrobat and Acrobat Reader. You can click the **Save as PDF** button in the toolbar to save an image in the PDF file format.
Filmstrip	This is another Adobe-created file format, used by Adobe Premiere to view or edit RGB animation files. In Photoshop Elements, you can open, but not save, files in this file format.
PSD	The native file format for Photoshop and Photoshop Elements. Enables you to preserve unique Photoshop Elements document information such as layers, group layers, and other settings.

File Format	Definition
Raw	This file format contains a stream of image information. It is a generic file format that can be used to transfer files between computers or applications.
Pixar	Pixar is the 3D computer graphics company that uses computers to make feature films. It is also the name of the file format used to store the custom, high-end graphics required by the company's sophisticated, high-end computer systems.
Scitex	Scitex is a type of computer used to process high-end images. Save your image in Photoshop Elements in the Scitex file format so that the image can be viewed on a Scitex computer.
Targa	The TGA file format is designed for computers that have a Truevision video board. Truevision boards are used for broadcast video and video production. This file format is also supported by many MS-DOS color applications. You can choose a pixel depth of 16, 24, or 32 bits per pixel.
Wireless Bitmap	Photoshop Elements enables you to open 3D images saved using this file format.

Glossary

A

Adobe Gamma control panel Adobe's software installed with Photoshop Elements. You can use it to calibrate the color management settings for Windows or Mac OS 9 computers. If you are using Mac OS X, you can use Apple's Display Calibrator software to calibrate the color management settings for your Macintosh computer.

Analog to Digital Converter (ADC) A chip or device containing one or more chips that converts analog data into digital data. For example, a charge couple device (CCD) converts light information into digital image information. CCDs are used in scanners and digital cameras.

angle bracket A character used with HTML to identify a tag: < and >.

animation Two or more images or text objects that play back and forth to create the illusion of motion. Photoshop Elements enables you to create an animated GIF, a commonly used file format for animation files viewable on Web pages.

anti-alias A software option that enables the program to smooth the edge pixels in an image, blending it with the background color.

aperture In a digital camera, the aperture setting determines the amount of light that is allowed to pass through to the CCD. Increasing the aperture setting can affect the depth of focus of the camera.

archive Also known as a *backup*. A folder, compressed file, disk, or CD-ROM containing a set of files and folders for a particular project, day, and so on.

ATM Acronym for *Adobe Type Manager*, ATM is Adobe's software for enabling operating systems and applications to work with Adobe's font technologies.

automate The technique of making an iterative or redundant task automatic. Choose an **Automate** command from the **File** menu.

B

background layer The bottom layer of an image file. *See also* Layer.

background color The color of the background of the image window in the Photoshop Elements workspace. The term can also refer to the background color of a Web page.

batch processing A term used to describe a way of automatically processing two or more files in Photoshop Elements. For example, you can use batch processing to convert image data or to rename files.

bitmap graphics A matrix of pixels that form an image. Digital pictures are created as bitmap graphics. Photoshop Elements enables you to edit bitmaps or to generate bitmap graphics using the Brush, Pencil, or Eraser tool. *See also* vector graphics.

BMP A standard bitmap file format supported by Photoshop Elements. BMP files are more commonly created and used with Windows PCs than with Macs.

brightness The luminance of a color across pixels in an image.

Browse A menu command in Photoshop Elements that opens the File Browser palette.

browser An application that can read Hypertext Markup Language (HTML) documents.

brush A drawing tool that can be selected from the toolbox. Can also be used to define the masked or unmasked areas of a layer or mask.

Burn A tool that resides next to the Dodge tool in the toolbox. Darken shadow, midtones, or highlight pixels with the Burn tool.

button A graphic element that performs a specific action in a software application or Web page, such as to go to another Web page or to bring up a dialog box. If clicked, a button initiates a transition to a unique set of information on the same or on a different Web page.

C

calibration The process of configuring one device, such as a monitor, to match predefined setting values, such as color settings, or to match the values of a second device, such as a printer or scanner.

canvas The actual workspace area of an image file. Noncanvas areas of an image window are marked with a gray color.

cast A light shade of a color, usually created by a reflection of a brighter color in an image.

CCD Acronym for *Charge Coupled Device*. CCDs are used with most popular digital cameras and scanners. CCDs translate light into digital data, which is in turn processed and stored as a file on the camera's storage card.

check box A graphic element that can be used on a Web page to indicate that a particular feature is on or off.

chroma Synonymous with hue and saturation color levels.

CIS Acronym for *Contact Image Sensor*. A low-cost image sensor used in some scanners.

Clipboard An area of memory managed by the operating system that stores cut or copied data from an application. Images stored in the Clipboard can be pasted into an image window.

Clone Stamp A tool located in the toolbox that enables you to copy part of a bitmap image and apply it elsewhere in the image window.

CMYK Acronym used to express *Cyan, Magenta, Yellow, and Black* color values. Each color component has a value between 0 and 255. Some applications and printers do not use the black channel of a CMYK image file. Photoshop Elements does not support opening or converting images to the CMYK color mode; Photoshop Elements uses only the RGB, Grayscale, Indexed Color, and Bitmap color modes.

Color Picker A window containing a palette of colors from which you can select. Click the foreground or background color swatch in the toolbox to open the Color Picker window.

ColorSync The name of Apple's color-matching software technology.

commands A task executed as the result of choosing a menu command. Most tasks are logged in the Undo History palette.

compositing The task of combining multiple images. For example, if you combine multiple images into multiple layers and channels in a Photoshop Elements image file, you are compositing images. The resulting single image is called a composite image.

contrast The difference between light and dark pixel values in an image or object.

convert Usually refers to changing the format of an image file from one file format to another by choosing the Save, Save As, or Save for Web menu command from the File menu.

Crop A tool that enables you to retain the subject of a photo while removing unselected image areas.

D

digital camera A consumer electronic device, similar to a traditional analog camera, that can capture digital images and store them to a removable card. High-end digital cameras can capture images directly to a computer's hard disk.

Dodge A tool that resides next to the Burn tool in the toolbox. The Dodge tool can lighten shadows, midtones, or highlight pixels.

download To copy a file or archive from another computer on a network or from the Internet to your computer's hard drive. For example, if you want to edit your Web pages, you can log in to your Web site and download a file to your computer using a network connection.

DPI Acronym for *dots per inch*, a measurement used to define printer resolution.

E

edit To change, adjust, or reorganize a text or image object.

editor An application or feature in an application that edits text or graphics.

effect One or more ways to enhance the way an image appears in the image window. Some effects can be added as layer styles. All effects are accessible from the Filter menu.

Embed An HTML tag used to add a sound or media file to a Web page. *See also* IMG SRC.

Eraser This tool erases pixels from an image. Photoshop Elements has three different kinds of eraser tools: Eraser, Background Eraser, and Magic Eraser.

Export A command used to convert the active image window into the selected file format, defined by a plug-in file installed on the hard drive.

Eyedropper A tool that can capture a color from an image and use that color as the foreground or background color in the toolbox.

F

file format A generic term for describing the way a file is saved. GIF, PSD, JPEG, and PNG are all different types of graphic file formats.

filter Photoshop Elements includes image-editing filters that adjust contrast, brightness, and produce other effects that can improve your images.

font A character set of a specific typeface, type style, and type size. Some fonts are installed with the operating system on your computer.

foreground The front-most layer of objects or images in an image window.

foreground color The upper-left color in the color well in the toolbox. If the pen, pencil, paintbrush, or other drawing tool is selected, the foreground color is used with the selected tool.

frames A feature of HTML that can be used to divide a Web page, enabling you to view and navigate more than one page in a browser window. Photoshop Elements enables you to create a Web photo album containing frames.

FTP Acronym for *File Transfer Protocol*. FTP is available in some browsers and can be used to upload or download files to the Web or to a network that has an FTP server.

G

gamma Also known as the gamma correction setting. Adjusts an image to prevent the midtones from appearing too dark on a computer screen. Switch gamma settings to view your Windows graphics on a Mac or to view your Macintosh graphics on a Windows platform.

GIF Pronounced "jif," the *Graphic Interchange Format* is one of the two most common graphic file formats used on the Web. The GIF format is most effective at compressing solid-color images and images with areas of repetitive color. In addition to supporting background transparency (which is great for animation), GIF files can represent up to 256 colors. The GIF format is best used with illustrations, text, and line art.

gradient A progression of colors that gradually blend or fade into each other. Create a gradient within an object or across frames and layers.

grayscale Represents a percentage of black, where 0 is white and 100 is black, and intermediate values are shades of gray.

H

halo An off-colored ring of pixels that appears around the borders of a graphic. Halos are most noticeable around the edges of a mask.

Hand A toolbox tool that enables you to move the contents of the image window in any direction.

hard disk A hardware component commonly used in computers to store files and folders of data.

hexadecimal A term to express red, green, and blue color values. Each color component is represented by a hexadecimal value, such as FF-FF-FF for white.

hide A term used to define the nonvisible state of an image layer, palette, or window.

highlight color The color used as a visual interface to identify selected text or graphics.

highlight A term used to describe a particular tonal range of pixels. Pixels distributed over the lighter shades of a 256 grayscale tonal range in an image. The highlight area is the opposite of the shadows area.

Hints Synonymous with ToolTips. Hints are located in the Hints palette. Click a tool in the toolbox to view its tool information in the Hints palette.

How To The new name of the Recipe palette in Photoshop Elements 2.0. The How To palette is a floating window containing a single task or a group of tasks that can be applied to a selected object or layer.

HTML Acronym for *Hypertext Markup Language*, which is the language used to create most Web pages.

hue/saturation Hue is an adjustable range of colors from 0 to 360, or plus or minus 180. Saturation values encapsulate color intensity within a range of 0 to plus or minus 100.

I

ICM Acronym for *Image Color Matching*. The name of Window's color-matching software technology.

image A bitmapped matrix of pixels that represents a picture.

IMG SRC The HTML tag used to define the location of an image file on the Web server.

Image mode Located in the Image, Mode menu, this command enables you to set the color mode of the image you are working with to RGB (full color), Indexed Color (a fixed set of less than 256 colors), Grayscale (256 shades of gray), or Bitmap (two colors).

Import The command used to acquire an image from a scanner or digital camera. It can also be used to convert a non-supported document into one of the file formats supported by Photoshop Elements.

Impressionist Brush One of the drawing tools located with the Brush tool in the toolbox. This tool combines pixel colors with the Brush Preset and Size settings. As it is applied to an image, this brush creates, smoothes, and blends the colors in an impressionist-like painting style.

Indexed Color One of the color modes supported by Photoshop Elements. This image mode uses an indexing algorithm to reduce the number of colors in the image using fewer than 256 colors and also reduce its file size.

Info palette Displays the location, size, and colors of a particular object in the image window.

interpolation The process used to calculate color when pixels are added or removed from an image during transformations. The Resample Image option in the Image Size dialog box enables you to choose the type of interpolation applied to the image. Bicubic interpolation creates the best results, but is usually the slowest method of interpolation. Bilinear and Nearest Neighbor are two additional options you can choose.

ISP Acronym for *Internet service provider*. To access the Internet, a computer must establish a connection to an Internet service provider. An ISP is a company that hosts phone or network access to the Internet.

K

JavaScript A scripting language created by Netscape to add complex Web features to Web pages.

JPEG Created by the *Joint Photographic Experts Group*, JPEG is a popular graphic file format used on the Web. The JPEG file format preserves broad color ranges and subtleties in brightness and image tones and supports millions (24 bits) of colors. It is best used with images and photographs. JPEG files can use lossy compression format. Lossy compression can remove some of the image data when a file is compressed. *See also* PNG.

JPEG 2000 A new file format supported by Photoshop Elements 2. The JPEG 2000 format enables you to adjust the compression level and image quality of the JPEG image; you can think of it as a sort of customized JPEG file format.

L

Lasso A selection tool that enables you to select a freeform set of pixels. Photoshop Elements has three kinds of lasso tools: Lasso, Polygonal Lasso, and Magnetic Lasso.

layer A particular plane in a document window that can be used to create simple or complex graphics. Rearrange, add, remove, hide, and lock any layer of an image in Photoshop Elements.

Layer Styles A collection of effects that can be applied to a selected object in the image window. Layer Styles are located in the Layer Styles palette.

lossless compression An image file compression format that can be used to compress a JPEG image. Lossless JPEG compression preserves the original image, without losing any image data. Photoshop Elements lets you choose between 10 levels of JPEG compression.

lossy compression An image file compression format that can be used to compress a JPEG image. Lossy compression could result in loss of image data. Photoshop Elements lets you choose between 10 levels of JPEG compression.

LZW Acronym for *Lempl-Zif-Welch*. A form of compression that works great with images that consist of a single color, such as a screenshot or a simple Web page. LZW uses lossless compression. Lossless compression preserves as much image data as possible while reducing the overall size of the image.

N

Marquee The Rectangular or Elliptical Marquee tool that enables you to select an area of pixels in an image.

mask A selection of pixels that can be modified in an image. You can create a mask by applying one of the selection tools.

megabyte Abbreviated as *MB*. A megabyte is equivalent to a million bytes, or more exactly, 1,048,576 bytes.

memory Also known as RAM (Random Access Memory). Refers to the amount of physical memory (in chips) installed on your computer. Virtual memory is the amount of memory or hard disk space allocated for use by the operating system and applications on a computer. Memory, as far as an application such as Photoshop Elements is concerned, is the amount of space required for an application to run its routines and functions.

menu A user-interface element originating from the operating system and containing commands for an application.

menu bar Located at the top of the Photoshop Elements work area, this user interface element enables you to view and select menus and menu commands.

midtones A term used to describe a particular tonal range of pixels in an image. The middle range of tonal shades of the 256 shades of gray used to represent light in a color image. Midtone-shaded pixels are located in between shadows, the darkest shades in the tonal range, and highlights, the lighter shades of the image.

O

opacity The degree of transparency applied to a layer in an image.

optimize To reduce the size or image quality of a document to decrease the loading time for a Web page.

options bar Contains additional settings for tools in the toolbox. The options bar is located at the top of the Photoshop Elements work area.

Q

Paint Bucket A fill tool that can be selected from the toolbox. Works with the color well to fill a selected object with the foreground color.

palette Similar to the term *floating palette* or *floating window*. A palette is a window containing a set of tools and iconic commands. Some palettes also contain a custom menu.

palette well Photoshop Elements stores all palettes in the palette well. If you don't want the palette to open from the palette well, deselect the Close Palette in Palette Well menu item from the More pop-up menu.

PDF Acronym for *Portable Document Format*. This file format is capable of preserving text and image information that can be viewed with a PDF viewer application such as Adobe Acrobat.

Pencil A drawing tool located in the toolbox. Use this tool to draw with a single pixel of color in the image window.

photo gallery A digital photo album. Choose the Create Photo Gallery menu command from the File menu, select from several different layouts, and customize all kinds of settings for your photo gallery. You can view the photo gallery on your hard drive, burn it to a CD-ROM or DVD-ROM, or post it to your Web site and share it with friends and family.

Photomerge A command located in the File menu that enables you to create horizontal or vertical panoramas.

panorama Two or more photos stitched together along a horizontal or vertical axis.

pixel An atomic element of color; pixels can be grouped together to form a picture or image.

PPI Acronym for *pixels per inch*. A measurement used to define screen resolution, such as 72 ppi or 96 ppi.

plug-in A special type of file that can be placed in a folder on your hard drive. If the plug-in preferences are configured correctly, all plug-ins will appear in the Filter menu.

PNG The *Portable Network Graphic* file format is a newer graphic file format growing in popularity on the Web. This format effectively compresses solid-color images and preserves details. The PNG format might require a plug-in to be added to a browser, but can support up to 32 bits of color, in addition to transparency and alpha channels. It uses a lossless form of compression. It is best used for creating high-color graphics with complex live transparency and for creating general low-color graphics. *See also* PSD, GIF, JPEG, and lossy compression.

preferences Application and document-specific settings that you can customize to increase your productivity with Photoshop Elements.

process A set of steps that, when followed, complete a task.

processor The central processing unit of a computer. A faster processor displays graphics more quickly than a slower processor does.

PSD Acronym for the native Photoshop and Photoshop Elements file format. Preserve layers, layer sets, channels, and masks by saving them in a Photoshop Elements PSD file.

R

radio button A user-interface element found in applications and Web pages that has either an on or off state.

RAM Acronym for *Random Access Memory*. *See* Memory.

recipe *See* How To.

Red Eye Brush A tool that can be used to replace colors in an image.

resolution The number of horizontal and vertical pixels that make up a screen of information. For example, 800×600 or 1024×768.

RGB *Red, Green, and Blue* values used to express a color. Each value can be within a range of 0 to 255.

rotate To flip or turn an image or selection of pixels horizontally, vertically, by 180 or 360 degrees, or to rotate freely.

rubylith A red hue that can be used in place of the traditional marching ants graphic to outline selections.

S

Save A command used to convert an image stored in memory into a file on the hard drive.

scale A term used to indicate the size—larger or smaller—of an original object or image.

scanner A computer peripheral that usually connects to the computer's USB port. A scanner can be powered by the USB port or powered by an external power source. Images are captured line by line and converted into digital data, viewable on your computer screen. Today's scanners can capture 24-bit or 36-bit images ranging from 600 ppi to 2400 ppi, or higher resolutions.

scroll bar A set of window controls consisting of directional arrows, a scroll button, and a vertical or horizontal bar that you can use to navigate an image window.

Selection Brush A new selection tool in Photoshop Elements 2. This tool enables you to add or remove pixels from a selection area in the image window. The selection area is either defined by marching ants or rubylith (a red hue) to define the editable and uneditable areas of the image window.

Send Via Email A menu command that enables you to resize a photo and send it to a friend using an email program installed on your computer.

shadows A term used to describe a particular tonal range of pixels—the darkest shades of pixels out of 256 shades of gray that represent light in an RGB image. Shadows are the opposite of highlights in an RGB image.

show Synonymous with *display*. The term means to make a palette or window visible in the work area, or to make a layer or image object visible in the image *hide*.

shutter speed A setting on a digital camera that can affect the simulated shutter speed on the camera. This affects how long the CCD will be exposed to light.

swatch Not a watch by any means. A swatch is a square of color stored in the Swatches palette. The Swatches palette consists of a group of standard default and customized colors associated with a particular graphic file. You can use a swatch of color to specify a particular color in a color palette and then apply the selected color with the Brush tool. You can also use a swatch to fill transparent areas.

T

tag A building block of HTML, such as <HEAD>. Tags work with a browser to determine how HTML content appears on a Web page. Tags usually appear in pairs. For example, the <HEAD> tag will eventually be followed by the </HEAD> tag.

text Also referred to as *type*. Alphabetic, non-alphabetic, and numeric symbols that define the characters in a font. Use the Type tool to add text to an image window.

toolbar Located just below the menu bar, the toolbar contains buttons that enable you to quickly access menu commands in Photoshop Elements.

toolbox A window that contains all the toolbox tools in the work area.

tool options bar *See* options bar.

Transform A set of tools that enable you to scale, distort, or skew all or part of an image in the image window.

TWAIN Acronym for *Technology Without An Interesting Name*. A special kind of plug-in file that enables Photoshop Elements to communicate with a scanner or digital camera device. Each device installs its own specific TWAIN plug-in file. Any installed TWAIN plug-ins can be accessed from the File, Import menu.

U

Undo A menu command that enables you to reverse a previous command in the image window. Set the number of undo levels in the General Preferences dialog box.

Undo History Photoshop Elements keeps track of every command or action that has been performed on a Photoshop Elements document. You can view the log of executed commands in the Undo History palette.

update To make current. Photoshop Elements automatically updates all windows whenever you change a value in one window or palette.

upload The process of copying a local file or folder to another computer.

URL Acronym for *Uniform Resource Locator*. Type a URL (such as `http://www.adobe.com`) into a browser window to go to a Web site or Web page on the Internet.

V

view box The rectangular border that denotes the viewable area of the image window in the Navigator palette.

vector graphics A type of graphic comprised of paths and points. Vector graphics use an algorithm to retain crisp, high resolution if they are scaled larger or smaller than their original sizes.

W

Web Also referred to as the World Wide Web. A group of computers running Web server software connected to an extended network around the world.

Web client A computer connected to the Internet and configured with a browser and plug-ins to enable users to surf the Web.

Web server A computer connected to the Internet and configured with server software to enable it to host one or more Web sites.

X – Z

ZIP Similar to LZW compression. ZIP uses lossless compression techniques to compress images. It works best with images that consist of large areas of a single color.

Zoom A tool that enables you to magnify the contents of the image window. Use with the Hand tool to move the page while it is magnified.

Index

A

accessing preferences
cache options, 21
display and cursor options, 19
file compatibility options, 19
file-saving options, 19
general preferences, 18
grid settings, 20
memory options, 21
plug-in settings, 20
preset resolutions, 20
scratch disk settings, 21
transparency options, 19
unit and column size options, 20

acquiring images, 10-11

Actual Pixels command (View menu), 240

Add/Remove Programs application, 231

additive color spaces, 35

Adjust Backlighting command (Adjust Lighting menu), 65, 238

Adjust Backlighting dialog box, 65

Adjust Brightness/Contrast command (Enhance menu), 60, 238

Adjust Brightness/Contrast menu commands
Brightness/Contrast, 62
Levels, 60

Adjust Color command (Enhance menu), 72, 238

Adjust Color menu commands
Color Cast, 72
Color Variations, 34
Hue/Saturation, 34

Adjust Fill Flash dialog box, 64-65

Adjust Lighting command (Enhance menu), 64, 238

Adjust Lighting menu commands
Adjust Backlighting, 65, 238
Fill Flash, 64, 238

adjustment layers, 63
Gradient adjustment layer, 76
Hue/Saturation adjustment layer, 76-77
Levels adjustment layer, 74-75
saving, 77

Adjustments command (Image menu), 238

Adobe Forums Web site, 15

Adobe Gamma control panel
color profiles, 28
Display Calibrator, 30-31
gamma settings, 29
monitor profiles, 29
monitor settings, 29
opening, 28
Step-by-Step radio button, 28
white point, 29-31

Adobe Online dialog box, 15

aging, removing signs of, 104-105

Airbrush tool, 186

aligning text, 173

All command (Select menu), 239

animation
Animated GIF format, 139
animated people, 146-149
cartoons, 145
creating, 142-143
file sizes, 143
in-between frames, 143
key frames, 143
people
animation options, 149
customizing subjects, 148
duplicating layers, 146
first frame, 147
hiding/showing layers, 146
in-between frames, 147
last frame, 147
Liquify command, 147
merging down layers, 148
motion blur, 148-149
previewing, 149
selecting subjects, 148
previewing, 144-145
resizing, 144
selecting images for, 140-141
shapes, 150-151
smooth animations, 149
troubleshooting display, 145

Annotations command (View menu), 241

applications, Add/Remove Programs, 231

applying
brushes, 185
effects, 154-155
filters, 154-155
layer styles, 200
patterns, 196-197
tools, 17

Arrange command (Layer menu), 239

Arrange Icons command (Window menu), 241

Artistic command (Filter menu), 160, 240

artistic filters, 155, 160-161

Artistic menu commands
Smudge Stick, 161
Sponge, 160

Attach to Email command (File menu), 209, 236

Attach to Email dialog box, 208

attaching photos to email, 208-209

Auto Color Correction command (Enhance menu), 68, 238

Auto Contrast command (Enhance menu), 68, 238

Auto Levels command (Enhance menu), 69, 238

Automatic Color Correction command (Enhance menu), 129

Automation Tools command (File menu), 237

Automation Tools menu commands, PDF Slideshow, 218

B

background
background images
blurring pixels, 53
selecting for animation, 141
layers
moving to background, 121
unlocking, 197
selecting, 5

backlighting, 64-65

Batch Processing command (File menu), 236

Bitmap command (Mode menu), 37

Bitmap dialog box, 37

Bitmap image mode, 37

bitmaps
defined, 183
file formats
BMP, 244
Wireless Bitmap, 245

black points, 61

blemishes, removing, 102-103

blending
color, 124-125
repaired image areas, 91

blending modes, 77, 87, 191

Bloat tool, 57, 105, 111, 156-157

Blur command (Filter menu), 53, 240

Blur menu commands, Motion Blur, 53

Blur tool, 91

blurring background pixels, 53

BMP (bitmap) file format, 244

bouncing ball animation, 151

brightness
increasing
brightness/contrast settings, 62-63
fill flash, 64-65
monitor brightness, 29
reducing, 62

Brightness/Contrast command (Adjust Brightness/Contrast menu), 62

Brightness/Contrast dialog box, 62-63

Bring All to Front command (Images menu), 241

Browse button, 6

Browse command (File menu), 6, 236

browsing files, 6-7

Brush menu commands, Reset Tool, 186

Brush Name dialog box, 203

Brush Strokes command (Filter menu), 240

Brush tool
applying, 185
color, 185
drawing circles, 187
drawing straight lines, 187
options, 185
resetting, 186
selecting, 184
stroke and fill settings, 187

brushes, 183
Airbrush tool, 186
brush pressure, 111
brush sizes, 157
Brush tool
applying, 185
color, 185
drawing circles, 187
drawing straight lines, 187

options, 185
  selecting, 184
  stroke and fill settings, 187
changing, 186
choosing, 91
custom brushes, 202-203
Red Eye Brush, 98-99, 113
Reset All Warning Dialogs, 21
resetting, 186
Selection Brush, 41-43, 83, 171

Burn tool, 71

buttons, 234-235
  Browse, 6
  Common Issues, 14
  Preview, 10
  Rotate, 7
  Save, 11
  Web buttons, 192-193

cache preferences, 21
calibrating color, 30-31
canceling crops, 47
capturing video frames, 12-13
cartoons, 145
Cascade command (Images menu), 241
changing
  blending modes, 87, 191
  fonts, 169
  shapes, 189
Choose Profile dialog box, 209
choosing
  brushes, 91
  file formats, 212-213
  fonts, 168
  profiles, 209
circular frames, 199
Clear command (Edit menu), 237

Clipboard, 23
Clone Stamp tool, 50-51
  removing blemishes, 103
  removing glare, 85
  removing scratches and stains, 90-91
  repairing smiles, 97
  repairing torn images, 88-89
  replacing missing areas, 92-93
Close All command (File menu), 236
Close All command (Window menu), 241
Close command (File menu), 236
closing
  Display Calibrator, 31
  files, 236
  palettes, 16
Cloud filter, 158-159
Clouds command (Render menu), 159
clouds, creating, 158-159
CMYK (cyan, magenta, yellow, black) color mode, 37
color, 27
  adjusting, 124-125
  Adobe Gamma control panel
    color profiles, 28
    Display Calibrator, 30-31
    gamma settings, 29
    monitor profiles, 29
    monitor settings, 29
    opening, 28
    Step-by-Step radio button, 28
    white point, 29-31
  blending, 124-125
  blending modes, 77, 191
  brightness
    increasing, 62-65
    reducing, 62

Brush tool, 185
color correction, 59
  adjustment layers, 63, 74-77
  Auto Color Correction, 68, 238
  Auto Contrast, 68, 238
  Auto Levels, 69, 238
  backlighting, 64-65
  brightness and contrast, 62-63
  Burn tool, 71
  color casts, 72-73
  color variations, 66-67
  composite images, 119
  Dodge tool, 70-71
  fill flash, 64-65
  gradient, 70
  hue/saturation, 69, 76-77, 87
  Magic Wand, 69
  partial images, 83
  Quick Fix dialog box, 78-79
  tonal range, 60-61
color modes, 5, 36-37
color profiles
  saving files with, 33
  selecting, 28
Color Settings dialog box, 32-33
color spaces, 34-35
contrast
  Auto Contrast, 68, 238
  Auto Levels, 69, 238
  increasing, 63
  reducing, 63
eye color, 99
foreground color, 159
gradients
  adjusting, 87
  creating, 86
  customizing, 77
  Gradient Editor, 77
  naming, 86

How can we make this index more useful? Email us at indexes@quepublishing.com

hue/saturation, 69, 76-77, 87
importance of, 31
monitors, 29
opacity, 191
swapping, 35
text, 172
tonal range, 60-61
transparency
  file optimization, 211
  preferences, 19
warming up lighting, 86-87

Color Cast command (Adjust Colors menu), 72

Color Cast Correction dialog box, 72-73

color casts, removing, 72-73

color correction, 59
adjustment layers, 63
  Gradient adjustment layer, 76
  Hue/Saturation adjustment layer, 76-77
  Levels adjustment layer, 74-75
  saving, 77
Auto Color Correction, 68, 238
Auto Contrast, 68, 238
Auto Levels, 69, 238
backlighting, 64-65
brightness and contrast, 62-63
Burn tool, 71
color casts, 72-73
color variations, 66-67
composite images, 119
Dodge tool, 70-71
fill flash, 64-65
gradient, 70
hue/saturation, 69, 76-77, 87
Magic Wand, 69
partial images, 83
Quick Fix dialog box, 78-79
tonal range, 60-61

color modes, 5

Color Picker dialog box, 34-35, 172

color profiles
saving files with, 33
selecting, 28

Color Settings command (Edit menu), 32, 237

Color Settings dialog box, 32-33

color spaces, 34-35

Color Variations command (Adjust Color menu), 34

colors. *See* **color**

column preferences, 20

combining
images with text, 174-175
palettes, 17

commands
Adjust Brightness/Contrast menu
  Brightness/Contrast, 62
  Levels, 60
Adjust Color menu
  Color Cast, 72
  Color Variations, 34
  Hue/Saturation, 34
Adjust Lighting menu
  Adjust Backlighting, 65, 238
  Fill Flash, 64, 238
Artistic menu
  Smudge Stick, 161
  Sponge, 160
Automation Tools menu, PDF Slideshow, 218
Blur menu, Motion Blur, 53
Brush menu, Reset Tool, 186
Distort menu
  Diffuse Glow, 124
  Liquify, 56-57, 89, 100, 156
Edit menu
  Clear, 237
  Color Settings, 32, 237
  Copy, 22, 44, 237

Copy Merged, 237
Cut, 237
Define Brush, 203, 237
Define Pattern, 204, 237
File Associations, 25
Fill, 187, 237
Paste, 22, 83, 237
Paste Into, 175, 237
Preferences, 237
Preset Manager, 237
Purge, 237
Show Clipboard, 23
Step Backward, 237
Step Forward, 237
Stroke, 187, 237
Undo, 237
Undo State Change, 237
Enhance menu
  Adjust Brightness/Contrast, 60, 238
  Adjust Colors, 72, 238
  Adjust Lighting, 64, 238
  Auto Color Correction, 68, 238
  Auto Contrast, 68, 238
  Auto Levels, 69, 238
  Automatic Color Correction, 129
  Quick Fix, 78, 125, 238
File menu
  Attach to Email, 209, 236
  Automation Tools, 237
  Batch Processing, 236
  Browse, 6, 236
  Close, 236
  Close All, 236
  Create Photomerge, 130, 236
  Create Web Photo Gallery, 214, 236
  Export, 236
  File Info, 11, 237
  Import, 10-12, 141, 236
  New, 184, 236
  New from Clipboard, 23, 44, 236
  Online Services, 236

Open, 9, 24, 236
Open As, 236
Open Recent, 236
Page Setup, 237
Place, 236
Print, 237
Print Layouts, 220, 237
Print Preview, 237
Quit, 14, 237
Revert, 236
Save, 23, 213, 236
Save As, 24, 33, 236
Save for Web, 144, 210, 236
Filter menu
Artistic, 160, 240
Blur, 53, 240
Brush Strokes, 240
Digimarc, 240
Distort, 162, 240
Noise, 163, 240
Other, 240
Pixelate, 240
Render, 240
Repeat Last Effect, 240
Sharpen, 240
Sketch, 240
Stylize, 240
Texture, 240
Video, 240
Help menu, Photoshop Elements Help, 14
Image menu
Adjustments, 238
Crop, 238
Duplicate Image, 238
Histogram, 238
Mode, 36, 238
Resize, 45, 144, 238
Rotate, 54, 238
Transform, 57, 238
Images menu, 241
Import menu, Frame From Video, 12, 141
Layer menu
Arrange, 239
Copy Layer Style, 178
Delete Layer, 239

Duplicate Layer, 126, 239
Flatten Image, 49, 239
Group with Previous, 175, 239
Layer Content Options, 239
Layer Style, 239
Merge Down, 49, 239
Merge Layers, 239
Merge Visible, 49, 239
New, 239
New Adjustment Layer, 63, 239
New Fill Layer, 239
Paste Layer Style, 178
Rename Layer, 239
Simplify Layer, 189, 239
Type, 239
Ungroup, 239
Mode menu
Bitmap, 37
Grayscale, 37
Indexed Color, 36
RGB Color, 36
Print Layouts menu
Contact Sheet, 224
Picture Package, 220
Render menu
Clouds, 159
Lighting Effects, 164
Resize menu, Image Size, 45
Rotate menu, Straighten Image, 55
Select menu
All, 239
Delete Selection, 239
Deselect, 83, 239
Feather, 83, 119, 239
Grow, 239
Inverse, 53, 239
Load Selection, 239
Modify, 239
Reselect, 239
Save Selection, 239
Similar, 239

Tools menu, Folder Options, 25
Transform menu, 57
View menu
Actual Pixels, 240
Annotations, 241
Fit on Screen, 240
Grid, 53-54, 123, 187, 240
New View, 240
Print Size, 240
Rulers, 123, 240
Selection, 240
Snap to Grid, 241
Zoom In, 240
Zoom Out, 240
Window menu
Arrange Icons, 241
Close All, 241
Effects, 154
Filters, 154
Hide Options, 241
Hide Palettes, 241
Hide Shortcuts, 241
Hide Status Bar, 241
Hide Tools, 241
Hide Welcome, 241
How To, 14
Images, 241
Layer Styles, 159
Navigator, 8
Reset Palette Locations, 21, 241
Show Options, 241
Show Palettes, 241
Show Shortcuts, 241
Show Status Bar, 241
Show Tools, 241
Show Welcome, 241
Welcome, 4
Common Issues button, 14
comparing image quality, 45
composite images
color adjustment, 124-125
color blending, 124-125
color correction, 83, 119

copying/pasting, 122
creating, 82-83, 118-119
defined, 83, 117
flipping, 123
organization of layers,
 120-121
reflections, 126-127
resizing, 123
rotation, 123

CompuServe GIF, 244

configuring preferences
cache options, 21
display and cursor options,
 19
file compatibility options, 19
file-saving options, 19
general preferences, 18
grid settings, 20
memory options, 21
plug-in settings, 20
preset resolutions, 20
scratch disk settings, 21
transparency options, 19
unit and column size options,
 20

**Contact Sheet command
(Print Layouts menu),
224**

**Contact Sheet dialog box,
224-225**

contact sheets, 224-225

contrast
Auto Contrast, 68, 238
Auto Levels, 69, 238
increasing, 63
monitor contrast, 29
reducing, 63

**Copy command (Edit
menu), 22, 44, 237**

**Copy Layer Style com-
mand (Layer menu), 178**

**Copy Merged command
(Edit menu), 237**

copying
images, 22, 44
layers, 48-49, 52
selections, 122

copyright notices
picture packages, 221
Web Photo Gallery, 216

correcting color. *See* **color
correction**

correcting images. *See*
repairing images

**Counter Clockwise tool,
111**

**Create Photomerge com-
mand (File menu), 130,
236**

**Create Web Photo Gallery
command (File menu),
214, 236**

**crooked teeth, straighten-
ing, 97**

**Crop command (Image
menu), 238**

Crop tool, 46-47

**cropping images, 11,
46-47**
panoramas, 133

cursor preferences, 19

**custom Photoshop instal-
lation**
Macintosh, 230
Windows, 231

**Custom Shape tool, 145,
189**

customizing
brushes, 202-203
fill settings, 187
filters, 155
gradients, 77
patterns, 204-205
Welcome screen, 181,
 194-195

**Cut command (Edit menu),
237**

cylindrical mapping, 137

D

darkening images
backlighting, 64-65
brightness/contrast settings,
 62-63

**decreasing opacity, 48,
191**

**default warning settings,
21**

**Define Brush command
(Edit menu), 203, 237**

**Define Pattern command
(Edit menu), 204, 237**

**Delete Layer command
(Layer menu), 239**

**Delete Selection command
(Select menu), 239**

deleting. See removing

**Deselect command (Select
menu), 43, 83, 239**

deselecting
images, 83
pixels, 43

**destructive filters, 155,
162-163**

dialog boxes
Adjust Backlighting, 65
Adjust Fill Flash, 64-65
Adobe Gamma
 color profiles, 28
 Display Calibrator, 31
 gamma settings, 29
 monitor profiles, 29
 monitor settings, 29
 Step-by-Step radio button,
 28
 white point, 29-30
Adobe Online, 15
Attach to Email, 208
Bitmap, 37
Brightness/Contrast, 62-63
Choose Profile, 209
Color Cast Correction,
 72-73
Color Picker, 34-35, 172

Color Settings, 32-33
Contact Sheet, 224-225
Define Brush, 203
Discard Color Information, 37
Feather, 43
Feather Selection, 119
File Browser, 6-7
File Info, 11
Frame From Video, 12-13
Hue/Saturation, 34
Image Size, 5, 45, 194
Indexed Color, 36
JPEG Options, 25
Levels, 60-61
Motion Blur, 53
New, 4, 184
New Layer, 86
Open, 9
Pattern Fill, 205
Pattern Name, 204
PDF Slideshow, 218-219
Photomerge, 130-133
Picture Package, 220
Preferences
    Display & Cursors panel, 19
    General panel, 18
    Grid panel, 20
    Memory & Image Cache panel, 21
    opening, 18
    Plug-Ins & Scratch Disks panel, 20-21
    Saving Files panel, 19
    Transparency panel, 19
    Units & Rulers panel, 20
Quick Fix, 78-79
Save, 11
Save As, 24, 33
Save for Web, 243
Select Import Source, 10
Stroke, 187
Style Settings, 115
TIFF Options, 25
Warp Text, 176-177
Web Photo Gallery, 214-217

Diffuse Glow command (Distort menu), 124
Digimarc command (Filter menu), 240
Discard Color Information dialog box, 37
Display & Cursors panel (Preferences dialog box), 19
Display Calibrator, 30-31
display preferences, 19
displaying. See viewing
Distort command (Filter menu), 162, 240
Distort command (Transform menu), 57
Distort menu commands
    Diffuse Glow, 124
    Liquify, 56-57, 89, 100, 156
documents
    creating, 4-5
    displaying information about, 9
    document view, 8
    naming, 4
    navigating, 8-9
    pasting images into, 22-23
    viewing, 8-9
    zooming in/out, 9
Dodge tool, 70-71, 97
dragging and dropping email attachments, 209
drawing
    circles, 187
    drawing tools, 234
    lines, 187
    shapes, 188-189
drop shadows
    creating, 115
    text, 173
Duplicate Image command (Image menu), 238

Duplicate Layer command (Layer menu), 126, 239
duplicating. See copying

E

easy Photoshop installation, 230
Edit menu commands
    Clear, 237
    Color Settings, 32, 237
    Copy, 22, 44, 237
    Copy Merged, 237
    Cut, 237
    Define Brush, 203, 237
    Define Pattern, 204, 237
    File Associations, 25
    Fill, 187, 237
    Paste, 22, 83, 237
    Paste Into, 175, 237
    Preferences, 237
    Preset Manager, 237
    Purge, 237
    Show Clipboard, 23
    Step Backward, 237
    Step Forward, 237
    Stroke, 187, 237
    Undo, 237
    Undo State Change, 237
editing images, 39
    color correction, 59
        adjustment layers, 63, 74-77
        Auto Color Correction, 68
        Auto Contrast, 68
        Auto Levels, 69
        backlighting, 64-65
        brightness and contrast, 62-63
        Burn tool, 71
        color casts, 72-73
        color variations, 66-67
        Dodge tool, 70-71
        fill flash, 64-65
        gradient, 70
        hue/saturation, 69, 76-77, 87
        Magic Wand, 69

How can we make this index more useful? Email us at indexes@quepublishing.com

partial images, 83
Quick Fix dialog box, 78-79
tonal range, 60-61
cropping, 46-47
image repair
  blending repaired areas, 91
  glare and unwanted reflections, 84-85
  missing areas, 92-93
  salvaging portions of images, 82-83
  scratches and stains, 90-91
  torn areas, 88-89
  warming up lighting, 86-87
image size, 44-45
layers, 48-49, 52
masks
  creating, 42-43
  defined, 41
  smoothing edges of, 43
photos of people, 95
  blemishes, 102-103
  eyes, 98-99, 105, 108-109
  facial expressions, 106-107
  hair color, 101
  hair styles, 100-101
  jaw line, 105
  mouths, 108-109
  noses, 108-109
  physiques, 110-111
  portraits, 112-115
  smiles, 96-97
  wrinkles, 104-105
pixels
  adding, 43
  deselecting, 43
  removing, 43
  selecting, 40-41
type masks, 171

effects. *See also* filters
  applying, 154-155
  defined, 153
  lighting effects, 164-165
  matte effect, 199
  picture frame effect, 198-199
  text effects, 180-181
Effects command (Window menu), 154
Effects palette, 154
effects tools, 234
Elliptical Marquee tool, 42
emailing photos, 208-209
Encapsulated PostScript (EPS) format, 245
Enhance menu commands
  Adjust Brightness/Contrast, 60, 238
  Adjust Colors, 72, 238
  Adjust Lighting, 64, 238
  Auto Color Correction, 68, 238
  Auto Contrast, 68, 238
  Auto Levels, 69, 238
  Automatic Color Correction, 129
  Quick Fix, 78, 125, 238
enlarging. *See* sizing
EPS (Encapsulated PostScript) format, 245
Eraser tool, 103
EXIF (Exchangeable Image File), 11
Export command (File menu), 236
eyedropper tools, 61
eyes
  enlarging, 105
  eye color, 99
  red eye, 98-99
  reshaping, 108-109

F

faces, editing
  blemishes, 102-103
  eye color, 99
  facial expressions, 106-107
  red eye, 98-99
  reshaping features, 108-109
  smiles, 96-97
  wrinkles, 104-105
Feather command (Select menu), 43, 83, 119, 239
Feather dialog box, 43
Feather Selection dialog box, 119
feathering images, 43, 83, 119, 239
File Associations command (Edit menu), 25
File Browser dialog box, 6-7
file formats
  Animated GIF, 139
  BMP, 244
  choosing, 212-213
  compatibility, 19
  CompuServe GIF, 244
  EXIF, 11
  Filmstrip, 245
  GIF, 212, 243
  JPEG, 25, 213, 243-244
  JPEG 2000, 211, 243
  PCT, 244
  PCX, 244
  PDD, 245
  Photo CD, 244
  Photoshop EPS, 245
  Photoshop PDF, 245
  Pixar, 245
  PNG, 213, 243
  PSD, 213, 245
  Raw, 245
  Scitex, 245
  Targa, 245
  TIFF, 25, 243-244
  Wireless Bitmap, 245

File Info command (File menu), 11, 237

File Info dialog box, 11

File menu commands
    Attach to Email, 209, 236
    Automation Tools, 237
    Batch Processing, 236
    Browse, 6, 236
    Close, 236
    Close All, 236
    Create Photomerge, 130, 236
    Create Web Photo Gallery, 214, 236
    Export, 236
    File Info, 11, 237
    Import, 10, 12, 141, 236
    New, 184, 236
    New from Clipboard, 23, 44, 236
    Online Services, 236
    Open, 9, 24, 236
    Open As, 236
    Open Recent, 236
    Page Setup, 237
    Place, 236
    Print, 237
    Print Layouts, 220, 237
    Print Preview, 237
    Quit, 14, 237
    Revert, 236
    Save, 23, 213, 236
    Save As, 24, 33, 236
    Save for Web, 144, 210, 236

file-saving options, 19

files
    browsing, 6-7
    file associations, 25
    file formats
        Animated GIF, 139
        BMP, 244
        choosing, 212-213
        compatibility, 19
        CompuServe GIF, 244
        EXIF, 11

        Filmstrip, 245
        GIF, 212, 243
        JPEG, 25, 213, 243-244
        JPEG 2000, 211, 243
        PCT, 244
        PCX, 244
        PDD, 245
        Photo CD, 244
        Photoshop EPS, 245
        Photoshop PDF, 245
        Pixar, 245
        PNG, 213, 243
        PSD, 213, 245
        Raw, 245
        Scitex, 245
        Targa, 245
        TIFF, 25, 243-244
        Wireless Bitmap, 245
    moving, 7
    naming, 24
    opening multiple, 7
    organizing, 191
    preferences, 19, 24-25
    renaming, 7
    saving
        file compatibility options, 19
        file-saving options, 19
        when to save, 213
    thumbnails, 6-7

Fill command (Edit menu), 187, 237

fill flash, 64-65

Fill Flash command (Adjust Lighting menu), 64, 238

fill settings, 187

Filmstrip file format, 245

Filter menu commands
    Artistic, 160, 240
    Blur, 53, 240
    Brush Strokes, 240
    Digimarc, 240
    Distort, 162, 240
    Noise, 163, 240
    Other, 240

    Pixelate, 240
    Render, 240
    Repeat Last Effect, 240
    Sharpen, 240
    Sketch, 240
    Stylize, 240
    Texture, 240
    Video, 240

filters, 153. *See also* effects
    applying, 154-155
    artistic filters, 155, 160-161
    Blur, 53, 240
    Brush Strokes, 240
    Cloud, 158-159
    customizing, 155
    destructive filters, 155, 162-163
    Digimarc, 240
    Distort, 162, 240
    Filters palette, 154-155
    Lighting Effects, 164-165
    Liquify, 156-157
    Noise, 163, 240
    Pixelate, 240
    Render, 240
    Repeat Last Effect, 240
    selecting, 154
    Sharpen, 240
    Sketch, 240
    Smudge Stick, 161
    Sponge, 160-161
    Stylize, 240
    Texture, 240
    Twirl, 161-163
    Video, 240

Filters command (Window menu), 154

Fit on Screen command (View menu), 240

Flatten Image command (Layer menu), 49, 239

flattening layers, 49

flipping
    images, 127
    selections, 123

How can we make this index more useful? Email us at indexes@quepublishing.com

Folder Options command (Tools menu), 25

folders
browsing, 6
Styles, 201

fonts
changing, 169
choosing, 168
color, 172

foreground
color, 159
moving layers to, 121

formats. *See* **file formats**

Frame From Video command (Import menu), 12, 141

Frame From Video dialog box, 12-13

frames (animation)
capturing, 12-13
cartoons, 145
circular frames, 199
creating, 142-143, 198-199
file sizes, 143
frames gallery, 216
in-between frames, 143
key frames, 143
mattes, 199
previewing, 144-145
resizing, 144
saving, 13

Full color management button (Color Settings dialog box), 32

gamma settings, 29

General panel (Preferences dialog box), 18

general preferences, 18

ghost text, 181

GIF (Graphics Interchange Format), 212, 243
CompuServe GIF, 244

glare
magnifying, 84
removing, 84-85

glass
creating reflections in, 126-127
removing glare from, 84-85

Gradient adjustment layer, 76

Gradient Editor, 77

gradients
adjusting, 70, 87
creating, 86
customizing, 77
Gradient adjustment layer, 76
Gradient Editor, 77
gradient layers, 70
naming, 86

Graphics Interchange Format. *See* **GIF**

Grayscale command (Mode menu), 37

Grayscale image mode, 37

Grid command (View menu), 53-54, 123, 187, 240

Grid panel (Preferences dialog box), 20

grids
preferences, 20
viewing, 53-54, 123, 187

Group with Previous command (Layer menu), 175, 239

Grow command (Select menu), 239

hair color, changing, 101

hair styles, changing, 100-101

Hand tool, 93

hands, removing wrinkles from, 105

help
Adobe support, 15
Common Issues, 14
help topics, 14-15
ToolTips, 17

Help menu commands, Photoshop Elements Help, 14

Hide Options command (Window menu), 241

Hide Palettes command (Window menu), 241

Hide Shortcuts command (Window menu), 241

Hide Status Bar command (Window menu), 241

Hide Tools command (Window menu), 241

Hide Welcome command (Window menu), 241

hiding
layers, 49, 201
palettes, 241
shortcuts, 241
status bar, 241
tools, 241

highlights, 61

Histogram command (Image menu), 141, 238

Horizontal Type Mask tool, 170

Horizontal Type tool, 168-169, 174, 176, 180

How To command (Window menu), 14

How To palette, 14

HSB (hue, saturation, brightness) color settings, 34

hue/saturation
    adjusting, 69, 87
    HSB (hue, saturation, brightness) color settings, 34
    Hue/Saturation adjustment layer, 76-77

Hue/Saturation command (Adjust Color menu), 34

Hue/Saturation dialog box, 34

ICC (International Color Consortium) profiles. *See* color profiles

Image menu commands
    Adjustments, 238
    Crop, 238
    Duplicate Image, 238
    Histogram, 141, 238
    Mode, 36, 238
    Resize, 45, 144, 238
    Rotate, 54, 238
    Transform, 57, 238

image modes, 36-37

Image Size command (Resize menu), 45

Image Size dialog box, 5, 45, 194

Image Size field (New dialog box), 4

images, 39. *See also* color
    acquiring, 10-11
    animation
        Animated GIF format, 139
        animated people, 146-149
        cartoons, 145
        creating, 142-143
        file sizes, 143

        in-between frames, 143
        key frames, 143
        people, 146-149
        previewing, 144-145
        resizing, 144
        selecting images for, 140-141
        shapes, 150-151
        smooth animations, 149
        troubleshooting display, 145
    backgrounds, 5
    bitmaps, 183
    blending with hand-drawn effects, 190-191
    brightening
        brightness/contrast settings, 62-63
        fill flash, 64-65
    browsing, 6-7
    clouds, creating, 158-159
    comparing image quality, 45
    composite images
        color adjustment, 124-125
        color blending, 124-125
        color correction, 83, 119
        creating, 82-83, 118-119
        defined, 83, 117
        organization of layers, 120-121
        selection transformation, 122-123
    copying, 22, 44
    cropping, 11, 46-47
    darkening
        backlighting, 64-65
        brightness/contrast settings, 62-63
    deselecting, 83
    emailing, 208-209
    enhancing perspective, 56-57
    feathering, 83
    flipping, 127
    image modes, 36-37

    images of people, correcting, 95
        blemishes, 102-103
        eyes, 98-99, 108-109
        facial expressions, 106-107
        hair color, 101
        hair styles, 100-101
        jaw line, 105
        noses, 108-109
        physiques, 110-111
        portraits, 112-115
        smiles, 96-97
        wrinkles, 104-105
    importing, 10
    layers
        adjustment layers, 63, 74-77
        copying, 48-49, 52
        creating, 48
        displaying, 49
        flattening, 49
        gradient layers, 70
        hiding, 49
        layer styles, 159, 200-201
        merging, 49
        moving, 49, 121
        opacity, 48
        organizing, 120-121
        overlapping, 121
        renaming, 121
        selecting, 120
        simplifying, 189
    masks
        creating, 42-43
        defined, 41
        smoothing edges of, 43
    matte effect, 199
    moving, 93
    objects
        moving, 51
        removing, 50-51
    opening, 24, 32, 118
    optimizing, 210-211
    panoramas
        correcting mismatched photos, 133
        cropping, 133

How can we make this index more useful? Email us at indexes@quepublishing.com

cylindrical mapping, 137
defined, 117
final touches, 137
indoor panoramas, 132-133
manually arranging photos in, 134-137
memory requirements, 133
outdoor panoramas, 130-131
perspective, 136
previewing, 135
removing images from, 135
selecting photos for, 128-129
shooting photos for, 131
pasting into current document, 22
pasting into new document, 23
pasting into other images, 83
patterns
    applying, 196-197
    creating, 204-205
    defined, 196
    naming, 204
photos
    emailing, 208-209
    hand-drawn effects, 190-191
    resizing, 208, 226-227
    Web Photo Gallery, 214-217
picture frame effect, 198-199
pixels
    adding, 43
    blurring background pixels, 53
    deselecting, 43
    pixelation, 53, 65, 119
    removing, 43
    selecting, 40-41

previewing, 9-10
printing
    contact sheets, 224-225
    picture packages, 220-223
reflections, 126-127
repairing, 81
    blending repaired areas, 91
    glare and unwanted reflections, 84-85
    missing areas, 92-93
    salvaging portions of images, 82-83
    scratches and stains, 90-91
    torn areas, 88-89
    warming up lighting, 86-87
resizing, 44-45
resolution
    changing, 45
    defined, 5
    preset resolutions, 20
    setting, 5
    viewing, 44
sampling, 51
saving, 23, 33
scaling, 52-53, 107, 226-227
scanning, 11
selecting, 22
sizing, 4, 44-45
slideshows, 218-219
straightening, 54-55
text
    adding, 168-169
    alignment, 173
    color, 172
    combining, 174-175
    drop shadows, 173
    fonts, 168-169
    ghost text, 181
    layer styles, 173, 181
    resizing, 169
    selecting, 172
    text effects, 180-181

text orientation, 173
    type masks, 170-171
    warp text, 176-179
    warping, 179
vector graphics, 183
viewing, 23
Web publishing, 207
    email, 208-209
    file formats, 212-213
    image optimization, 210-211
    slideshows, 218-219
    Web Photo Gallery, 214-217
zooming in/out, 50
Images command (Window menu), 241
Images menu commands, 241
Import command (File menu), 10, 12, 141, 236
Import menu commands, Frame From Video, 12, 141
import sources, 10
in-between frames, 143
increasing brightness/contrast, 63
Indexed Color command (Mode menu), 36
Indexed Color dialog box, 36
Indexed Color image mode, 36
Indexed mode, 195
indoor panoramas, 132-133
installing Photoshop, 229-231
International Color Consortium (ICC) profiles. See color profiles
Inverse command (Select menu), 53, 239

J-K

jaw line, editing, 105

JPEG (Joint Photographic Experts Group), 25, 213, 243-244
JPEG 2000, 211, 243

JPEG Options dialog box, 25

key frames, 143

L

labels, 221

Lasso tool, 41

Layer Content Options command (Layer menu), 239

Layer menu commands
Arrange, 239
Copy Layer Style, 178
Delete Layer, 239
Duplicate Layer, 126, 239
Flatten Image, 49, 239
Group with Previous, 175, 239
Layer Content Options, 239
Layer Style, 239
Merge Down, 49, 239
Merge Layers, 239
Merge Visible, 49, 239
New, 239
New Adjustment Layer, 63, 239
New Fill Layer, 239
Paste Layer Style, 178
Rename Layer, 239
Simplify Layer, 189, 239
Type, 239
Ungroup, 239

Layer Style command (Layer menu), 239

Layer Styles command (Window menu), 159

Layer Styles palette, 159

layers
adjustment layers, 63
Gradient adjustment layer, 76
Hue/Saturation adjustment layer, 76-77
Levels adjustment layer, 74-75
saving, 77
background layers, 197
copying, 48-49, 52
creating, 48
displaying, 49
flattening, 49
gradient layers, 70
hiding, 49
layer styles, 159
applying, 200
hiding, 201
saving, 201
scaling, 201
Simple Inner, 191
Styles folder, 201
text, 173, 181
Wow Neon, 191
Wow Plastic, 191
merging, 49
moving, 49, 121
opacity, 48
organizing, 120-121
overlapping, 121
renaming, 121
selecting, 120
simplifying, 189
tonal range, 141

Layers palette, 48-49

legs, reshaping, 111

Levels adjustment layer, 74-75

Levels command (Adjust Brightness/Contrast menu), 60

Levels dialog box, 60-61

lighting
lighting effects, 164-165
reflections, 127
shadows, 165
warming up, 86-87

Lighting Effects command (Render menu), 164

Lighting Effects filter, 164-165

lines, drawing, 187

Liquify command (Distort menu), 56-57, 89, 100, 156

Liquify filter, 156-157

Load Selection command (Select menu), 239

lowering opacity setting, 87

M

Mac OS X buttons, 193

Macintosh computers
Photoshop installation, 229-230
removing Photoshop elements from, 231
system requirements, 229

Magic Eraser tool, 85

Magic Wand tool, 69, 158

Magnetic Lasso tool, 40-41, 52

magnifying glare, 84

mailing photos (email), 208-209

manually arranging panorama photos, 134-137

mapping panoramas, 137

marching ants, 41

masks
creating, 42-43
defined, 41
smoothing edges of, 43
type masks, 170-171

matte effect, 199

measurement units, 20

Memory & Image Cache panel (Preferences dialog box), 21

How can we make this index more useful? Email us at indexes@quepublishing.com

memory preferences, 21

menu commands. *See* commands

Merge Down command (Layer menu), 49, 239

Merge Layers command (Layer menu), 239

Merge Visible command (Layer menu), 49, 239

merging
layers, 49
shapes, 189

merging down warped text, 179

midtones, 61

Minimize command (Images menu), 241

missing areas, replacing, 92-93

Mode command (Image menu), 36, 238

Mode menu commands, 36-37

modes
blending modes, 87, 191
color modes, 5, 36-37

Modify command (Select menu), 239

modifying images. *See* editing images

mold damage, removing, 90-91

moles, removing, 102-103

monitors, 29

Motion Blur command (Blur menu), 53

Motion Blur dialog box, 53

mouths, reshaping, 108-109

Move tool, 122

moving
files, 7
images, 93
layers, 49, 121
objects from images, 51
type masks, 171

multiple files, opening, 7, 118

multiple reflections, 127

N

naming
documents, 4
files, 24
gradients, 86
layers, 121
patterns, 204

navigating
documents, 8-9
help topics, 14
palettes, 17

Navigator command (Window menu), 8

Navigator palette, 8-9

New Adjustment Layer command (Layer menu), 63, 239

New command (File menu), 184, 236

New command (Layer menu), 239

New dialog box, 4, 184

New Fill Layer command (Layer menu), 239

New from Clipboard command (File menu), 23, 44, 236

New Layer dialog box, 86

New View command (View menu), 240

Noise command (Filter menu), 163, 240

Noise filters, 163

noses, reshaping, 108-109

O

objects
distorting, 57
moving in images, 51
removing from images, 50-51

Online Services command (File menu), 236

opacity
decreasing, 191
layers, 48
lowering, 87

Open As command (File menu), 236

Open command (File menu), 9, 24, 236

Open dialog box, 9

Open Recent command (File menu), 236

opening
Adobe Gamma control panel, 28
Color Settings dialog box, 32
files
file associations, 25
multiple files, 7
Filters palette, 154
images, 24, 32, 118
New dialog box, 4
palettes, 16
Preferences dialog box, 18
Welcome screen, 4

optimizing images, 210-211

organizing
files, 191
layers, 120-121

orientation of text, 173

Other command (Filter menu), 240

outdoor panoramas, 130-131

overlapping images, 121

P

Page Setup command (File menu), 237

Paintbrush graphics (PCX) file format, 244

painting tools, 234

palettes
- closing, 16
- combining, 17
- Effects, 154
- Filters, 154-155
- How To, 14
- Layer Styles, 159
- Layers, 48-49
- navigating, 17
- Navigator, 8-9
- opening, 16
- Undo History, 103

panoramas
- correcting mismatched photos, 133
- cropping, 133
- cylindrical mapping, 137
- defined, 117
- final touches, 137
- indoor panoramas, 132-133
- manually arranging photos in, 134-137
- memory requirements, 133
- outdoor panoramas, 130-131
- perspective, 136
- previewing, 135
- removing images from, 135
- selecting photos for, 128-129
- shooting photos for, 131

Paste command (Edit menu), 22, 83, 237

Paste Into command (Edit menu), 175, 237

Paste Layer Style command (Layer menu), 178

pasting
- images
  - into current document, 22
  - into new document, 23
  - into other images, 83
- selections, 122

Pattern Fill dialog box, 205

Pattern Name dialog box, 204

patterns
- applying, 196-197
- creating, 204-205
- defined, 196
- naming, 204

PCT file format, 244

PCX (Paintbrush graphics) file format, 244

PDD (Adobe Photo Deluxe) file format, 245

PDF (Portable Document Format), 245

PDF Slideshow command (Automation Tools menu), 218

PDF Slideshow dialog box, 218-219

people
- animating
  - animation options, 149
  - customizing subjects, 148
  - duplicating layers, 146
  - first frame, 147
  - hiding/showing layers, 146
  - in-between frames, 147
  - last frame, 147
  - Liquify command, 147
  - merging down layers, 148
  - motion blur, 148-149
  - previewing animation, 149
  - selecting subjects, 148

repairing photos of, 95
- blemishes, 102-103
- eyes, 98-99, 108-109
- facial expressions, 106-107
- hair color, 101
- hair styles, 100-101
- jaw line, 105
- mouths, 108-109
- noses, 108-109
- physiques, 110-111
- portraits, 112-115
- smiles, 96-97
- wrinkles, 104-105

perspective
- enhancing, 56-57
- panoramas, 136
- skewing, 57

Phosphors field (Adobe Gamma control panel), 29

Photo CD file format, 244

Photo Gallery, 214-217

Photomerge dialog box, 130-133

photos. *See also* images; panoramas
- emailing, 208-209
- hand-drawn effects, 190-191
- matte effect, 199
- picture frame effect, 198-199
- printing
  - contact sheets, 224-225
  - picture packages, 220-223
- repairing, 95
  - blemishes, 102-103
  - eyes, 98-99, 108-109
  - facial expressions, 106-107
  - hair color, 101
  - hair styles, 100-101
  - jaw line, 105
  - mouths, 108-109
  - noses, 108-109

How can we make this index more useful? Email us at indexes@quepublishing.com

physiques, 110-111
portraits, 112-115
smiles, 96-97
wrinkles, 104-105
resizing, 208, 226-227
slideshows, 218-219
Web Photo Gallery,
214-217

Photoshop Elements Help command (Help menu), 14

Photoshop EPS (Encapsulated PostScript) format, 245

Photoshop installation, 229-231

Photoshop PDF (Portable Document Format), 245

physiques, reshaping, 110-111

Picture Package command (Print Layouts menu), 220

Picture Package dialog box, 220

picture packages, 220-223

Pixar file format, 245

Pixelate command (Filter menu), 240

pixelation, 53, 65, 119

pixels
adding, 43
blurring background pixels, 53
deselecting, 43
pixelation, 53, 65, 119
removing, 43
selecting, 40-41

Place command (File menu), 236

plug-in preferences, 20

Plug-Ins & Scratch Disks panel (Preferences dialog box), 20-21

PNG (Portable Network Graphics), 213, 243

Polygonal Lasso tool, 41

Portable Document Format (PDF), 245

Portable Network Graphics (PNG), 213, 243

portraits, 112-115. *See also* photos

preferences
accessing, 18
cache options, 21
default warning settings, 21
display and cursor options, 19
file compatibility options, 19
file-saving options, 19
general preferences, 18
grid settings, 20
memory options, 21
plug-in settings, 20
preset resolutions, 20
rebuilding, 21
saving, 21
scratch disk settings, 21
transparency options, 19
unit and column size options, 20

Preferences command (Edit menu), 237

Preferences dialog box
Display & Cursors panel, 19
General panel, 18
Grid panel, 20
Memory & Image Cache panel, 21
opening, 18
Plug-Ins & Scratch Disks panel, 20-21
Saving Files panel, 19
Transparency panel, 19
Units & Rulers panel, 20

Preset Manager command (Edit menu), 237

preset resolutions, 20

Preview button, 10

previewing
animation, 144-145
images, 9-10
panoramas, 135
video, 13

Print command (File menu), 237

Print Layouts command (File menu), 220, 237

Print Layouts menu commands
Contact Sheet, 224
Picture Package, 220

Print Preview command (File menu), 237

Print Size command (View menu), 240

printing
contact sheets, 224-225
picture packages, 220-223

profiles
choosing, 209
color profiles
saving files with, 33
selecting, 28
monitor profiles, 29

PSD file format, 213, 245

publishing to Web, 207
email, 208-209
file formats, 212-213
image optimization, 210-211
slideshows, 218-219
Web Photo Gallery, 214-217

Pucker tool, 89, 101, 108-111

Purge command (Edit menu), 237

Q-R

quality of images, comparing, 45

Quick Fix command (Enhance menu), 78, 125, 238

Quick Fix dialog box, 78-79

Quit command (File menu), 14, 237

rasterized images, 183

Raw file format, 245

RBG mode, 195

rebuilding preferences, 21

Reconstruct tool, 111, 157

reconstructing images. *See* repairing images

Rectangular Marquee tool, 175

red eye, 98-99

Red Eye Brush tool, 98-99, 113

reducing
    brightness, 62
    contrast, 63
    distortion, 115

Reflection tool, 111

reflections
    creating, 126-127
    enhancing, 127
    lightening, 127
    multiple reflections, 127
    removing, 84-85
    resizing, 127

removing
    blemishes, 102-103
    brushes, 203
    color casts, 72-73
    glare, 84-85
    objects from images, 50-51
    Photoshop elements, 231

pixels, 43
red eye, 98-99
reflections, 84-85
scratches and stains, 90-91
warp effect, 179
wrinkles, 104-105

Rename Layer command (Layer menu), 239

renaming
    files, 7
    layers, 121

Render command (Filter menu), 240

Render menu commands
    Cloud, 159
    Lighting Effects, 164

repairing images, 81
    blending repaired areas, 91
    glare, 84-85
    missing areas, 92-93
    photos of people, 95
        blemishes, 102-103
        eyes, 98-99, 108-109
        facial expressions, 106-107
        hair color, 101
        hair styles, 100-101
        jaw line, 105
        mouths, 108-109
        noses, 108-109
        physiques, 110-111
        portraits, 112-115
        smiles, 96-97
        wrinkles, 104-105
    reflections, 84-85
    salvaging portions of images, 82-83
    scratches and stains, 90-91
    torn areas, 88-89
    warming up lighting, 86-87

Repeat Last Effect command (Filter menu), 240

replacing missing areas, 92-93

Reselect command (Select menu), 239

Reset All Warning Dialogs button, 21

Reset Palette Locations command (Window menu), 241

Reset Tool command (Brush menu), 186

resetting Brush tool, 186

reshaping
    eyes/nose/mouth, 108-109
    physiques, 110-111

Resize command (Image menu), 45, 144, 238

Resize menu commands, Image Size, 45

resizing
    animation frames, 144
    photos, 44-45, 208, 226-227
    reflections, 127
    selections, 123
    text, 169

resolution
    changing, 45
    defined, 5
    preset resolutions, 20
    setting, 5
    video, 13
    viewing, 44

Revert command (File menu), 236

RGB (red, green, blue) color settings, 34

RGB Color command (Mode menu), 36

RGB Color image mode, 36

rollover, 193

Rotate button, 7

Rotate command (Image menu), 54, 238

Rotate menu commands, Straighten Image, 55

How can we make this index more useful? Email us at indexes@quepublishing.com

rotating
  selections, 123
  smiles, 97
  thumbnails, 7

ruler
  preferences, 20
  viewing, 53-54, 123

Rulers command (View menu), 123, 240

S

salvaging portions of images, 82-83

sampling images, 51

saturation
  adjusting, 69, 87
  HSB (hue, saturation, brightness) color settings, 34
  Hue/Saturation adjustment layer, 76-77

Save As command (File menu), 24, 33, 236

Save As dialog box, 24, 33

Save button, 11

Save command (File menu), 23, 213, 236

Save dialog box, 11

Save for Web command (File menu), 144, 210, 236

Save for Web dialog box, 243

Save Selection command (Select menu), 239

saving
  adjustment layers, 77
  brushes, 203
  files, 19, 213
  images, 23, 33
  layer styles, 201
  preferences, 21
  video frames, 13

Saving Files panel (Preferences dialog box), 19

scaling images, 52-53, 107, 201, 226-227

scanning images, 11

Scitex file format, 245

scratch disks, 21

scratches, removing, 90-91

searching help topics, 15

Select Import Source dialog box, 10

Select menu commands
  All, 239
  Delete Selection, 239
  Deselect, 83, 239
  Feather, 83, 119, 239
  Grow, 239
  Inverse, 53, 239
  Load Selection, 239
  Modify, 239
  Reselect, 239
  Save Selection, 239
  Similar, 239

selecting
  animation images, 140-141
  Brush tool, 184
  filters, 154
  images, 22
  layers, 120
  pixels, 40-41
  Shape tool, 188
  text, 172

Selection Brush tool, 41-43, 83, 171

Selection command (View menu), 240

selection tools, 234
  Elliptical Marquee, 42
  Lasso, 41
  Magnetic Lasso, 40-41, 52
  Polygonal Lasso, 41
  Selection Brush, 41-43

Set Vanishing Point tool, 136

setting preferences
  cache options, 21
  display and cursor options, 19
  file compatibility options, 19
  file-saving options, 19
  general preferences, 18
  grid settings, 20
  memory options, 21
  plug-in settings, 20
  preset resolutions, 20
  scratch disk settings, 21
  transparency options, 19
  unit and column size options, 20

shadows
  changing, 60
  creating, 165
  drop shadows, 115, 173

Shape tool, 188-189

shapes
  animating, 150-151
  changing, 189
  drawing, 188-189
  merging, 189
  Shape tool, 188-189

sharing contact sheets, 225

Sharpen command (Filter menu), 240

Shift Pixels tool, 111

shortcuts bar, 16, 234-235

shoulders, reshaping, 111

Show Clipboard command (Edit menu), 23

Show Options command (Window menu), 241

Show Palettes command (Window menu), 241

Show Shortcuts command (Window menu), 241

Show Status Bar command (Window menu), 241

Show Tools command (Window menu), 241

Show Welcome command (Window menu), 241

showing. *See displaying*

shrinking torn paper, 89

Similar command (Select menu), 239

simple gallery, 217

Simple Inner layer style, 191

Simplify Layer command (Layer menu), 189, 239

simplifying layers, 189

sizing
- brushes, 157
- eyes, 105
- images, 4, 44-45
- photos, 208, 226-227
- reflections, 127
- selections, 123
- text, 169
- thumbnails, 6

Sketch command (Filter menu), 240

Skew command (Transform menu), 57

skewing perspective, 57

slideshows, 218-219

smiles
- repairing, 96-97
- rotating, 97

smoothing edges of mask, 43

Smudge Stick filter, 161

Smudge Stick menu command (Artistic menu), 161

Smudge tool, 97, 105

Snap to Grid command (View menu), 241

Sponge filter, 160-161

Sponge menu command (Artistic menu), 160

stains, removing, 90-91

standard Photoshop installation, 231

Step Backward command (Edit menu), 237

Step Forward command (Edit menu), 237

Straighten Image command (Rotate menu), 55

straightening images, 54-55, 97

Stroke command (Edit menu), 187, 237

Stroke dialog box, 187

stroke settings (brushes), 187

Style Settings dialog box, 115

styles
- layer styles, 159
  - *applying, 200*
  - *hiding, 201*
  - *saving, 201*
  - *scaling, 201*
  - *Simple Inner, 191*
  - *Styles folder, 201*
  - *text, 173, 181*
  - *Wow Neon, 191*
  - *Wow Plastic, 191*
- Web Photo Gallery, 214

Styles folder, 201

Stylize command (Filter menu), 240

subtractive color spaces, 35

supported file formats
- Animated GIF, 139
- BMP, 244
- choosing, 212-213
- compatibility, 19
- CompuServe GIF, 244
- EXIF, 11
- Filmstrip, 245
- GIF, 212, 243

JPEG, 25, 213, 243-244
JPEG 2000, 211, 243
PCT, 244
PCX, 244
PDD, 245
Photo CD, 244
Photoshop EPS, 245
Photoshop PDF, 245
Pixar, 245
PNG, 213, 243
PSD, 213, 245
Raw, 245
Scitex, 245
Targa, 245
TIFF, 25, 243-244
Wireless Bitmap, 245

swapping colors, 35

T

tables gallery, 217

Tagged Image File Format (TIFF), 25, 243-244

Targa file format, 245

tears, repairing, 88-89

teeth, straightening/whitening, 97

text
- adding to images, 168-169
- alignment, 173
- color, 172
- combining with images, 174-175
- drop shadows, 173
- fonts
  - *changing, 169*
  - *choosing, 168*
  - *color, 172*
- ghost text, 181
- layer styles, 173, 181
- resizing, 169
- selecting, 172
- text effects, 180-181
- text orientation, 173
- type masks, 170-171
- warped text, 176-179

How can we make this index more useful? Email us at indexes@quepublishing.com

Texture command (Filter menu), 240

theme gallery, 217

thumbnail view (files), 6-7

thumbnails
formatting, 215
rotating, 7
sizing, 6

TIFF (Tagged Image File Format), 25, 243-244

TIFF Options dialog box, 25

Tile command (Images menu), 241

tonal range
analyzing across layers, 141
black point, 61
correcting, 60-61
highlights, 61
midtones, 61
shadows, 60
white point, 61

toolbox, 233-234

tools, 233-234. *See also* **brushes**
applying, 17
Bloat, *57, 105, 111, 156-157*
Blur, *91*
brushes
Airbrush, 186
brush pressure, 111
brush sizes, 157
Brush tool, 185-187
changing, 186
choosing, 91
custom brushes, 202-203
Red Eye Brush, 98-99, 113
Reset all Warning Dialogs, 21
resetting, 186
Selection Brush, 41-43, 83, 171

Burn, *71*
Clone Stamp, *50-51*
removing blemishes, 103
removing glare, 85
removing scratches and stains, 90-91
repairing smiles, 97
repairing torn images, 88-89
replacing missing areas, 92-93
Counter Clockwise, *111*
Crop, *46-47*
Custom Shape, *145, 189*
Dodge, *70-71, 97*
Elliptical Marquee, *42*
Eraser, *103*
eyedropper tools, *61*
Hand, *93*
Horizontal Type, *168-169, 174-176, 180*
Horizontal Type Mask, *170*
Lasso, *41*
Magic Eraser, *85*
Magic Wand, *69, 158*
Magnetic Lasso, *40-41, 52*
Move tool, *122*
options, *17*
Polygonal Lasso, *41*
Pucker, *89, 101, 108-109, 111*
Reconstruct, *111, 157*
Rectangular Marquee, *175*
Reflection, *111*
Set Vanishing Point, *136*
Shape, *188-189*
Shift Pixels, *111*
Smudge, *97, 105*
ToolTips, *17*
Turbulence, *111*
Twirl Clockwise, *101, 111, 113*
Type, *172, 174*
Vertical Type Mask, *170*
Warp, *56-57, 105, 109-110, 157*
Zoom, *45, 50*

Tools menu commands, Folder Options, 25

ToolTips, 17

torn images, repairing, 88-89

Transform command (Image menu), 57, 238

Transform menu commands, 57

transforming selections, 122-123

transparency
file optimization, 211
preferences, 19

Transparency panel (Preferences dialog box), 19

troubleshooting animation, 145

Turbulence tool, 111

Twirl Clockwise tool, 101, 111-113

Twirl filter, 161-163

twirling hair, 101

Type command (Layer menu), 239

type masks, 170-171

Type tools, 167, 172-174
Horizontal Type, *168-169, 174-176, 180*
Horizontal Type Mask, *170*
Type, *172-174*
Vertical Type Mask, *170*

U

Undo command (Edit menu), 237

Undo History palette, 103

Undo State Change command (Edit menu), 237

undoing changes, 157

Ungroup command (Layer menu), 239

uninstalling Photoshop elements, 231

Units & Rulers panel (Preferences dialog box), 20

unlocking background layers, 197

V

vector graphics, 183

Vertical Type Mask tool, 170

video
frames, 12-13
previewing, 13
resolution, 13

Video command (Filter menu), 240

View menu commands
Actual Pixels, 240
Annotations, 241
Fit on Screen, 240
Grid, 53-54, 123, 187, 240
New View, 240
Print Size, 240
Rulers, 123, 240
Selection, 240
Snap to Grid, 241
Zoom In, 240
Zoom Out, 240

viewing
Clipboard, 23
documents, 8-9
grids, 53-54, 123, 187
images, 23
layers, 49
picture packages, 223
resolution, 44
ruler, 53-54, 123
slideshows, 219

W

waists, reshaping, 110-111

warming up lighting, 86-87

warnings, 21

Warp Text dialog box, 176-177

Warp tool, 56-57, 105, 109-110, 157

warped text, 176-179

Web buttons, 192-193

Web Photo Gallery, 214-217

Web publishing, 207
email, 208-209
file formats, 212-213
image optimization, 210-211
slideshows, 218-219
Web Photo Gallery, 214-217

Web sites
Adobe Forums, 15
file formats, 243

Welcome command (Window menu), 4

Welcome screen, 3
customizing, 181, 194-195
opening, 4
options, 5

white point, 29-31, 61

whitening teeth, 97

Window menu commands
Arrange Icons, 241
Close All, 241
Effects, 154
Filters, 154
Hide Options, 241
Hide Palettes, 241
Hide Shortcuts, 241
Hide Status Bar, 241

Hide Tools, 241
Hide Welcome, 241
How To, 14
Images, 241
Layer Styles, 159
Navigator, 8
Reset Palette Locations, 21, 241
Show Options, 241
Show Palettes, 241
Show Shortcuts, 241
Show Status Bar, 241
Show Tools, 241
Show Welcome, 241
Welcome, 4

Windows computers, installing Photoshop on, 229-231

Wireless Bitmap file format, 245

work area, 3, 16-17

Wow Neon layer style, 191

Wow Plastic layer style, 191

wrinkles, removing, 104-105

X-Z

Zoom In command (View menu), 240

Zoom Out command (View menu), 240

Zoom tool, 45, 50

zooming in/out, 9, 50

How can we make this index more useful? Email us at indexes@quepublishing.com